THE GREAT FIRE OF ROME

WITNESS TO ANCIENT HISTORY

Gregory S. Aldrete, *Series Editor*

ALSO IN THE SERIES:

Jerry Toner, *The Day Commodus Killed a Rhino: Understanding the Roman Games*

Debra Hamel, *The Battle of Arginusae: Victory at Sea and Its Tragic Aftermath in the Final Years of the Peloponnesian War*

Robert Garland, *Athens Burning: The Persian Invasion of Greece and the Evacuation of Attica*

Stefan G. Chrissanthos, *The Year of Julius and Caesar: 59 BC and the Transformation of the Roman Republic*

Nathan T. Elkins, *A Monument to Dynasty and Death: The Story of Rome's Colosseum and the Emperors Who Built It*

THE GREAT FIRE OF ROME

Life and Death
in the Ancient City

Joseph J. Walsh

Johns Hopkins University Press
Baltimore

© 2019 Johns Hopkins University Press
All rights reserved. Published 2019
Printed in the United States of America on acid-free paper
2 4 6 8 9 7 5 3 1

Johns Hopkins University Press
2715 North Charles Street
Baltimore, Maryland 21218-4363
www.press.jhu.edu

Library of Congress Cataloging-in-Publication Data

Names: Walsh, Joseph J., 1953– author.
Title: The Great Fire of Rome : life and death in the ancient city / Joseph J. Walsh.
Description: Baltimore : Johns Hopkins University Press, [2019] |
Series: Witness to ancient history | Includes bibliographical references and index.
Identifiers: LCCN 2019009854 | ISBN 9781421433707 (hardcover : alk. paper) |
ISBN 9781421433714 (pbk. : alk. paper) | ISBN 9781421433721 (electronic) |
ISBN 1421433702 (hardcover : alk. paper) | ISBN 1421433710 (pbk. : alk. paper) |
ISBN 1421433729 (electronic)
Subjects: LCSH: Great Fire, Rome, Italy, 64. | Rome—History—Nero, 54–68. |
Fire extinction—Rome—History. | Nero, Emperor of Rome, 37–68.
Classification: LCC DG285.3 .W35 2019 | DDC 937/.6307—dc23
LC record available at https://lccn.loc.gov/2019009854

A catalog record for this book is available from the British Library.

*Special discounts are available for bulk purchases of this book.
For more information, please contact Special Sales at 410-516-6936
or specialsales@press.jhu.edu.*

Johns Hopkins University Press uses environmentally friendly book
materials, including recycled text paper that is composed of at least
30 percent post-consumer waste, whenever possible.

For Gayla—
Colleague, editor, and spouse extraordinaire

CONTENTS

Acknowledgments ix

Prologue 1

I
Perils of Life in Rome 8

II
Inferno 42

III
The Day After 73

IV
Neropolis 96

V
Legacy 112

APPENDIX A.
Sources 129

APPENDIX B.
Proposed Timeline of the Great Fire 134

Notes 137

Suggested Further Reading 161

Index 169

ACKNOWLEDGMENTS

I am indebted to several scholars for their advice and for their generosity in helping me access sites in Rome essential to my research for this book. Sister Maria Panagia Miola, SSVM, helped me access inscriptions and reliefs in the Vatican, and Maddalena Scoccianti guided me through excavations in the vicinity of the Circus Maximus. Clementina Panella and Russell (Darby) Scott helped me make sense of the archaeology of the Great Fire. James Rives and Jerry Toner read sections of this book and provided invaluable feedback and bibliography. Angela Christman offered input on the history of martyrdom in Christianity. Martha Taylor directed me to this series and offered her usual sage advice, support, and encouragement. Greg Aldrete, Witness to Ancient History's series editor, also offered invaluable advice and displayed considerable patience as I worked on the book, as did Matt McAdam and Catherine Goldstead, editors at Johns Hopkins University Press. Barbara Lamb provided thorough, thoughtful, and savvy editorial guidance.

I thank Loyola University Maryland's Center for the Humanities, the office of Dean of the College of Arts and Sciences, and Loyola's Classics Department for their support of my research for this project. Robert Cronan of Lucidity Information Design showed exemplary professionalism and, again, patience, in making the maps in this book.

Gayla McGlamery, my dearest colleague and spouse, has dedicated innumerable hours to reading, rereading, and improving my drafts. I'd be lost without her, and but for her this book would not have been completed. It is dedicated to her.

Of course, all blunders that have survived my colleagues' sensible advice and superior judgment are mine.

THE GREAT FIRE OF ROME

Prologue

THIS BOOK TELLS THE STORY of the greatest of the Great Fires, the Great Fire of Rome. Ancient Rome's size, significance, and power were enormous in comparison to that of other cities of its era, and this fire obliterated the better part of the city. It would be well over a millennium before another urban fire of this scale occurred, and no city of Rome's evident and considerable superiority to its contemporaries ever suffered such a devastating conflagration. Nor does the story of any other great historical fire offer such star power in human terms—Nero, Saints Peter and Paul, Aeneas, Raphael, Michelangelo—or in architectural—St. Peter's Basilica, the Vatican, the Colosseum, the Circus Maximus.

Readers of this text will get a glimpse of what a horrifying experience the disaster was for those who endured it and for those who perished in it. But the book also examines the daily lives of those victims and survivors in that simultaneously magnificent and dangerous city, lives marked by perils as well as pleasures. It explores how the city and its residents prepared for, sustained, made sense of, and, ironically, invited the disaster. The Great Fire's extraordinary aftermath and legacy—as important as the event itself—will also receive their due.

In the ancient Mediterranean and Europe, Rome was not *a* city—it was *the* city. The heart of a vast and complex empire, Rome itself was unprecedentedly vast and complex. Never had so many fantastically wealthy and abysmally poor people gathered together in one place, and the city's fabric and configuration reflected the presence of both. Rome contained splendid temples for worship, impressive basilicas for public business, gardens and fountains for relief, and, among its many splendid venues for entertainment, one of the largest sports facilities in human history, the Circus Maximus. Some residents lived in impressive urban mansions, others in tenement slums that would rival the grimmest in the most overcrowded cities today for danger, discomfort, and misery. Shops were everywhere and sold everything then available. Rome was a vibrant, motley, exhilarating, exhausting place, which wore its importance on its sleeve. A city where anything could happen—and did.

Unfortunately, much of what happened was bad.

Peril was everywhere in Rome. Its inhabitants contended daily with the threat of collapsing buildings, flood, crime, food poisoning, disease, and, of course, fire—the price of living in *the* city.[1] The Great Fire of 64 CE, however, was unlike anything Rome's residents had ever experienced. It started in the shops at the Circus, spread the length of that huge racetrack, and soon commenced an inexorable march through the city. No building, no neighborhood, no person was safe from conflagration; it even consumed a significant part of the emperor Nero's ever-expanding palace. After raging for six days, the fire spent itself just short of the Esquiline Hill, towards Rome's northeastern edge. Or so it seemed, for a second fire broke out, further demoralizing Rome's weary and despondent population.[2] The city's inhabitants must have felt as if the fires would never end. When they finally subsided, vast swaths of Rome were in ruins. The historian Tacitus claimed that the city of Rome had never suffered a catastrophe "more severe and destructive." The greatest city of the ancient world had endured its greatest blow.[3]

Disasters reveal character, in both senses of the word.

People experiencing disasters have hard choices to make and often little time to make them. Courage contends with fear, selflessness with self-interest, decency with shamelessness. Our very sense of who we are and what we stand for is at stake. As each individual's character is put to the test, some pass, some fail, and for many the assessment is vexingly—or comfortingly—ambiguous. You can spend a lifetime agonizing over whether you did what you should have done. You can also reinterpret, rewrite even, the narrative of your response, if it is too troubling.

This book explores individual responses to the Great Fire of Rome, and in the process perhaps something of the character of Rome's residents is revealed. We do not have the names of the hundreds of thousands of residents of Rome who endured the fire, but the historian Tacitus did describe average Romans' experiences of the conflagration, including their terror, despair, struggles, and strategies to survive, and, of course, their moral crises. It is difficult to read about the fire and the victims' responses to it without wondering how one would have responded if faced with such a dire and testing situation.

A society's response to disaster tells us a great deal about that society's character, that is, its nature. Not all societies respond to disasters in the same way. Some are vigilant and prepared for the worst; others are not the least so. A drought in a community with little food in its storehouses can turn into a catastrophe. The same drought in a community that has saved years of food for hard times may scarcely leave a mark. Vulnerability to disaster can vary immensely and have exceedingly different consequences. How societies respond to disaster can also vary considerably, as do the ways in which societies make sense of disaster. Are the gods punishing us for something? Has our negligence caused the disaster? Is it just chance, life? Is some individual or segment of society responsible for the event, for our lack of preparedness for it, or for our woefully inadequate response to it? Is it the king's fault, the president's, the prime minister's? Mine? The answers to these questions, in turn, reveal a great deal about the character of the affected societies—from how they think, to what they value, to the nuts and bolts of how they live their lives.

This book, then, also focuses on what Roman preparation for, response to, and processing of the Great Fire tells us about Roman society and particularly about the urban experience of the residents of ancient Rome. In the ancient world, a conflagration of this nature and magnitude could only have taken place in the city of Rome. The magnitude has much to do with Rome's unparalleled size, of course, but it also has to do with the particular character of the great city and the lives people led there. As Rome became the center of the Mediterranean world and western Europe, it expanded horizontally and vertically to accommodate an unprecedented concentration of people. The city that emerged set the stage, even provided the preconditions, for the Great Fire.

This text, therefore, considers both Rome as the context for the fire and how the unrelenting dangers and distresses of that context provided residents with a kind of mental preparation, training even, for catastrophe. If ancient Rome had been designed—rather than, for the most part, expanding organically and haphazardly—we might suspect that a master planner had set things up for a devastating fire, so perfect were conditions for conflagration. A sense of the fabric of ancient Rome—its streets, apartment houses, slums, shops, and what they were made of and contained—is required to understand how the fire started, spread, and devastated the city. Just as important, an understanding of the trying conditions of life in Rome will help us understand the mentality of its residents, people inured to danger, accustomed to navigating an urban landscape configured to frustrate, and so with expectations calibrated to preserve some equanimity in that unnerving environment. Indeed, because one wonders how anyone could endure living in such a hazardous and at times terrifying place, this book also touches on a few aspects of Rome that provided some compensation for living amidst worry, insecurity, and pain.

Several other themes emerge in the chapters that follow because, like the configuration of the city, they too are intertwined with the fire. First is the character and personality of Nero, star of the grand and terrifying spectacle. He would most certainly be pleased to be identified as the star, since he was in his own view above all a performer, and his role in the fire was the greatest act in the play that was his life. In the wake of the fire, he transformed Rome, and in some respects today's Rome still reflects that transformation. And, of course, the ancient accusation that he started the fire still hangs over him. We must ask if he is guilty, although the asking is much easier than the answering.

It is impossible to examine the Great Fire without examining the Romans' relationship to history. For them, the past existed alongside the present, defining it and providing a lens through which to understand and assess current events and the contemporary state of their world. Noteworthy, too, is Roman historians' preoccupation with morality. They rarely viewed crises in strictly political or economic terms. For them, crises were at heart moral. Corruption, decadence, wickedness, foolishness, and the like explain why nations falter and even fall. This moralizing perspective informed ancient historians' views regarding disasters as well, not just society's responses to them, but even their very causes. This approach may seem utterly alien to modern readers—how could the causes of a natural disaster, for example, be in part moral?—but this mode of thinking is not entirely extinct, and indeed not entirely incompatible with the way twenty-first century researchers approach disasters. According to today's scholarly consensus, an earthquake by itself does not cause a disaster; rather, it is much more our vulnerability to the earthquake (which is only the triggering event) that transforms that event into a full-fledged catastrophe. A 6.9 earthquake in the Bay Area of California in 1989 killed 67 people; a weaker earthquake of 6.6 in Bam, Iran, on the other hand, killed 26,271 people in 2003.[4] The vastly different levels of vulnerability to earthquake in the two communities account for the vastly different casualty numbers. This approach may not, strictly speaking, entail moral judgment, but it nonetheless places partial responsibility for the disaster in human hands—we are, to this way of thinking, agents of our own disasters.[5] There are still today religious figures who view catastrophes as divine retribution for a whole host of sins, just as some Romans did.

The Romans' moral understanding of history and processing of events make it difficult for us to trust ancient historians and other ancient writers and thus to nail down the whys and hows of ancient events. More problematic yet, it can be difficult to know *what* happened and even, at times, *if* something happened at all. The most basic facts regarding an event can be in dispute. Only a small fraction of written and material evidence from the ancient world survives, and what there is comes from a time when the technology was so primitive that narratives of actual occurrences relied on rumors and suspect testimony. The Great Fire provides a superb example. In piecing together the narrative, one confronts controversies, puzzles, and even mysteries—a murder mystery, in fact, if human hands intentionally started that deadly inferno.

Mythology also crops up in this volume again and again, for it, like history, helped the ancient Romans make sense of the world. For instance, stories of the gods and heroes were integral to the theatrical Nero that Nero created. In a sense, he was playing and living a role in a mythological narrative of his own composition, but inspired by the tales of Apollo and other gods ubiquitous in Greek and Roman literature. These narratives informed the punishment he inflicted on the Christians and the logic behind his Domus Aurea (Golden House), the extraordinary palace he constructed on land the Great Fire had conveniently cleared for him. Tacitus employed the mythological tales of Rome's foundation to shape his readers' understanding of the Great Fire.[6] It would be misleading, though, to distinguish the role mythology played from that of history, as we might do today. For the Romans, narratives of the past could be equally and simultaneously myth and history, for there was no need to disentangle or even distinguish the two. In any event, mythological and historical narratives served the same function—to help the Romans define themselves and their relationship to the world and the gods, to make sense of their existence. Perhaps we are not so different as we would like to think. Facts and data seem to have little purchase today for the many who embrace narratives that confirm their sense of who they are and of how the world works, however detached from reality those narratives may be. And the internet offers an unlimited supply of such narratives: unsubstantiated, implausible, and even fantastic, but nonetheless credible and compelling to many. The line between myth and history is blurred in our world as well.

Our exploration of the Great Fire also reveals the distinctive and substantial role that buildings played in ancient Rome. These buildings were victims of the Great Fire, but they were also its accomplices, as the nature of their placement, construction, and materials allowed a localized fire to grow into a grand inferno. Even more noteworthy and revealing is the role buildings played in Romans' construction of their past, present, and future. Buildings today inform and reflect who we are and what we value, but they did so for the Romans to a much greater degree, and the Romans were much more conscious of buildings' potential to do that. Architecture simply meant more to them than it does to us, and it did more for them. Buildings expressed values and beliefs; they helped the Romans define themselves to others and to themselves; they communicated pride, dignity, status, success, and power. Buildings were an open declaration to the world, as they can be today, but a more powerful and vital declaration than in the modern world, where we have so many other ways to express who we are and to publicize our values, wealth, accomplishments, and meaning. We have the internet, television, movies, billboards, recordings, magazines, newspapers (and we inhabit a world where a much larger percentage of the population can read). None of these existed in ancient Rome. In rebuilding Rome along new lines after the fire, Nero was not just improving the old city; he was creating a new one, with a new identity and significance, one that would more closely and satisfyingly reflect *his* identity and significance.

The vulnerability of Roman buildings to fire and other catastrophes was, in part, an effect of the relatively primitive state of Roman technology, at least compared to the technology of advanced countries today. Another effect was that communication was relatively primitive. Rome did have a sophisticated culture of books and letter writing, but few could read or afford books and letters. The Roman government disseminated its messages through coins, inscriptions, buildings, and the like, and in Rome itself the government published a daily gazette, the *Acta Diurna* (*Daily Deeds*). The *Acta*, however, tended to focus more on accidents, births, deaths, and divorce and wedding announcements than on the sort of news we encounter on the front page or website of the *New York Times*. Unfortunately, all of these Roman modes of communicating published the government's and its supporters' reading of things. Nor were they of much use in relating breaking news, especially the sorts of reports that could mean the difference between life and death in the midst of a disaster. Word of mouth—

rumor—therefore played an indispensable and powerful role in helping Rome's residents navigate day-to-day life in the city and also survive disasters. This was Romans' only option, really, which meant that the amount of verifiable, impartial, reliable information, particularly as events unfolded, was alarmingly meager—and rumor continued to shape events in the wake of the Great Fire, as Nero and the earliest Christians discovered. Here too, however, we should not feel too smugly superior to the ancient Romans: Rome's roiling rumor mill was likely more trustworthy than the preposterous narratives and explanations so much of the internet traffics in. We modern, rational people may, after all, be entering a post-fact world, in which technology enables word-of-mouth rumors and fabrications to go viral.[7]

All disasters matter and have a lasting impact. Few, however, can rival the Great Fire of Rome for the breadth, significance, longevity, and improbability of its consequences and legacy. Some of the fire's aftereffects were intentional. The devastated sections of Rome were rebuilt expressly employing design and material principles intended to avert the recurrence of a fire of that magnitude. The layout and very stuff of much of the city was purposefully transformed, and, to a noteworthy degree, a new Rome emerged. Nero intentionally transformed his palace as well, creating a revolutionary marvel of architecture that gobbled up an almost comically vast portion of the city's center.

Nero could not have imagined, however, that his actions in response to the fire's devastation would set the precedent for Roman persecution of the Christians, significantly affect the character of Christianity in antiquity and beyond, contribute to the artistic and cultural revolution of the Renaissance, and result in the construction of Rome's two most emblematic buildings, St. Peter's Basilica and the Colosseum. One other legacy he might not have imagined: the Great Fire of Rome helped make Nero *the* Roman emperor, a "Superstar," as a recent scholarly publication characterized him,[8] a status he has retained into the twenty-first century. He is still fiddling while Rome burns, but in the guise of Barack Obama, George W. Bush, Donald Trump, Justin Trudeau, Stephen Harper, Angela Merkel, Theresa May, and virtually any political figure you can conjure up whose opponents wish to attack. From a historical standpoint, a great fire (like any catastrophe) does not end when the flames are extinguished. That merely marks the beginning of new chapters in the disaster's story.

-I-
Perils of Life in Rome

THESE DAYS THE STANDARD IMAGE of ancient Rome is that of an advanced, modern, clean, urban landscape filled with beautiful architectural wonders.[1] Even a movie like *Gladiator*, for all its blood and guts and savagery, presents the city of Rome as a sort of ancient Singapore—glitzy, tidy, and orderly. The presence of a street performer or two scarcely matters—our big cities have them as well. Moreover, our experience of the archeological remains of the ancient city tends to confirm this impression. The Colosseum we visit is a ruin, but a clean and orderly one, and the remains of the forum and Palatine are all stone, brick, greenery, and charming decorative lizards. Charts, maps, models, and reconstructions reinforce our sense of ancient Rome as a city of spick-and-span splendors unsoiled by the presence of human beings, with their sweat, spit, trash, and excrement. And there is something to this image—Rome was indeed full of magnificence and beauty—but it was also a city of filth, discomfort, and peril, and it provided the context, and the very fuel, for the Great Fire. Fire, though, was only one thread in a tapestry of threats to health and life.

The configuration of the city, how Romans lived in that context, and the things and even materials the city consisted of—the very stuff of the city—did more than contribute to making Rome a trying and dangerous place to live. They were the cause.

The Romans are famous for their rectilinear city planning, and justly so. When they founded a new city on virgin ground, or on the ground of an earlier city they had leveled, they would lay it out on rational principles and in straight lines. The contours and configuration of Rome itself, however, had been established well before Romans learned from the Greeks how to design according to a grid. Rome started off, that is, as a jumbled mess, developing naturally and untidily to meet the needs of various moments, with little thought to the long-term expansion of the city. Manhattan provides an instructive parallel. A map of the island reveals two cities. The better part of the island to the north consists, for the most part, of a rigidly geometrical grid. This New York is the legacy of the Commissioners' Plan of 1811, a plan that would remind ancient Romans of the rectilinear grids they employed in founding numbers of towns and cities throughout their empire. The southern tip of the island, however, is more chaotic, largely the result of ad hoc development and developments in the city's early days. Ancient Romans would recognize this configuration as well, but from their own experience of the city of Rome.

Rome started off as a series of tiny, distinct hamlets that grew into villages and then eventually grew together into a town. That early growing was done without much in the way of planning or regulation, and so the city's earliest street patterns were a tangled muddle. As the city expanded, temples and other public buildings were added, and some streets were leveled and paved. Like all ancient towns of prosperity and aspiration, Rome was transformed by public projects. There is no indication, however, that the Roman government prioritized regularization of the numerous winding streets and lanes around which many of Rome's residences were gathered.

As the Romans became the preeminent people of the Mediterranean and a socioeconomic revolution transformed Italy, a population explosion added overcrowding to the disorder of Rome's layout, and that disorderly, tangled web of twisting streets and alleys had to accommodate waves of newcomers.[2] Rome had no public transportation system, which made it imperative to squeeze as much as possible into as little space as possible. Romans built tight and high. The result was a sprawling but jam-packed and confusing urban landscape.[3] "My neighbor Novius and I can touch hands by reaching out through our windows," dryly noted the poet Martial (c. 40–c. 103 CE) on the proximity of his apartment house to the one across the street.[4] Exacerbating the overcrowding, much land in central Rome was dedicated to public buildings of one kind or another—temples and shrines all over the place, the Roman Forum, other fora emperors built, warehouses, theaters, the Circus Maximus, and other venues for spectacles. Ultimately the emperors snatched the entire Palatine Hill for themselves. That is, a huge chunk of central Rome was taken out of play.

Most streets accommodated one wagon, and most sidewalks accommodated, perhaps, two pedestrians—if, that is, shops did not move their wares and services out onto the sidewalk and even into the streets, as was the custom. The emperor Domitian (rule: 81–96 CE) garnered praise from Martial because he got all those barbers, cooks, wine sellers, butchers, and, we assume, dozens of other sorts of business folks, out of the streets they had been blocking. Before Domitian's measures, Martial grumbled, Rome outdoors had been "just one big shop."[5] Streets and sidewalks tended to be narrow and twisting, and looming over many were apartment houses. In the first century BCE, Cicero considered Rome's "apartment houses piled high" and its "lousy roads and the ridiculously narrow lanes" a laughable embarrassment.[6] And so the streets of Rome were perpetually congested. The vast majority of its approximately one million people (in our period) walked through its narrow streets, and like all Mediterranean peoples, the Romans preferred to conduct their lives outdoors, however crowded and turbulent those outdoors were. Congestion and commotion were the norm in the streets of Rome.

In this overcrowded and jumbled environment, Romans inhabited, essentially, three types of dwelling: urban townhouses (*domus*; plural, *domus*), apartment houses (*insula*; plural, *insulae*), and workplace quarters (*taberna*; plural, *tabernae*).[7] Only the very wealthy could afford townhouses, which generally had the same configuration as those at Pompeii: a series of rooms around an open courtyard (*atrium*), possibly two stories and possibly with a garden in the back surrounded by another set of rooms. These homes would have no windows to the outside world, receiving their light and air from the courtyard. Most Romans, however, lived in apartments, which, like apartments today, could vary immensely in quality.[8] Some of the most elegant could have high ceilings, rooms on more than one floor, lighting from a courtyard, a breeze from the street side to the court side, a toilet, and even wall paintings.[9] The apartments at the lowest end, which in Rome vastly outnumbered the luxury sort, had low ceilings, little breeze, little light, often only one room, no paintings, and no toilet. Perhaps most significant for our purposes (and more on this below), the elegant apartment houses were usually built of sturdier materials, such as brick and concrete, while the cheaper apartments, particularly in pre-Fire Rome, could be ramshackle half-timbered structures consisting largely of wood or with half-timbered construction above the lowest floors. One can, of course, construct cheap and unstable structures in brick or concrete as well. Apartment buildings could reach ten floors or perhaps more, although most were likely only a few stories high. Lastly, many Romans lived behind, above, or in their shops, generally in cramped quarters. These shops could be part of a *domus* or an *insula* or built into any variety of other structures, even the Circus Maximus, as we shall see.

Roman neighborhoods tended to be more mixed than neighborhoods in modern cities. Inhabitants living in plush townhouses often rented some of their street-front space to shop owners and other businesses. Even wealthy Romans had an eye out for the extra buck. The rich and poor were not as rigidly segregated as they often are today. Two tendencies for separation can be discerned, though. Professions tended to gather together, which made life much easier for their customers. In a world without MapQuest and a city without street signs, it was easier to find, for instance, a perfume shop by going to the *vicus turarius* (perfumers' neighborhood), where they tended to collocate. Certain businesses and professions gathered together because they needed to be in a specific part of the city, or, more likely, on the fringes of the city. Undertakers and fullers (who used urine to process wool) gathered on the outskirts of Rome with good reason, for example. The other tendency was for the wealthy to live on Rome's hills or their slopes, and for everyone else to dwell in the valleys. The hills had purer air and were breezier, dryer, and less prone to suffer from Rome's frequent flooding. As in all great cities, neighborhoods could become less or more fashionable as circumstances and values changed, although this propensity was less pronounced in ancient Rome than in modern cities, such as New York, where the character and prosperity of neighborhoods can change in a blink.

The government oversaw vast public projects—the Colosseum and the Pantheon, for example—and set aside spaces for fora, parks, covered colonnades, bathhouses, and other such facilities that offered relief from the city's oppressiveness—not that these couldn't get crowded as well. When it came to private dwellings and businesses, however, the government generally undertook little in the way of urban planning or construction, although regulations did bring some order, at least, to the conduct of day-to-day life. Emperors had the power to seize private land, if they really wanted to, but some were reluctant to do so. Roman law did not have what we would recognize as eminent domain, and normally the authorities avoided appropriating or even purchasing compulsorily.[10] Disasters offered emperors opportunities to expropriate land and reconfigure sections of the city, as well as to introduce new regulations—that is, to do some genuine comprehensive urban planning, for which the Great Fire provided the most significant opportunity.[11]

Such was the overcrowded and precarious setting for Romans' lives. Life in that environment had its pleasures, of course, and those of Rome were exceptional, but life was also an ongoing battle with inconvenience, adversity, and insecurity. It is impossible to discuss here all the facets of life in Rome that could make its residents miserable and jeopardize their health and lives. We do not have time, for example, to examine how innumerable tiny inhabitants such as flies, fleas, mosquitos, bedbugs, tics, tape-, round-, and whipworms (just to mention a few!) bedeviled the nerves and flesh of Rome's human inhabitants and undermined their health. Those creatures could, among other things, spread disease, occasion infections and fevers, enervate their victims, and deprive them of rest and sleep. What follows below, then, is a brief examination of just a few aspects of life in Rome that made the place exasperating, exhausting, and downright dangerous.

Flood

A visitor to modern Rome gets no inkling of how frequent and terrible floods were for the ancient Romans. Huge embankments along the Tiber isolate today's city from the river and protect its inhabitants from floods. Indeed, the Tiber has little impact on the life of the city, other than funneling Rome's wearisome traffic onto the few bridges that link the two banks of the river. You can live your entire life in Rome without having any more contact with the Tiber than looking down upon it as you pass over one of those bridges or viewing it from the walls of the embankments, and some Romans do. Unfortunately for ancient Rome's residents, the embankments were not erected until the nineteenth century,[12] and their lives were inevitably intertwined with the river in largely disagreeable and occasionally deadly ways.

By 64 CE, the year of the Great Fire, the Tiber's water was polluted and undrinkable, but Rome's elaborate aqueduct system compensated for that deficiency. There was no remedy, however, for the frequent and often deadly floods the river inflicted on the city. Rome is famous for its "seven hills"—there is even a 1957 romantic movie titled *The Seven Hills of Rome*—but most of its life was conducted in the valleys, which weave among the hills. Rome's shops, markets, warehouses, meeting halls, and entertainment venues clustered in the valleys, where the vast majority of its inhabitants lived. When the Tiber overflowed its banks, those valleys would become, essentially, branches of the river. Some of the floods were nuisances, vexing yet endurable for those determined or compelled to live in the political and economic hub of their world. These floods would occasion economic losses—wares destroyed, food spoiled, shops closed, shipping delayed, productivity reduced—and impose inconveniences and discomforts on a population already challenged by day-to-day life in that frustrating city. Even these relatively minor floods could last for days, as would the stench from the mixing of the Tiber's contaminated waters with Rome's own filth.

Major floods could be catastrophic. Within the lifespan of some of those who experienced the Great Fire, three floods had been so vast and the waters so high that Rome's inhabitants needed boats to get around the city (5, 15, and 36 CE). Survivors of the Great Fire had to endure another major flood just five years later, when the city was not even close to putting the effects of the fire behind it. Rome's residents could expect to witness several floods in their lifetime, a couple of them most likely severe, and these floods could last as long as the nine days of the Great Fire. And when the waters finally receded, the aftermath of the flooding would prolong the misery.

The social and economic impact of the major floods could be immense. People would drown, as would some, perhaps many, of Rome's huge population of domesticated and commercial animals. (Six inches of quickly moving water suffice to knock a person over, and a mere couple of feet of water can carry off a car.)[13] Rome's people, dogs, cattle, and other beasts were overmatched, and indeed our sources tell us of floods so sudden and powerful that residents of Rome were swept off their feet and away to their deaths. Describing a flood of the late republic, Dio gave a harrowing précis of the impact:

> The Tiber . . . suddenly rose so high that it flooded all the valleys in the city and even overwhelmed much of Rome's heights. Indeed, the residences, which had been constructed of brick, got thoroughly soaked and collapsed, and all the draught animals drowned in the flood. As for the people . . . those who had not fled to the highest points were caught in their homes or on the roads and perished. Since the horror of the flooding lasted so many days, the houses that survived the flood itself became unsound and injured many people, some right away, but some later.[14]

People could be isolated—trapped, really—for days without food, potable water, support, or company. As is generally the case with disasters, but particularly in cities with extreme economic stratification such as ancient Rome, the poor suffered more than the rich. Although Roman neighborhoods were more mixed than those in most modern cities, by Nero's day the poor tended to live in those inundated valleys, and the rich on those famous hills or their slopes. In addition, the rich in their dry mansions would have the resources to wait out even the most catastrophic flooding reasonably comfortably, including inundations that lasted a week or more. The poor endured or perished.

We might expect Rome's vaunted sewer system to reduce the flooding and alleviate the suffering the floods brought, and it did in some instances and to some degree. Rome's sewers were, after all, intended and designed not to dispose of waste, but to lessen flooding. They were not really a sewer system, but rather a drainage system. Unfortunately, they were woefully inadequate to the job when the Tiber raged, and in the ongoing war between the Tiber and Rome's state-of-the-art (for its day) drainage system, the Tiber generally won the big battles. If the river rose high enough, the entire drainage system would flow back.

Other strategies to mitigate the danger and damage of floods, such as periodic raising of the ground level in the flood plain, may have helped, but only somewhat. The flooding of Rome remained a fact of life throughout antiquity and beyond, until the embankments were finally erected on the Tiber in the nineteenth century.

Could the ancient Romans have built embankments comparable to those today? This book is not an exercise in counterfactual history, and we cannot know for certain, but the people who erected the Colosseum, the Pantheon, the empire's vast aqueduct systems, and ports out of whole cloth could have done so, I believe, had they decided to put their determination, ingenuity, and resources to the project. The ancient biographer Plutarch (before 50–after 120 CE) tells us that Julius Caesar had planned to divert the Tiber below Rome into a navigable channel to allow oceangoing ships to reach Rome, and to build grand breakwaters along the Italian coast near Rome. Controlling the river and sealing off bodies of water was not out of the question for a man of Caesar's ambition and power.[15] His assassination, however, terminated those plans. There is also some archaeological evidence that the Romans may have planned to create some sort of embankment, although these remains likely had more to do with upgrading the port. In any event, if this construction reflected an intention to address flooding, nothing came of it.[16] That the cost of such an embankment would have been considerable and that the project would have been challenging and disruptive were certainly obstacles, but a more significant impediment to taming the Tiber, I would suggest, was the Romans' worldview.[17]

The Romans felt they should mitigate the impact of floods and other disasters, if possible, but they considered disasters an unavoidable part of life, intrinsic to it, and only a fool would think it possible to eliminate them entirely. Just as the average Roman in the street expected to endure discomfort, risk, and quite possibly calamity, so did Rome's leaders. Most of those leaders, of course, lived on the slopes and summits of Rome's hills, frequently high enough that their *domus* were dry when the rest of city was inundated. Inadequate half measures therefore made sense. The authorities also seemed more focused on mitigating than preventing the damage. Nor would addressing the floods give Rome's leadership the most bang for their public-project buck. Grand enterprises should enrich life in Rome and the city's appearance, but from the aristocrats' and emperors' points of view, such projects should above all redound to their sponsors' glory, prestige, and honor. Every time Romans attended games in the Colosseum—or even walked past or spied the building from a distance—they were reminded of Vespasian's and Titus's lavish benefaction.[18] People do not feel gratitude for every day that passes without a flood. When floods do not occur, people tend to forget that they happen and forget those who have taken measures to mitigate the risk. Besides, as the impact and memory of a disaster fade, communities become less likely to invest in preventing the next one, as we see only too well in today's world.[19]

Collapsing Buildings

Many prosperous and technologically sophisticated modern cities are subject to fire and flood, though with nothing comparable to Rome's vulnerability. Residents of these cities, even the poorest, however, generally do not need to worry that their apartment buildings might collapse. Ancient Romans did, and with good reason.

As improbable as ongoing building collapses may seem to us, the ancient evidence leaves little doubt that this was a constant threat in Rome. The geographer Strabo, writing some time at the end of the first century BCE or the first decades of the first CE, observed that "construction goes on unceasingly, because there are so many building collapses and fires and so much selling and reselling."[20] Even more telling, and startling, is the historian Livy's description of the pack animals of Rome's great Carthaginian adversary Hannibal tumbling down mountain cliffs: "Since the path was narrow with steep precipices on both sides, the crammed column pushed many off into the abyss, some armed soldiers among them. And the pack animals with their loads tumbled down just like collapsing buildings."[21] Since Livy reasonably did not expect many of his readers to have seen animals falling off mountain cliffs, he needed a comparison familiar to them so that they could imagine what it was like. What he came up with, of all things, was buildings collapsing, precisely because he could assume that his Roman readers, at least, were well aware of and very likely had seen buildings fall.

Floods and fires caused a great many buildings to collapse. We do not know how many Romans perished when their buildings collapsed in Rome's many fires, but their number must have been significant. In addition to the dangers of fire and smoke was the horrifying prospect of being buried in the smoldering rubble of your home. Floods might have been even more pernicious because, by weakening the foundations and lower levels of buildings, they allowed some collapses to occur days, weeks, or even months after the event—that is, after the inhabitants had moved back in, lulled into a false sense of security. Water has been a great enemy of buildings since humankind started constructing them, and it can be patient.

One reason for these frequent collapses should not surprise: money. To save when constructing buildings, some property owners would cut as many corners as possible, by employing cheap materials, employing cheap and possibly poorly skilled labor, and rushing the construction. The most notorious and devastating example of this occurred in 27 CE in Fidenae, a town only a few miles from Rome. A certain Atilius cut corners in the construction of the foundation and superstructure of an amphitheater. The building collapsed, taking the lives of tens of thousands who had shown up to see gladiatorial fights.[22] On top of such iffy construction practices, apartment owners tried to jam as many floors and thus people into their apartment houses as possible, even if the numbers of both exceeded the structural capacity of the building. In one of his short poems, Martial advised a certain Maximus that true freedom entails accepting a humble life free of luxury. This life includes an apartment with a ceiling so low that Maximus would not be able to stand up straight in it.[23] Rome's overcrowding meant that there would always be someone game to rent just about any room in just about any building. The satirist Juvenal, in the late first- or early second-century CE, suggested that Romans could buy a nifty house in any small town for the equivalent of a year's rent for "some gloomy apartment" in Rome itself.[24]

The overcrowding led to laws prohibiting landlords from demolishing their buildings, however much a landlord might want to replace an apartment house with a larger and more upscale one and thereby increase revenues (at least emperors recognized that Rome's poor and struggling needed some place to live). One appalling way to get around this prohibition was for owners to allow their property to decay to the point of collapse; then they could rebuild as they wished. Of course, people were living in those dilapidated buildings landlords were strategizing to bring down. There is not a hint in our sources that Roman property owners felt any responsibility for their tenants. Juvenal complained of Roman landlords' indifference to their tenants' safety: "Who fears, or ever feared, the collapse of his house in cool Praeneste, or rural Gabii, or Tivoli perched on its hillside, or Volsinii, nestling amid its woodland ridges? But here in Rome we inhabit a city largely shored up with gimcrack stays and props: that's how our landlords postpone slippage, and—after masking great cracks in the ancient fabric—assure the tenants they can sleep sound, when the house is tottering."[25] It is worth noting, too, that Juvenal here indicated that this collapsing is specific to Rome. The great republican politician and sometime philosopher Cicero, surely one of ancient Rome's most humane denizens, in a letter expressed delight at the prospect that the collapse of some of his urban properties could result in profit. Not a word of concern about the inhabitants of those properties.[26] Rome's elite frowned on downright cruelty to the lower orders, but otherwise they were largely indifferent to the fate of those below them, certainly more indifferent than they were to the prospect of profit. This attitude made perfect sense for people who despised Rome's common folk, as Cicero and his ilk tended to do. In letters to his best friend, Atticus, Cicero referred to Rome's lower classes as "dregs of the city" (*sentinam*; literally, "bilge water"!) and "that horrible and voracious rabble, a mob of leeches draining the treasury." Cicero's contempt was not restricted to Rome's many underemployed and struggling residents, "takers" in some modern political parlance that Cicero would agree with. In one of his speeches, he included artisans and shopkeepers—that is, small business people—among the urban dregs.[27]

In response to the interminable collapse of buildings, Augustus limited the height of construction to 70 Roman feet (slightly smaller than the modern foot). Nero reduced that height limit as well, and in the early second century the emperor Trajan lowered the height limit to 60 feet.[28] This might have helped, but some landlords squeezed more floors into shorter buildings by lowering the ceilings and perhaps installing too many floors for the buildings to carry safely, whatever the buildings' height. Also, it is unclear how rigidly the restrictions were enforced. In Rome, as in many places, the gap between law and intention, on one side, and practice and reality, on the other, could be considerable.

Crime

Once night fell, Rome was the Wild West. Muggers prowled the streets looking for victims, and they would resort to lethal force if necessary or even if merely so inclined. Such violence made cold-hearted sense. Romans often wore money belts below their clothes, and jewelry tended to be wound around people's throats and fingers. Thieves would instantly—which meant, violently—incapacitate their victims and then rip or cut off their valuables. The Roman version of bars stayed open late, and the drunks the taverns produced occasionally attacked those they encountered.[29] Sometimes groups of young men, due to their numbers or status, felt themselves entitled to harass, beat, and rob Rome's other residents. When charioteers prowled about without a care making life miserable and unsafe for Rome's other residents, for example, Nero had to put a stop to their lawlessness.[30]

Occasionally even members of the aristocracy added to the street violence the common robbers and brawlers perpetrated. Just as some British aristocrats of the eighteenth and nineteenth centuries had a taste for dissolution, street mayhem, and danger, so did their ancient Roman equivalents. Cruel and transgressive thrills were to be found aplenty at night in Rome's murky and wine-soaked streets. Most notoriously, Nero, while emperor, supposedly enjoyed donning a disguise, heading out into the streets of Rome under cover of darkness, and attacking people returning from dinner parties. If the victims refused to endure a beating, he would stab them and then dump their bodies down the sewers to be washed into the Tiber and out to sea. Risky behavior on his part—and indeed, on one such jaunt a senator whose wife he had assaulted wound up beating him severely—but that was the point. Still, after the incident with the senator, Nero did what all sensible Romans of means did at night—he brought along bodyguards.[31] Unfortunately, the poor and middling classes did not have the resources to bring an entourage along when they left their homes. If at all possible, the best nocturnal policy for residents of Rome was to stay at home, although, as is true today, that was not always possible.

Nor was any person physically safe by day, even in Rome's teeming streets. The agricultural writer Varro (116–27 BCE) tells us of a man fatally knifed in a crowd. As the perpetrator melted into the throng, he was heard exclaiming that he had assassinated the wrong man. Varro was not surprised that such a tragedy occurred in Rome.[32] Meanwhile, pickpockets, cutpurses, and other sorts of thieves were operating in Rome's busy streets. Romans had to be alert at all times.

Romans might seek security at home, but they were not entirely safe there, either. A contemporary of Augustus, Dionysius of Halicarnassus, complained of slaves becoming wealthy through robbery and housebreaking,[33] and Martial warned that thieves break into money boxes, the closest thing many Romans had to a safe.[34] Even the poor, who had little worth stealing, were not immune. The Elder Pliny reported that window flower/garden boxes, a bit of country and consolation to those living in urban poverty, had largely disappeared as residents felt forced to shut and bar their windows because of an unnerving and "savage" wave of break-ins.[35] Locked and barred doors, guards, and guard dogs—the usual defenses against burglars—might keep out strangers, but if our sources are to be trusted, acquaintances, associates, and even relatives were also a danger.

Apparently, Romans poisoned each other at an alarming rate, particularly those of property. Poisoning was not confined to the city of Rome, of course, but just as Rome seemed to have the best and most of everything else, it had the best and most poisoners. In the big city, poisoning was even a profession of sorts—Nero assigned students to his favorite poisoner, Lucusta, for some expert training.[36] The champion poisoner of ancient Rome, however, may have been Nonius Asprenas, a friend of Augustus who was accused of poisoning 130 (!) dinner guests.[37] He was acquitted, which may have had something to do with the fact that Augustus attended the trial.[38] There may have been many, many more poisonings than we know about, because the Romans did not have the medical knowledge to detect poison with certainty. But there may have been far fewer than our sources report. Rome's rumor mill was quick to suspect poisoning when someone died suddenly or unexpectedly, especially when someone else stood to profit from that death. Some of those poor souls probably died of an undiagnosed disease or condition, or from food poisoning, which was a persistent threat.

One might wonder what the police and the district attorney's office were up to while all this mayhem transpired. Couldn't they have done something to diminish Rome's perpetual crime wave? The answer may astonish the modern city dweller: they did not exist. Rome's criminal justice system was largely do-it-yourself. The emperor would go after groups he deemed dangerous or disruptive and have them suppressed, arrested, or banished—like Nero with the charioteers—but emperors and their agents had little to do with conventional crime, even of the violent sort (murder, rape, assault, robbery), unless it involved some important member of the aristocracy or of the political bureaucracy. As for everyone else—good luck! Rome's firefighters, the *vigiles*, were empowered and expected to address crime, if they came across any on their patrols, and the emperor would employ them and other forces to restore public order if he thought it needed, but that was the extent of these quasi-military units' involvement in fighting crime.

Emperors might take steps to reduce crime under special circumstances. Augustus, for example, posted guards around the city during his most splendid shows and spectacles, since the streets would otherwise be largely deserted and left to hooligans and their depredations.[39] Augustus's principal concern, however, was most likely not the public's security, even though he was particularly obsessed with public order and control. Rather, he wanted to ensure that as many people as possible would attend and enjoy his shows with peace of mind and that the city would be on its very best behavior during these events—that is, that the shows would be great successes and remembered as such. Once these shows had ended, the guards went back to their barracks, and life on the streets of Rome returned to its normal unease.[40] Tacitus's characterization of Augustus's motives in establishing an official to oversee law and order in Rome typifies the authorities' attitude: "Soon after he took control of the state, because of the size of the population and the sluggishness of the legal system, he appointed a former consul to control the slaves and that segment of society that is prone to reckless violence unless it fears violent consequences."[41] (Those dregs again.) Suppress turbulence in the streets (the unruly, riotous poor) and threats to the Roman order (slaves inclined to rebellion)? Yes. Pursue muggers, thieves, and even rapists and murderers? No.

There was no 911 to call, no governmental agency or office to investigate crimes once they were committed, and no district attorney to prosecute criminals. If you were being attacked, you needed to call your neighbors for help and hope they would respond; if persons unknown had murdered a relative of yours or robbed your home, you had to figure out who it was, and if you discovered the culprit, you or someone close to you had to prosecute the villain. As one would expect, this system, if system it was, was ineffective in preventing, solving, and prosecuting crime, and it was ripe for abuse.[42] As was true for pretty much every problem in ancient Rome—and, one might venture to say, everywhere in every time—wealthy victims were much more likely to gain satisfaction. They had the connections to access first-rate legal guidance, the resources to drag the culprit to court, and the credibility to convince the jury or the presiding magistrate, invariably members of Rome's elite, who very likely looked at the lower orders much as Cicero did.[43]

Pollution

Rome had too many people packed too closely, and it lacked the modern technologies that today, in some cases at least, mitigate the effects of overcrowding and congestion. The resulting pollution assailed just about every organ and sense in the body. A few examples follow.

Ears

The city's racket was inescapable. As in most Mediterranean communities, by day people lived their lives outside their homes, where they brought along their arguments, laughter, pleas, cries, and insults. Rome was an aggressively social city, and most of that socializing took place in the open. Shop owners tended to push their businesses out onto the sidewalks and even the streets—butchers, cooks, you name it—and other entrepreneurs would be roaming about hawking their wares. Even barbers would ply their craft on the sidewalks as crowds jostled by—suggesting a more immediate danger to the ears.[44] Amidst such mobs and such competition, sellers would need to tout their goods and services loudly. The rich, with their litters and entourages, would push their way through the crowds, increasing the crush and the noise; one must imagine frequent shouts of "Get the hell out of the way," "Who the hell do you think you are?," and "Damn it all! That's my foot you're crushing." Adding to the din would be the philosophers, poets, and pundits of all sorts enlightening the passing public. Martial bemoaned, "There's no place in this city where a poor man can think or rest—mornings, teachers and their classes rob your life; at night, it's the millers and bakers; and round the clock, the hammering of the bronze-smiths."[45] Major construction projects, like those after the Great Fire, could go on for years, and there is no indication that workers made any effort to abate the racket. Those who lived in urban mansions might be buffered somewhat from the din of the liveliest and noisiest city of antiquity, but the vast majority of Romans living in cramped apartments just had to endure it.

Even worse, you might live near an establishment that generated a great deal of noise. Seneca complained of living above a bathhouse and hearing absolutely everything that transpired below:

> All sorts of racket hem me in from every direction. I live above a private bath . . . as they exercise, the body-builders toss their lead weights around . . . I hear groans, and whenever they hold their breath they let it out with hissing and rasping gasps. When the sounds of some unathletic sort of guy, content with a cheap massage, come my way, it's the slapping of hands on his shoulder that I hear . . . If on top of that some ballplayer starts counting his score, well, I've had it. Imagine, too, some guy itching for a fight . . . and another who likes to sing in the bath . . . Now add to these guys the hair-plucker with a high and shrill voice that he noisily employs to draw attention to himself, jabbering nonstop and never shutting up,

other than when he's plucking someone's armpit and so making his victim do the shouting for him. And now the cacophonous and varied cries of folks hawking sausages, pastries, and drinks.[46]

It is evident that Seneca's apartment had little in the way of soundproofing, and neither did anyone else's.

Night was little better. In much of the city too many people were jammed into too small apartments. If the family of four living in the tiny apartment above you was up arguing, if their toddler was crying, if members of the family arose to go to the bathroom many times in the night (very likely a common occurrence, as the section on disease suggests), you were part of it. Your neighbors could overhear what *you* were up to as well. It was a life with no privacy.

Just as bad was the racket on the street. Most shops were closed at night, and most sensible people were in their homes, but robbers and drunks, sometimes in groups, could be rambling about the city streets with little consideration of others' need to sleep. Worse yet, the streets of Rome had become so impossibly crowded that Julius Caesar allowed most wagons to enter the city only shortly before dusk, and they had to be out of town before dawn. That meant that the provisioning of about one million inhabitants started at dusk and lasted through the night. There is no evidence, moreover, that the drivers, loaders, and unloaders of all those vehicles gave a fig about keeping the noise down, just like modern roofers and other repair people, for example, who show up for work at 6:30 or 7 a.m. The hammering, yelling, and radios turned to '80s rock commence immediately. In ancient Rome, though, the racket could go all night.[47]

Rome's many festivals exacerbated the overcrowding and increased the din. Tourists and revelers would pour into town to attend the spectacles. Chariot racing, animal fights, gladiatorial combat, and dramatic performances were among the attractions. Julius Caesar's first-century BCE spectacles assaulted more than the senses: "So huge a crowd from all over poured into the city to see all these shows that lots of the visitors had to stay in tents pitched along the streets and roads. Quite a few people were often crushed to death by the crowd." Even Rome's elite were not safe: "Among the victims were two senators."[48] Once emperors took command of these festivals—Caesar was dictator, not an emperor, though he in some respects functioned as a model for emperors—they grew even bigger and more sensational. The din and possible danger of festival crowds would only grow, although emperors, as we have seen, could exert some control over the streets.

Nose

Rome stank.

The city's methods of waste disposal were the major culprit. As we have seen, Rome's sewers were designed primarily to drain water. Some filth would be washed away with that water, but not all. Most residences did not have bathrooms, let alone toilets that connected to the sewers, and so most people relieved themselves into chamber pots. When the pot threatened to overflow or its stench became intolerable, the standard strategy was to toss the muck out the window—a strategy that also made perfect sense. You live, say, on the fourth floor of some ramshackle apartment house, and you are already sleep deprived because of all the racket coming from the streets and from neighbors living above, below, and next to you. The reek from the chamber pot is so strong that it, too, is contributing to making sleep impossible. What is the likelihood you will carry the disgusting sloshing pot down three flights of stairs, trudge to a public toilet or ditch designated for excrement, deposit your filth there, walk back to your building with the dripping vessel, and then drag your exhausted self back up the three flights of stairs, all in the middle of the night? Not to mention the fact that only a fool would go out on the streets of Rome after dark alone. Unsurprisingly, this mode of waste disposal created hazards for those walking below, including the occasional pot that would come flying along with the excrement. Juvenal reported: "Consider . . . how often leaking, broken pots come hurtling down from windows above, how loudly and heavily they crash and damage the sidewalk. You'd be considered a chump, someone incapable of taking precautions against accidents, if you go out to dinner without making a will . . . so, you'd best hope and pray, you unfortunate wretch, that the women of Rome are satisfied with dumping just the contents of their pots on you."[49]

Tons of human waste wound up in the street, as did the waste of Rome's abundant four-legged inhabitants and of the pack and draught animals that brought supplies to the city at night.[50] A downpour might wash some of it away, but a light rain would mix it with the other filth and dirt in the street to produce a disgusting gunk (fig. 1). Juvenal complained of his legs (not just feet!) being covered with mud,[51] mud consisting of a good deal more than just soil and water. Still, for much of the year Rome has very little rain. At those times, the waste would wind up as part of an insalubrious dust, kicked up by the city's innumerable pedestrians and wagons, and winding up in Romans' eyes, throats, and worse—some of this dust would find its way into the city's open fountains

Pompei - Nuovi Scavi - Via dell' Abbondanza - Prospetti di case con balconi e tettoie

Figure 1. Pompeii street image on an Italian postcard, circa 1920–23, featuring stepping stones. Such stepping stones enabled Roman pedestrians to avoid stepping in the filthy streets, which in Rome were often flooded as well. Courtesy of Wikimedia

and into the food being prepared right by or even on the sidewalk. And, of course, Romans had to breathe air contaminated with that dust.

Rome's residents were not quite drowning in feces and urine. The Romans did take some sensible and even clever steps to remove or segregate at least a portion of the muck. Jars were placed around town for pedestrians to urinate into; fullers then fetched the jars and used the urine to process and bleach wool. Ditches were dug here and there for pedestrians to defecate into; *stercorarii* (excrement haulers) picked up and brought the excrement to the countryside to fertilize the land. The Romans also positioned rather elegant bathrooms here and there around the city, and the ones in the public bathhouses were available to pedestrians when they were open. It all sounds rather modern, but it was also woefully inadequate. In the fourth century CE, the public latrines numbered a mere 144 in that immense city, and that is likely more latrines than Rome had in our period. Moreover, residences with toilets were few and far between, and the public toilets, jars, and ditches would have been of little use to people at home in their apartments. For all of ancient Rome's wealth and sophistication, chamber pots and windows remained the reigning waste disposal technology in the city. Officials were charged with seeing to the removal of the layers of filth that covered Rome's streets, but our sources suggest that their success was uneven. The emperor Caligula (37–41 CE) humiliated the future emperor Vespasian by having soldiers pile muck from the street in the folds of his toga, because he had been neglecting his duty to remove it.[52] Vespasian may have indeed neglected his duty, but keeping Rome's streets clean and clear was a formidable challenge—new layers of filth were added daily. We are also most likely talking about periodic efforts merely to keep conditions from getting too out of control, which they at times nonetheless did.[53]

One last enemy of the nose deserves mention. The prominence of Roman bathhouses and the ubiquity of perfumes might suggest a world of fragrant cleanliness. But many if not most residents of Rome would not be able to make it to a bathhouse every day, even in summer when Rome is a hot, sweaty city, and baths in homes were exceedingly rare in the metropolis. Clothes were not washed with the frequency of clothes today, either. After bathing, a lower-class Roman with only one or two outfits very likely put on the same grimy, smelly clothes she or he had worn to the bathhouse. The liberal use of perfume (among those who could afford it) is more an indication of how strong the body odors were that the fragrances were meant to mask than evidence of a sweet-scented society. There was no real remedy for body odor, and even Nero, a fan of fragrances, could not escape a reputation for malodorousness.[54]

And so, the odor of sweat, urine, and ordure must have been unavoidable at all times and overpowering at some. Moreover, the exposed and often festering waste created an environment hazardous to the general health of Rome's residents. The stink itself might not kill you, but its sources could.

Lungs

Rome may have been a preindustrial city, but its inhabitants found their own ways to generate air pollution. Romans cooked on open fires, used open fires to heat their abodes (though most people did without), and heated their vast public bathhouses and the numerous smaller private ones with smoke-spewing furnaces.[55] Rome's constant outbreaks of building fires added to the smoke. The most significant ones, like the Great Fire, exacerbated the pollution considerably. And, of course, the city's significant population of livestock supplemented the smog with their methane gas emissions. The tendency of pollution to linger in Rome's air aggravated the situation, as it can today. Anyone who has lived in Rome for a period has experienced how modern pollution can sit over the city for days on end. The lower-lying areas in particular, where most ancient

Romans lived, can feel like troughs of stagnant, unwholesome air. Ancient Rome was no different.[56] It is no surprise that the poet Horace advised turning one's back on Rome's "smoke and wealth and racket," just after mentioning the city's "harsh clouds."[57] Like today, all that smog irritated the eyes and throat, but it is even more alarming that Rome's residents had no choice but to inhale the noxious air and so draw toxic particulates into their lungs.

Stomach

Rome's educated and prosperous classes were obsessed with food, and their writings are full of (often censorious) descriptions of outlandish dishes. Suetonius related the ingredients of one of the emperor Vitellius's favorites: pikes' livers, the brains of both pheasants and peacocks, flamingo tongues, the sperm of lampreys (and doubtless a few other choice ingredients), which he had brought to Rome from the corners of the empire.[58] Only those few at the peak of Rome's economic pyramid experienced sumptuous banquets and such gastronomic novelties, however, and our sources suggest that some of Rome's elite actually preferred a simpler and, they felt, healthier diet. Most Romans, in any event, had more basic concerns when it came to filling their bellies—acquiring healthy food and enough of it.

Rome had an unprecedentedly complex and comprehensive system to supply its residents with food. This provisioning was as essential as the water supply to making a preindustrial city of Rome's scale possible. Still, the system was vulnerable to a degree it is difficult for inhabitants of prosperous modern cities to imagine. The staples were mostly imported from the rest of Italy and from overseas, and though Roman literature is full of wisdom concerning farming, the scientific and technological revolution that enables first-world modern agriculture to produce vast amounts of food and to weather adversity relatively easily was centuries away. Disasters both natural (such as drought and blight) and human made (such as war and even pirates) could imperil shipping, and fires and floods could destroy what the authorities had stored up in the city. Periodic food shortages and the attendant empty stomachs were simply a part of life, as were the soaring food prices and even the occasional rioting that came with them. Hungry crowds, and even those just apprehensive about the security of the food supply, could take desperate action: "When unremitting droughts had caused the grain supply to shrink, a mob stopped the Emperor Claudius right in the middle of the forum and showered him with insults and bits and pieces of bread so vehemently that he barely escaped to the palace by a back door." In this case, according to Suetonius, accosting the emperor worked. Claudius responded by doing everything possible to guarantee the importation of sufficient quantities of grain, even in winter, by insuring transport ships and offering bonuses for the construction of new ones.[59]

Wealthy Romans who imported foreign delicacies and kept private fish ponds to supply their dinner tables, such as the infamous Vedius Pollio, a friend of Augustus who condemned misbehaving slaves to be devoured by the lampreys in one such pond,[60] were of course immune to the rising prices. Locked in their townhouses, they could also avoid the food riots. Rome's lower and middling classes were not so fortunate. Even in times of plenty, some Romans would struggle to put enough food on the table. Many poor Romans counted on seasonal or occasional work, such as harvesting crops in the vicinity of the city, unloading cargo ships (sailing came to a virtual standstill in winter, at least for those with any sense or choice—Claudius's insurance was an exception), and laboring on Rome's massive government building projects, all of which would eventually end. The good times came and went. Rome's famous grain subsidies and giveaways might help some get through the lean times, but only adult male citizens could claim the food.[61] What of Rome's women and children, and the many foreigners, slaves, and other ineligibles who resided in that cosmopolitan city? Nor does grain put a roof over your head or clothes on your back. In all cultures, one of the simplest and most obvious ways to cut corners when times are tough is to eat less. Hard on all who must take that dire step, but particularly damaging to children.

Even in times of plenty, Romans' diet presented two dangers to their health: a lack of balance, and the danger of spoiled, adulterated, or otherwise contaminated food. Grain and bread were the cornerstones of the Roman diet, particularly in the city. The government dole consisted of grain, which is much less prone to spoilage than fruit and vegetables. When Rome's residents panicked about the food supply and the prospect of shortages, the concern was almost invariably about the availability of grain. Vegetables and fruit might provide nutritional variety (and flavor), but for most Romans in nothing like the quantities a healthy balance would require. The result was widespread malnourishment.[62]

Roman officials closely monitored the weights and measures employed in the city's many public markets, and so crafty Roman merchants, always with an eye to an edge, would adulterate grain (again, the Romans' staple). Modern refrigeration did not exist, and neither did modern notions of food hygiene. Spoilage and contamination were endemic to Rome's food supply. Nor would

Rome's urban folk really know where much of their food had come from; there were no labels indicating ingredients or place and date of origin. Cicero complained that at a banquet he wisely avoided the oysters and lampreys, but was bushwhacked by a beet.[63] Ten days marked by diarrhea, vomiting, and intestinal pain ensued. Martial told us of the regifting of a sausage,[64] again, in a world without refrigeration. He was joking, we hope, but how often would people actually receive or purchase food well past its "expiration" date?[65]

Disease

Rome, then: city of a million or so anxious, sleep-deprived, under- or malnourished residents squeezed into a filthy petri dish of an environment prepped to breed every sort of nasty microbe imaginable, and walking, flying, and swimming creatures well-suited to make sure the microbes had their run of the place. A full list of the ailments and diseases Romans were subject to would take pages: a smorgasbord of pulmonary and intestinal ailments, typhoid fever, rickets, hepatitis, meningitis, malaria, just to name a few.[66] The great second-century CE doctor and medical writer Galen was impressed that Rome seemed to offer doctors an unending supply of patients suffering from jaundice and edema to treat and study.[67] One can only imagine the number of Romans suffering from diarrhea at any given moment—and in answering the call that cannot be refused, keeping their families and neighbors up many a night.

Although our sources are inconsistent in reporting them, epidemics were common in ancient Rome. As Walter Scheidel put it, "the size, density, and connectedness of the city must have invited microbial onslaughts."[68] Onslaughts indeed. Suetonius reported that in 65 CE, the year after the Great Fire, thirty thousand Romans died of plague. Another epidemic followed around fifteen years later, which Jerome (c. 347–420 CE) asserted killed some ten thousand people a day.[69] Rome's constant flooding increased the likelihood of disease and epidemics. Combine the Tiber's polluted waters with the muck of Rome's filthy streets, allow it all to stew for days, as was often the case with Roman floods, and then administer to an overcrowded, unhealthy, weary population, and you have a perfect brew for all sorts of maladies.[70]

The young and the old were particularly vulnerable to Rome's vast array of diseases. Infant mortality was woefully high. The most famous instance of this was the offspring of Cornelia, daughter of Scipio Africanus (Hannibal's conqueror) and the mother of two of the Roman Republic's greatest rabble-rousers, Tiberius and Gaius Gracchus. She gave birth twelve times, but only three of her children made it to adulthood. Since our source did not tell us what killed the nine who did not survive, we cannot with complete certainty attribute their deaths to some malady or disease, but illness surely took some if not all of them.[71]

Disease was not the only medical peril Romans were subject to. The rough-and-tumble city offered its inhabitants innumerable opportunities to suffer wounds, contusions, and broken and sprained limbs. Overcrowded streets, ramshackle buildings, endemic crime, ongoing and mostly unregulated building projects, among other aspects of life in the city, made Rome a cornucopia of injury. It is understandable that Galen was impressed with the considerable variety of types of dislocation the city offered—a boon to his medical experience and his writings.[72]

The Romans devoted plenty of attention to the preservation and restoration of health, but to limited effect. There was no certification for doctors. Any glib con man could go into the medical business, and many did. Most people could not afford doctors anyway and had to rely on folk medicine and superstition, just as their ancestors had done. Some examples. Writing in the first century CE, Pliny the Elder reported that for joint pain some folks thought goat dung boiled in vinegar with a bit of honey does the trick, but boar's dung is the way to go for contusions and spasms. Some advocated an alternative delivery system to treat internal damage and the like: powdered dung ingested with vinegar. He added that Nero enjoyed this cocktail when at the chariot races, though he preferred a version mixing dung ash with water—a kind of sports drink, apparently.[73]

Pliny also provided an example of folk birth control: "There is a third species of spider . . . known as the 'wooly spider.' They say it has a huge head that has two tiny worms in it, when you cut it open. When the worms are tied to a woman with a ribbon of deer hide before sunset, the woman will not be able to get pregnant, according to Caecilius in his commentary. The effect lasts for a year."[74] It is safe to say that the only chance this contraceptive had of working would have been in scaring off potential sexual partners. Some herbs used to mitigate pain might have been effective, but just as common were bizarre and futile prescriptions, such as these two methods of addressing toothache that Pliny recommended: (1) catch a spider with your left hand (not the right!), squish it up in rose oil, then pour the concoction into the ear closest to the pain; (2) wrap raven's dung in wool and wear it as an amulet.[75]

The fatal flaw in the Romans' response to illness, however, was their complete ignorance of microorganisms. Bacteria and viruses were unknown and would remain so for well over a millennium. The ancients did try to come up with rational explanations for sickness. The theory of the four humors, to give just one example, posited that health depends on the balance of four fluids in the human body—phlegm, blood, black bile, and yellow bile—or of the body's four essential components—hot, cold, dry, and wet. No superstition here, and the reasoning makes a great deal of sense, if one thinks about it. For one thing, some ancient doctors, like their modern counterparts, recognized that balance and moderation in life enhance health and so advised their patients to eat and sleep well, exercise, and avoid too much alcohol—sound advice one hears in doctors' offices today. Unless doctors understand the extent to which microbial creatures cause illness and disease, however, they will be helpless when confronting most bacterial and viral infections and clueless as to how to check their spread. Ancient doctors did not even know such creatures exist, and had any theorized that tiny, tiny living beings, invisible and imperceptible to us, caused diseases, they most likely would have been considered fantasists and quacks.

It is no surprise, then, that some—perhaps many—Romans considered much of the medical profession (if that term can be applied) downright dangerous. The poet Martial employed a bit of gallows humor: "Recently, Diaulus was a doctor; now he's an undertaker. What he's doing as an undertaker is no different from what he used to do as a doctor."[76]

Fire

And, of course, there was fire.

The Rome of the Great Fire was a city of wood. That might surprise us, since when we visit the city today its ancient remains are mostly brick and stone—often lovely marbles brought to Rome from throughout the Mediterranean. But a great deal of the city's domestic architecture was wooden, and even buildings that largely consisted of more fire-resistant materials had beams and other structural elements of wood, and the furniture and accouterments within all buildings tended to be largely of wood.[77] Wool, grain, oil, and human and animal excrement were just a few of the other flammable materials ubiquitous in the city. The fact that Romans cooked and heated with open flames and that their standard mode of lighting was oil-filled lamps, which could easily tip and spill or fall and break, meant that there were abundant opportunities for fires to start, spread, and feed on all those flammable materials. A mere splash could spell doom for your *insula* (fig. 2). We have

Figure 2. Roman oil lamp. Such clay lamps were ubiquitous in Rome and the principal source of nighttime light for most inhabitants. Oil was poured into one hole to feed the wick that protruded from the other hole. Unfortunately, the design allowed for easy spillage, and the material allowed for easy breakage. These lamps posed a considerable risk of fire. Castor and Pollux (Dioscuri), terracotta Roman oil lamp, 1st century AD, Staatliche Antikensammlungen, Munich; photo by Carole Raddato; courtesy of Wikimedia Commons

no statistics, but it is likely that there were small fires in Rome every day and that these fires at times grew into middling or even sizeable fires. The layout of the city, moreover, exacerbated the situation considerably, as we shall see in this text's account of the Great Fire. We might, therefore, expect the city to dedicate a considerable portion of its resources to preventing and fighting fire.

When Rome was still a Republic, however, it had no fire department. This may strike us as astonishing. In the first century BCE, the last century of republican government, the city was already immense by ancient standards, extremely overcrowded, and subject to constant and occasionally significant fires. The Greek biographer Plutarch's explanation for how the wealthiest man in Rome at that time, Crassus, acquired much of his vast fortune shows how wild and frightening the situation was. Crassus or his agents would on the spot purchase buildings that were still ablaze and the buildings abutting the flaming structure at a fraction of the buildings' worth. Once the deal had been concluded, Crassus's personal fire brigade would step in and seek to halt the damage. One can imagine the opening conversation.

Crassus (or agent): I'd like to buy your apartment house for 50,000, but we have to seal the deal immediately.
Desperate and Outraged Owner: But the building is worth at least 100,000!
Crassus (or agent): Well, it was twenty minutes ago, and now that I think of it, the damage the building has suffered while you have dallied has reduced the offer to 45,000.
Desperate and Flustered Owner: But . . .
Crassus (or agent): 40,000 now . . .
Desperate and Defeated Owner: OK, OK! At least I'll be able to salvage something from this disaster.

Crassus's men would then extinguish the fire. Or, perhaps, even more devilish, let it blaze a bit to allow the impending fate—and plummeting worth—of the abutting properties sink in with *their* owners. Once the fire was out, Crassus would set to salvaging what could be salvaged, renovating what could be renovated, and building anew where financially advantageous. He had purchased five hundred slaves who were trained builders and architects precisely for this operation, whose scale was immense.[78] Plutarch's account furnishes us with several things worth noting. First, Crassus was ruthless in the face of fellow Romans' losses—a reminder of how little Rome's aristocrats cared about anyone else when an opportunity for profit presented itself. Next, he was doing this in the open, and it was perfectly legal. Third, the scale of the operation and the fortune he derived from it suggests the shocking frequency of fires in Rome; indeed, Plutarch attributed Crassus's ability to amass a fortune this way to the inevitability of fires and collapses in Rome's landscape. Last, and most startling, is the absence of what we would recognize as a municipal fire department or some other sort of public entity to address fires in Rome.[79]

After a day in 6 CE when several serious fires had broken out in the city, Augustus established Rome's first municipal fire department. What had changed, really, was not that fire had suddenly become a greater problem, but that Rome now had a new form of government. Politics in the Roman Republic was like a grand and nasty game of Monopoly, which, like many games of Monopoly, went on for centuries as Rome's politicians jostled for power and prestige. A standing department of burly firefighters equipped with axes, the contestants feared, might become a dangerous tool in the hands of the magistrate/competitor who at the moment controlled it. Starting towards the end of the second century BCE, the competition among Rome's politicians intensified, and the contestants became increasingly ambitious, ruthless, and violent, until Augustus, whose ambition, ruthlessness, and violence were second to no one's, had taken the whole board. All the key properties—military, fiscal, religious, architectural, and even psychological—were now under his control. Game over. Since Augustus wound up with unprecedented control over Rome, he could afford to address the scourge of urban fires without fear of undermining his own position—the priority of Roman politicians in every era, and, alas, one could argue, of politicians in every culture. In fact, being under the emperor's control, the firefighters could be called upon to address unrest in the city, thereby contributing to the city's—and the emperor's—security. Political change, then, made the establishment of a fire department acceptable. Augustus dubbed the firefighters *vigiles* (the awake ones, the watchmen), and their chief, *praefectus vigilum* (Director of the Watchmen).[80]

We might be surprised that the title *vigiles* says nothing about fire. To give just a few modern examples, American fire services tend to be called Fire Departments; British ones, Fire Brigades or Services; Canadian ones, Fire Services or Departments. The Latin term has led some to consider them primarily a police force, and the emperors did employ them to preserve or restore public order when the need arose. The term, however, actually reflects how they operated as firefighters—they spent most of their time patrolling Rome looking for signs of fire; if they found fire, they would try to extinguish it and prevent its spread.

Unfortunately, our sources tell us almost nothing about how they did this, even though those sources constantly mention fires. We know more about the equipment they used. Let's work through some of their equipment, then, and see what it tells us about Roman firefighting techniques.[81]

- Water buckets (*hamae*; singular, *hama*): Patrolling *vigiles* brought water buckets along. They were used to fetch water from Rome's many public fountains, some of which were strategically located to fight fires. We have to imagine groups of *vigiles* running to fetch water, then running the water back to the site of the fire, then doing that again, and again, and again. Or, they would set up a bucket line, as we know later firefighters did. This would be possible only if the patrols were quite large, which would reduce the *vigiles*' ability to cover the city, or after word had been sent to the fire stations and more *vigiles* had arrived. Either way, if the fire had grown to any size, the bucket strategy would have been of limited efficacy.
- Pickaxes (*dolabrae*; *dolabra*): The other piece of equipment patrolling *vigiles* carried with them was a pickaxe. Pickaxes were presumably used very much as they are used today—to hack through doors and walls to rescue people, to get access to the fire, and the like.[82]

Other equipment would have to be fetched from the fire station.

- Rags (*centones*; *cento*): Most likely patchwork quilts of otherwise useless material that would be used to smother fires.
- Pumps (*siphones*; *sipho*): The Romans used pumps to bring water to fire. We even have archaeological remains of several ancient pumps. Unfortunately, this evidence suggests that their power would have been quite limited, and we should not imagine anything remotely like the powerful streams that blast from modern hoses. The principal barrier to effective hoses was that the Roman world lacked rubber.
- Ballistae (*ballistae*; *ballista*): Now things get particularly interesting. Ballistae were Roman artillery machines that hurled large projectiles at the enemy; Julius Caesar used them in his campaigns in France and Britain. They could, of course, be used to batter the walls of besieged cities, and it was this capacity to destroy even large, well-built structures that made the ballista so important to Roman firefighting. A military writer of the fourth century CE indicated that each ballista required a unit of ten enlisted men and one NCO to operate;[83] we can assume something similar for each firefighting ballista.

Most of the equipment described above might be effective against small, confined fires. Once a fire had started to spread, however, the *vigiles*' best chance to control it was to create a firebreak—that is, destroy everything combustible in the line of the fire, sometimes even through controlled burning, to starve the fire of fuel and thus halt it. Hence the ballistae. This is perfectly rational firefighting, and it is a technique used today to fight forest fires. But it was also used even into the twentieth century to fight urban fires. The Great San Francisco Earthquake of 1906 caused a great many fires to break out, and those fires wound up destroying more of the city than the earthquake itself had done. In desperation, San Francisco's firefighters employed dynamite to create firebreaks—essentially, to level part of the city to halt the fire's spread—but in one of those tragic ironies that often accompany disasters, their attempts did more to start new fires than to halt the already existing ones.[84] The Romans had no dynamite, of course, but the principle was the same: heavy military weaponry to bring buildings down. Preservation through destruction.

The limitations of this equipment, of ancient firefighting technology, explains a surprising feature of Rome's fire department—its immense size. We do not know precisely how many firefighters there were in Rome in 64 CE—the Romans most likely did not have a precise count, either—but our best guess is something in the neighborhood of 3,920, a number that was most likely doubled in 205 CE, and almost all of those *vigiles* would have been used in the field. Let's put that number into perspective. In 2013, New York City's fire department had a little over 15,000 employees, of whom slightly more than 10,000 were actual uniformed firefighters; London's Fire Brigade had slightly over 5,000 firefighters. But each of those cities had in excess of eight million inhabitants. To use a city with a population comparable to ancient Rome's one million, Austin, Texas, had slightly more than 900,000 residents in 2014 and a fire department of slightly over 1,100, that is, less than one-third the size of ancient Rome's, a discrepancy that increases when we consider that a good many of those 1,100 were doing clerical and support work.

In relation to population and in comparison to today's developed cities, then, Rome's fire department was immense. The size of the *Vigiles* also reveals something about how differently the Romans thought from the way we do, particularly about their usual first response to a problem, which was to throw lots of people at it. Their economy and social system explain this response. First, theirs was a slave economy, and the state, the emperor, and the upper classes had an almost unlimited store of people they could compel to address any task. Second, the number of people in Rome who were scraping together a living, who subsisted on part-time and seasonal jobs, was substantial. People with muscle and without options were plentiful.

In so many things—water technology and architecture are two examples—the Roman Empire and its capital city were way ahead of their time, and most of human history offers nothing so advanced and so seemingly modern. This was the case for the *Vigiles* as well. But not having the benefit of the technological and scientific revolutions of the nineteenth century, they were also considerably behind our own time. And the limited evidence suggests that the *vigiles* did not consider rescuing people a priority. Their principal charge was to prevent fires from spreading. As so often in ancient Rome, the inhabitants were on their own.

One of the great ironies of life in ancient Rome was that, although the city was endowed with a remarkable—indeed, unprecedented—volume of flowing fresh water, the technology did not allow the Romans to take full advantage of that resource. Buckets and feeble pumps. The succession of fires, grand and middling, that our sources mention, provides the proof.[85] Still, we do not and never will know how many small fires would have become significant had not the *vigiles* and their basic tools extinguished them, and the emperors' continuing substantial investments in their fire service suggests that those investments had an impact. This text even suggests that the *vigiles* may have scored a couple of critical victories in their battle against the Great Fire. Rome was a city of fires, to be sure, but it could have been even worse.

And yet people actually lived in Rome.

Some had no choice, of course. Rome was where their homes, families, and livelihoods were, and picking up and moving one's life elsewhere in the ancient world was more difficult and riskier than it is today.[86] Inertia would also have played a role. But Rome had compensations—some of them found nowhere else in the ancient world and some found nowhere else to the same degree as in Rome. In both quality and quantity, Rome was unique.

As densely developed as most of ancient Rome was, the city had an impressive array of gardens and parks, particularly on the city's outskirts. Rome's ubiquitous bathhouses offered relief as well. Our best information on the number of bathhouses in Rome comes from the fourth century CE: 11 elegant, massive imperial complexes, and another 856 establishments,[87] some of them public and some private, and which, we must assume, varied greatly in services, accouterments, elegance, and clientele. Rome's bathing facilities, particularly the grand ones emperors built, were much more than just places to wash. They were civic centers, meeting places, gyms, recreational facilities, warmth in the cold of winter, cool in the heat of summer, art galleries, tanning salons, schools, part-time bordellos in some cases, and, as Seneca's letter above suggests, eateries and beauty salons. The most sumptuous complexes offered an opportunity to inhabit and relish a fairyland of beauty, elegance, and excess normally accessible only to Rome's wealthiest—indeed, to live the gorgeous, pampered life of an emperor in his palace, if only fleetingly.

Rome also offered the enjoyment of antiquity's most spectacular and sophisticated public entertainments—the greatest shows in the greatest venues with the greatest performers. Chariot racing, gladiatorial combat, exhibitions of exotic animals (usually including their deaths), men fighting animals, animals fighting animals—literally, lions and tigers and bears, not to mention elephants and giraffes—theatrical performances (traditional plays but also bawdy and violent skits), music, parades, spectacular sacrifices and other dazzling religious ceremonies, and the most bizarre and imaginative public executions on earth. Much of this entertainment appalls us, but with the resources of the empire and the engagement of the emperor behind it, it was riveting and thrilling, and absolutely first-rate. One example. The celebratory opening of the Colosseum, a building with curious ties to the Great Fire,[88] included—among many other delights—star-studded gladiatorial combat, the slaughter of five thousand animals in a single day, at least one mock sea battle, aquatic performances by horses, bulls, and other animals, and a woman having sex with a bull—over one hundred days of such attractions, with massive attendance. We may suspect that our sources have exaggerated somewhat, and we can hope that the bull spectacle was the product of special effects (at which the Romans excelled), but the festival must have been astonishing for its scale, imagination, variety, and shock value.[89] Only in Rome.

As it is today, Rome was also a city of architectural wonders and world-class art. Many of the emperors' architectural projects brilliantly combined beauty, majesty, and technical and artistic virtuosity. Some of these structures embellish Rome to this day: the Colosseum, the Pantheon, and Trajan's Column and Market, among others. The Temple of Peace provides an illuminating example. The Elder Pliny considered it one of the three most beautiful buildings in Rome, worth seeing on its own merits. It doubled, however, as one of Rome's preeminent art galleries, housing a terrific collection of what were already for the Romans old-master paintings and sculpture—works by a veritable Who's Who of Greek artists, including Pheidias, Polykleitos, and Leochares. There was no denying that many of the city's works of art had been plundered from elsewhere, and that conquest had funded many of the city's most magnificent buildings. The sack of Jerusalem and destruction of the Temple, for example, helped pay for the Colosseum, and the "peace" the Temple of Peace commemorated was the one the Romans secured in the same war by devastating Judea and killing tens or even hundreds of thousands of Jews. These were buildings, one might say, erected on the rubble and corpses of others. Many of Rome's foreign residents, including slaves who wound up in bondage as a result of Roman imperialism, likely viewed structures celebrating it with a mixture of amazement, sadness, and anger. Romans, however, were not in the least embarrassed by their conquest of the world around them and felt that they had earned their mastery and the right to be surrounded by the fruits that came with it. Even the poorest citizens walking around the city would encounter unambiguous reminders of Rome's and their own superiority to everyone else, and all Romans shared ownership in those buildings and monuments, and therefore in the accomplishments they commemorated. The visual greatness of the city suggested Rome's and thus your greatness, no matter how poor you were, no matter how little you had actually contributed to that greatness.

Rome offered yet another spectacle unparalleled in antiquity—its people. No other city attracted so many people from so many places of so many sorts with so many quirks. Greeks, Egyptians, Jews, Syrians, Africans, Germans, Spaniards, Thracians—you name them—were all represented in the city. Considering the ethnic complexity of the city, it is not entirely surprising that in the first century BCE Julius Caesar had "actors performing in all languages." Augustus did so as well.[90] Rome had a remarkable concentration of doctors, teachers, scholars, and intellectuals, whose presence helped make Rome a culturally vibrant and sophisticated city. But those are only a few of the professions and trades Rome's inhabitants plied.

Rome had by far the most specialized trades of any city in the ancient world, including occupations such as duck dealers (*anatiarii*), wig makers (*capillamentarii*), inserters of eyes into sculpted busts and statues (*fabri oculariarii*—not real eyes, of course), forehead readers (*metoposcopi*—essentially palm readers, but reading customers' future through their foreheads), veterinarians who specialized in mules (*mulomedici*), manufacturer/purveyors of opulent clothing with gold decoration (*aurivestrices*), bakers of bread especially designed to help the digestion (*pistores magnarii pepsiani*) and, of course, the pluckers of armpit hair (*alipili*), who, as we saw above, kept poor Seneca from sleeping. Not to mention the sex workers, the folks scratching together a living through various kinds of street hustling and hawking of wares and other activities, and the professional poisoners. Every service, every product, every refinement conceivable was available in Rome.[91] The diversity of people, professions, and products helped increase Romans' sense of *urbanitas*. Like its English derivative *urbanity*, *urbanitas* suggested the sophistication and savvy only life in a great city can confer. Like residents of complicated, vexing modern cities, Romans griped incessantly about the trials of urban life, for which the sources cited above give abundant testimony. And no wonder. Still, there was no alternative, if you wanted or needed to be at the epicenter of wealth and power at the time. Rome was the place to be.[92]

Despite Rome's consolations and pleasures, most Romans led hard and precarious lives in that harrowing city. An afternoon strolling in lovely public gardens would likely be punctuated by a walk through some of Rome's revolting streets back to a cramped, dismal apartment. Who knew what you would be stepping on and breathing in along the way? If you headed back too late and wound up walking in darkness, you might not get back at all. And would there be sufficient and healthy food when you got home? What if that insalubrious city made you or your children sick? You most likely could not afford a doctor, and doctors did not know what they were doing anyway. Nor could those magnificent buildings protect you when the city was flooding, an epidemic had broken out, your apartment building was collapsing, fire was devastating your neighborhood, or your unheated apartment turned cold and dank on chilly winter days or unbearably hot during scorching summer heat waves. Life in that great city was an ongoing series of trials.

Those unending discomforts and perils helped shape the experience, mindset, and expectations of Rome's residents on the eve of the Great Fire. Most people today who live in prosperous modern communities anticipate and enjoy a high level of comfort and security. Indeed, in the mental landscape of those lucky few, comfort and security are the default. When disaster strikes, we are surprised, perhaps even shocked, that it is striking us.

For inhabitants of the ancient Mediterranean world, even the most powerful and prosperous, disaster was an inevitable part of life. Nothing was certain, and nothing secure. As the mythical Oedipus's life was starting to unravel—he had, after all, unwittingly killed his father, slept with his mother, and sired children/siblings—the playwright Sophocles had him protest (or whine?), "I am a child of good luck," as though he should be immune to misfortune. Any ancient viewer or reader of the play would have cringed or smirked or sighed at such a claim, not just because the facts of Oedipus's case so clearly put the lie to his assertion but also because the facts of life as they themselves experienced them did the same. Recognition of our shared vulnerability to tragedy and disaster was one of antiquity's most profound insights. This is not to say that the Romans were immune to tragedy and suffering, that their acceptance of the certainty of misfortune inoculated them against pain and sorrow. Rather, they acknowledged that the pain and sorrow catastrophes inflicted upon them were inescapable.

This mindset may also in part explain why, until the Great Fire, a calamity of unprecedented devastation to the city, the Romans had taken only inadequate measures to prevent and prepare for disaster, especially fire. To be sure, when Rome was a republic, its aristocracy, the only ones with the resources and power to effect such measures, did not think the welfare of the great mass of Rome's disadvantaged was their or the state's responsibility, except when such concern was deemed politically advantageous. When Augustus put the republic out of its misery and emperors came to exercise power, they tended to consider it in their interest and, to give the best of them credit, their responsibility to see to it that Rome functioned reasonably well for its residents and that its poor did not starve. Augustus instituted the most significant reforms: he reorganized the city into fourteen districts (*regiones*), subdivided those districts into neighborhoods (*vici*), appointed officials to oversee the districts, and allowed Rome's residents to elect other officials to oversee the neighborhoods; he appointed boards to tend to the water and food supplies and to the roads; and, of course, he created the *Vigiles*. But for all those laudable measures, Augustus failed to address the tinderbox of domestic structures ubiquitous in the city. Rome's leaders in all ages tended to consider the sufferings of their subjects the business of those subjects. If anything, emperors seemed to think their role was not so much to prevent tragedy as to help people in the wake of it, to restore order and confidence, repair damage, and perhaps even play the role of consoler-in-chief.[93] And for all the Romans' ingenuity and architectural sophistication, theirs was a preindustrial society, whose scientific and technological knowledge and resources were limited. Tragedy and disaster were to be weathered, to be regretted, to be mitigated, perhaps, but not to be averted. The best defense against calamity was a philosophical acceptance of the inevitable.

Of course, it was not quite as simple as that, as the ancients knew perfectly well. The "Father of History," as Cicero dubbed him, Herodotus (fifth century BCE), told a story that at first blush confirms the lesson of Oedipus's fate, namely, that none of us is in control of our destiny. The Athenian lawgiver and sage, Solon, visited the wealthiest man of his day, Croesus, King of Lydia. Croesus had his staff give Solon a tour of his immense wealth and then asked him who was the most fortunate (*olbiotaton*) man he had ever encountered, quite reasonably expecting to hear, "Why, you, Croesus!" Croesus was irritated when Solon's selections were veritable nobodies, and asked, essentially, "What about me?" Solon famously replied that things change, even for the wealthy and powerful, and even *their* luck can turn against them. No one can be considered fortunate, Solon averred, until that person had completed life without suffering a catastrophic setback. But Herodotus's Solon was not so simple as to think that the poor and weak have the same prospects in life as the rich and powerful. Less well remembered are Solon's comments on precisely that disparity: "The exceedingly wealthy but unfortunate (*anolbios*) man . . . is better able to satisfy his desires and to endure great disaster when it befalls him."[94]

The stories of Croesus and Oedipus remind us that disasters are great levelers. The encounter between Croesus and Solon suggests something else just as profound and true about disasters, however: one's chances of coming out the other end of a disaster and its aftermath with property, family, and life intact are considerably better if you are wealthy. As they are today. As they were in the Great Fire.

-II-
Inferno

The People

No one would have been shocked on July 19, 64 CE, when a fire broke out in the shops under the arches of the Circus Maximus.[1] Some shops were packed with flammable goods, and others were eateries with open fires and stacks of wood used to prepare food for the prostitutes, astrologers, and other fortune-tellers who frequented the area. Every veteran of Rome knew that fires were a daily fact of life in the great city, and parts of the Circus itself had experienced a major fire just thirty years earlier. However awful the consequences of these fires could be for some, the city nonetheless seemed to limit and absorb them, and go on. This fire was different. Just as there had never before been a city like Rome, there had never been a fire like the one that started that evening.

The fire that began in the shops soon spread the full length of the Circus Maximus, a structure of astonishing size: over 600 meters long and 100 meters wide, six football fields in length and one in width. Before long, the entire structure was ablaze, with flames rising hundreds of feet in the air as they found and fed upon the two wooden upper tiers of stands. The conflagration must have been spectacular. If the fire could have been confined to the Circus, as had been the case with the Circus fire a few decades earlier, it would have represented a considerable blow to one of Rome's most important buildings, but not the city's greatest catastrophe. Once the fire jumped to the low-lying adjacent neighborhoods, however, broad swaths of Rome were doomed.[2]

Like most of the city, those neighborhoods consisted largely of ramshackle timber-frame tenement houses built too high, too close together, and too cheaply, forming a vast, jumbled warren of snaking alleys and streets. The buildings' proximity to each other, even when on opposite sides of the narrow streets, made it easy for the fire to hop from one to another. Too, the inhabitants' possessions were made mostly of flammable materials, as were the wares of the shops that occupied the ground floor of most buildings. Even the sturdier-built structures of more durable and fire-resistant material offered wood and other substances aplenty to feed the flames and help them spread. The stone and brick of Rome's impressive warehouses may have seemed resistant to fire, for example, but their contents often required little more than a spark to generate flame. Rome was a vast storehouse of kindling waiting for that spark.

From the lower-lying neighborhoods, the fire then climbed some of Rome's famous hills; the lower slopes of the Palatine, home to many of Rome's wealthiest and most prominent citizens, were soon in flames. Not even Nero's residence remained unscathed. Next, the fire coursed back down into Rome's urban valleys. No one could predict in what directions this vast and intense conflagration would spread next, and it was nearly impossible for Rome's inhabitants to know its extent and direction at any given moment (fig. 3).

The same layout and materials that made it easy for the fire to spread made it difficult for its residents to escape. Even on a clear, untroubled day, Rome's bewildering maze of narrow, winding streets limited views to a block or so. As smoke from the fire enveloped sections of the city, it reduced visibility even further. The smell of burning materials, perhaps occasionally even of the flesh of the inferno's human and animal victims, would have obliterated all the other odors in that normally pungent city, but it would have been difficult for inhabitants fleeing through Rome's urban canyons to discern what direction the smells were coming from. In July, Rome's breezes tend to come out of the south and southwest, which would blow the fire northward towards the heart of the city, but the city's winds can gust from any direction, and the Great Fire was of such magnitude and intensity that it would have generated its own powerful and shifting drafts. Modern records indicate that July is one of the hottest and driest months in Rome. Rain is quite rare, and temperatures average 88–89 degrees Fahrenheit. Nature did its part to aid catastrophe.

Many of Rome's streets must have become blistering, stupefying wind tunnels. The canyons of apartment houses that composed so much of the city would have distorted perception of the various noises the fire caused: its own roar, the crash of the many collapsing buildings, the bellows and barks of Rome's

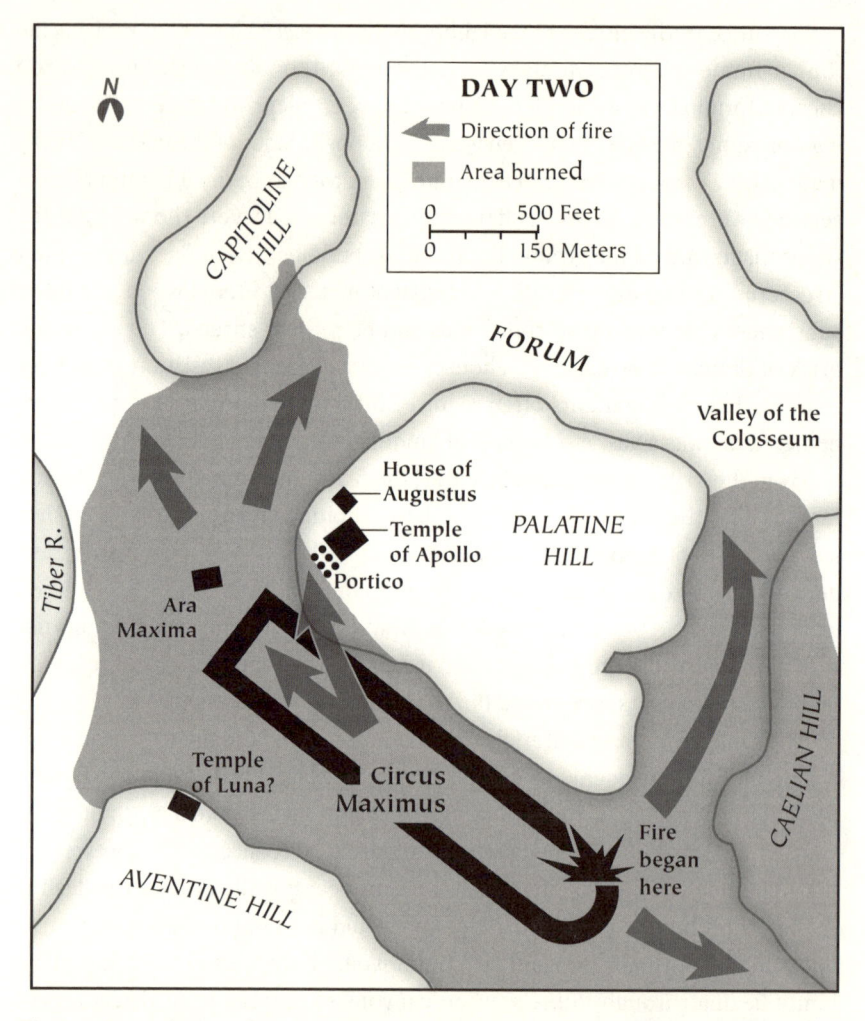

Figure 3. Map of Day 2 of the Great Fire. The details are an approximation of where and when the fire spread based on our limited sources. Lucidity Information Design, LLC

terrified animal population, the cries of Rome's desperate human fugitives. The searing heat made it even more difficult to read the situation and one's surroundings. Rome's inhabitants found themselves overwhelmed and disoriented by the assault on their senses, and accurate, life-and-death information would have been difficult, if not impossible, to come by. Miscommunication and rumor are endemic to modern disasters, despite the technological sophistication of our modes of transmitting information, and even experts with all the available evidence can be reduced to guesswork as a calamity unfolds. Ancient

Romans had to rely exclusively on rumor and their own senses for information. Generally, the authorities did not feel it was their responsibility to provide the common folk with information in the midst of a disaster, and so it is not surprising that our sources say nothing about officials informing and directing the population of Rome amidst the chaos and terror of the Great Fire. They themselves probably understood very little anyway. And so, just as you were on your own in your attempts to escape, you were on your own in your attempts to get accurate and perhaps even life-saving information. For Romans seeking to elude the Great Fire, people desperate for any scrap of accurate information amidst the pandemonium, there was only word of mouth—the breathless utterance of someone running past, the confident report based on no actual information, assertions fueled by panic and adrenaline, and the confused and confusing shouts and cries of other terrified people fleeing for their lives.

Fire was not the only danger. Buildings collapsed all the time in Rome, as we have seen, and fire was one of the most common causes of those collapses. The city's many ramshackle tenements could scarcely sustain any damage and remain standing. During the Great Fire, your flight could be cut short by a building collapsing into the street and upon you, leaving you crushed—or worse, trapped—under a heap of burning rubble. The collapsed and collapsing buildings could block escape, causing you to turn back into the wall of people right behind you. Waves of terrified Romans were surging through the labyrinthine city, fleeing in every direction, doubling back when blocked or when panic took them, at times rushing into other human hordes. The rich had gangs of burly and armed bodyguards to open the way through the crowds, with no regard for the safety of anyone else.[3] Exacerbating the crush and clogging the avenues of escape, slaves might also be carrying the often bulky property of the rich, of far greater importance to Rome's elite than the safety of their poor neighbors, and bearing in litters the elderly and children of their masters. Of course, there also were the looters.[4] Some might have been normal people yielding to the temptation to profit from the chaos—many of Rome's poor lived in a state of unrelenting and hopeless economic desperation. Others were hardened criminals, who in Rome were indeed a hard and ruthless lot. They would not hesitate to pummel or even kill anyone who stood in their way, nor would they hesitate to attack people fleeing the fire and relieve them of whatever money and possessions they had managed to grab.

You could easily escape the flames only to have your fellow Romans crush you. Rich and poor alike fell to the flames and the crowds, but chances were better for the prosperous—those bodyguards, for one thing. And although the poor and the rich were not as segregated in ancient Rome as in modern cities, the rich were still likely to live amidst townhouses and on the slopes or heights of hills, which would be less densely packed with people and tenements than the valleys and would provide a better view of the unfolding conflagration. No one is immune to disasters, as Oedipus reminds us, but in Rome's highly stratified society, money increased your odds of surviving them.

Fear and despair, coupled with the physical and mental exhaustion of trying to stay ahead of the fire, broke the will of some. Others who could have escaped simply gave up and embraced their end. Some who had lost relatives in the fire chose to join them in death, perhaps, in part, overcome by guilt over having failed to save them. With scarcely any time to consider, many a Roman had to make the most agonizing decisions: Should we leave the slow behind? What about the infirm and the elderly? Could saving your parents cause your children to lose their lives? and What did you owe your neighbors in this ultimate trial of character? These questions would torment anyone at any time in any culture, but they addressed the very core of what it meant to be Roman. The moral glue to Roman society was *pietas*, the recognition and fulfillment of your obligations to your own—to your country, to your gods, to your community, and to your family, each member of which had different claims upon you. It is no accident that Aeneas, mythological father of the Roman people, was commonly represented as carrying his father on his shoulder and leading his son by the hand as he fled from the conflagration that engulfed Troy—until the Great Fire of Rome in 64, the first of the two pivotal fires in the Romans' history and consciousness.[5]

Virgil's *Aeneid*, the Romans' national epic, tells the story. The Trojan Paris had taken the Greek king Menelaus's wife, Helen, and a massive Greek expedition sailed to Troy to get her back and exact revenge. After a ten-year siege, the Greeks finally sacked and burned Troy, killed or enslaved the bulk of Troy's population, and recovered Helen. Only Aeneas and his followers managed to escape. Virgil has the refugees flee blazing and doomed Troy and sail halfway across the Mediterranean to Italy, for in the Romans' view, the gods allowed the Greeks to sack Troy to compel the Trojan remnants to resettle in Italy and there, through intermarriage with locals, create the Roman people.

Aeneas's extraordinary escape from the flames consuming Troy, along with his rescue of his son and father and statuettes of their household gods, had become *the* encapsulation of *pietas* for Romans. Rome's first emperor, Augustus, had made the image of Aeneas carrying his father and leading his son from burning Troy part of his public relations, and so the image had proliferated in Rome itself and beyond—through statues grand and small, coins, reliefs, paintings, and the like, in both the private and public spheres.[6] Some Romans fleeing the flames surely had representations of Aeneas's flight from Troy decorating their townhouses or apartments—smaller figures were available to those of limited means—and it is not out of the question that, during their own flight, some saw statues, paintings, or mosaics depicting Aeneas's paradigmatic performance of *pietas*—reminders of what was expected of all Romans. Such heroics may easily be enacted in poetry and sculpture, but amidst real flames? Some inhabitants of Rome literally dragged their infirm relatives through the burning and chaotic streets, less romantic than Aeneas but just as noble; others just saved themselves. For some, the catastrophe was as much moral as physical.

Troubling, too, were reports that gangs of men were preventing attempts to fight the fire and were even nurturing it. They claimed to be acting on orders from someone in authority. Were they? If so, on whose orders? What sort of orders? And *who* were they? They could have been roaming vandals, pyromaniacs, looters who made such claims to scare off any resistance, or even average Romans driven mad by the cataclysm enveloping them. How could an ordinary citizen, disoriented by the chaos, exhausted by the effort to escape the maze of death that Rome had become, with nerves strained to the breaking point, tell who these people were? Looting almost certainly occurred during the Great Fire. If these gangs were indeed acting on orders, were they instruments of a Neronian plan to destroy the city, as was later alleged? Or were they *vigiles*, doing their duty to the best of their very limited ability? If the latter, they would have been fighting the fire through controlled burning intended to create firebreaks,[7] as they did in employing military equipment to knock down and burn granaries.[8] Military equipment was needed to flatten the formidable granaries, and burning would have been the most certain way to deprive the fire of the buildings' mass of flammable materials. Could there have been different bands of men, some bent on mischief, but others attempting to check the course of the fire?

Whoever they were, and whatever they were up to, they certainly were not about to pause to clarify anything. Fleeing Romans asking questions could expect a forearm in the face as a response. There was no time for explanation or debate. Who knows, anyway, if anyone could hear accurately what breathless, rushing bands of men were yelling amidst the deafening pandemonium? If the lion's share of these bands of men were *vigiles* doing their duty, their very equipment—hooks, grapples, axes, even artillery!—could have suggested to those they encountered that they were vandals, criminal gangs, or even invaders. Their very strategy—destroying parts of the city to save the rest—would have reinforced the impression their arsenal suggested. Amidst the smoke, din, and terror, desperate Romans could have misunderstood the *vigiles*' actions and perhaps even misheard their words. Residents of Rome certainly knew that the *vigiles* existed and for what purpose, but few would have known what a firebreak was. While it is true that Rome constantly endured fires and saw the *vigiles* in action, it had been a decade since the last significant fire in Rome—one in which the employment of military artillery to create firebreaks might have made sense—and that one was confined to one Roman neighborhood, the Aemilian district in the Campus Martius.[9] Most residents of Rome would never have seen the counterintuitive firefighting tactic of preservation through destruction in action, and even if they had, amid the flames, collapses, crowds, and chaos, would they have had the presence of mind to process the *vigiles*' actions? An elbow in the nose from a busy and burly firefighter might have been the only communication they received from the authorities. Rumor would handle the rest.

Once the Great Fire was well under way, its searing temperatures would have set buildings afire without a touch of a single flame. It would dry up and heat nearby structures and their contents to the point at which apparently spontaneous ignitions would have occurred—a perfectly natural phenomenon not to be conflated with the fictional human spontaneous combustion of Charles Dickens's *Bleak House* or television's *South Park*. Ancient Rome was full of materials subject to such ignition, including the manure of the city's numerous human and animal inhabitants.[10] Absent modern science, how would observers of these spontaneous ignitions have made sense of the sight? The only reasonable explanation had to be arson. Some scoundrels were bent on spreading the fire. Whatever the truth, the imaginations of the city's beleaguered population must have run wild, and the feeling that everything and everyone was conspiring against them must have been strong, triggering the desire—the need, perhaps—to explain how this could be happening, to find something or someone to blame for this unprecedented conflagration, stronger yet.

Where to flee to? On the one hand, those the fire menaced would have been principally concerned with escaping the peril literally before their eyes. But once they had managed to extricate themselves from an immediate threat of death, they had to consider how to escape the massive hell that Rome had become. Climbing the heights would have been a logical choice since the hills were less densely built up. Depending on the hill, there tended to be more public buildings, parks, mansions, and open spaces—fewer close-packed knots of *insulae*, and so less fuel for the fire. On the other hand, Roman fires at times climbed and ravaged the peaks of the city's hills. The Capitoline Hill, for example, often endured major fires. You could get trapped on a hill, surrounded by rising and inexorable flames. The best course was to get out of the center of the city entirely. Many fled across the Tiber to the river's western bank, where the neighborhood of Trastevere and the Vatican are situated today. Several bridges connected the two banks, and the western bank was the safest place to be if you could manage to get there. Others tried to get to the great parks and gardens, largely owned by the emperor, that rimmed the northern and eastern edges of the city. Another, though less secure, option was the Campus Martius, the Roman army's old parade and training ground. By Nero's time, it accommodated some important imperial structures and other buildings, but several of these had substantial open spaces, and it was, in any event, more sparsely developed than the city center. Many escaped Rome by the great roads that led to Italy's other major cities. Ironically, once you got out of Rome proper, these roads were lined with tombs and monuments to the dead.[11] We can only guess at how many fatigued and battered refugees, sitting by or on some tombstone amidst a sea of grave markers and mausoleums, gazed somberly at these reminders of death and considered the newly lost loved ones who had just joined the old.

Sooty, exhausted, often burned, with cuts, bruises, and broken bones and spirits from their flight, the fire's survivors crowded into the sides of Rome's grand roads and cemeteries, the open spaces on the other side of the Tiber, the parks on the city's outskirts, and the Campus Martius. They were now safe, but their senses made peace impossible: you could see the fire's impact on the flesh, faces, and clothes of your fellow refugees, hear their wails and lamentations and perhaps even deranged ramblings, smell charred flesh and organs and the stink of sweat and desperation, feel your own burns and wounds, and taste air fouled by smoke, soot, and death. All the while, for days, the Great Fire continued to make its monstrous presence felt: its massive plumes of flame and smoke were within sight, the roar of the great blaze within earshot, and its smoke could still drift in your direction and inflame your eyes and throat, as did waves of intense heat. There was no fleeing reminders of the horror, and however inured Romans were to the city's usual sensory overload, they had never experienced anything so traumatizing and revolting as this.

The Fire

While Rome's residents were fighting for survival, so was the fire.[12] To survive, a fire must obtain and consume flammable materials, and as we have seen, ancient Rome provided these in abundance. The Great Fire found its first nourishment in the shops under the arches on the exterior of the Circus Maximus. Their flammable wares "fed" the fire,[13] according to Tacitus, and the dwellings above those shops provided additional fodder for the fire's appetite. They likely provided the fire's first victims as well. As the fire rose, it found a veritable banquet of wood at the upper levels of the building. The Circus's lowest tier was stone, but the upper two tiers at that time were wooden. The fire started at the corner towards the Palatine and Caelian Hills and swept the length of the Circus towards the northwest and the Tiber, feeding on that immense structure and growing as it went. But even the Circus would eventually be consumed and provide no more sustenance. For the fire to survive, other sources of fuel were needed, and the fire found them in the tenements along the paths of least resistance, the very paths Rome's harried residents were using to escape.

From the Circus, the fire could go in four directions: (1) towards and up the Aventine Hill to the south; (2) towards and up the Palatine Hill to the north; (3) northwesterly into the adjoining lowlands along the Tiber; and (4) northeasterly into the adjoining but somewhat narrow valley between the Caelian and Palatine Hills. It apparently tried all four. Tacitus is frustratingly vague in describing the fire's course, and our other ancient sources do not attempt it. At least Tacitus does give us a sense of the fire's tendencies in expanding beyond the Circus Maximus: "First, the fire furiously swept over the level ground. Then it climbed the hills, but it surged back to ravage the lower-lying areas." Which "level ground" and which "hills"? Alas, he does not tell us. Other things he and other sources do tell us, however, along with the archaeological and epigraphical record, enable us to reconstruct the course of the fire, although little is certain and much is debated.[14]

Tacitus's first "level spaces" are most likely the lowland and valley between the Caelian and the Palatine. The first "hills" are the Aventine and Palatine, on either side of the Circus. The lowest slopes of the Aventine, again, to the south of the Circus, most likely suffered some damage, but the fire does not seem to have climbed very high. This makes sense because the summer breezes in Rome tend to blow towards the north. The lower slopes of the Palatine, those facing the Circus, suffered considerable damage. The fire then turned northward into the lowlands along the Tiber, attacking the Palatine's westerly slopes along the way. It seemed headed straight for the Campus Martius but only reached its southern corner. Its advance was not halted, however; it made two right turns towards the east, away from the Tiber, one into the dip between the Palatine and the Capitoline Hills, and one northeasterly around the northern edge of the Capitoline. The slopes of both hills were now being assaulted from more than one side. Meanwhile, coursing northward on the other, eastern side of the Palatine, the fire attacked the Palatine's slopes on that side, as its swath of destruction widened when it reached the valley where the Colosseum now stands. This enormous eastern prong of the conflagration made a left turn into the Roman Forum, along the northern slope of the Palatine, and headed straight for the Capitoline Hill. At this stage, the Great Fire formed a sort of horseshoe around the southern, eastern, and western sides slopes of the Palatine, executing a pincer movement towards the hill's northern flank, the horseshoe's gap.

The buildings in this vast, low-lying horseshoe provided an enormous buffet of flammable materials—wood, cloth, olive oil, animal and human excrement, to name only a few of the substances waiting to feed the fire—and its path was open. As Tacitus put it, "There were no mansions with formidable walls, or temples enclosed by barriers, or anything else that could arrest the fire"—only more fuel—and he claimed that the flames could not be prevented from "consuming" the Palatine, although it seems that the crest of the hill was actually spared.[15]

In Tacitus's, Suetonius's, and Dio's telling, the Great Fire encountered no or at least no effective opposition in its earliest phases.[16] Tacitus claimed that the flames successfully "anticipated any countermeasures."[17] It certainly must have seemed that way to those experiencing the fire, and it was natural for our ancient sources, with their conviction that the fire caused absolute material, human, and moral devastation, to focus on the places the fire reached and ravaged. It can be just as revealing to consider the places it did not reach, however, and why.

Four key sectors of the city center that were in the path of the Great Fire early on avoided destruction, at least in part: the summit of the Palatine Hill, the heights of the Capitoline Hill, half of the Roman Forum, and most of the Campus Martius (fig. 4). Why? The most reasonable explanation is that some units of the *Vigiles*, despite their technologically primitive equipment and the overwhelming scale and intensity of the blaze, scored a few significant victories against the fire.[18] Taken together, these four areas could be considered the heart and soul of ancient Rome, which explains why the *vigiles* would have focused on saving them and not others.

52   THE GREAT FIRE OF ROME

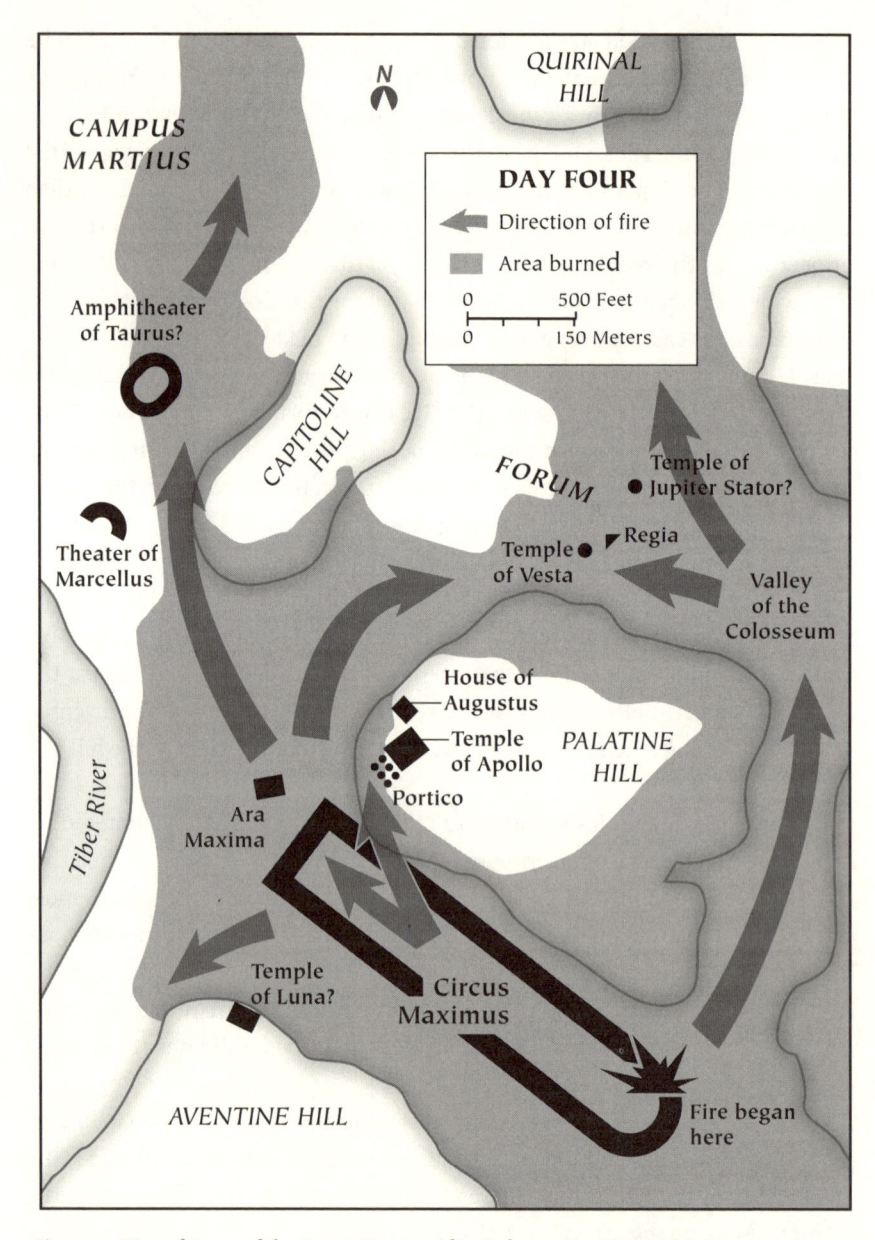

Figure 4. Map of Day 4 of the Great Fire. Lucidity Information Design, LLC

The principal temple of the Roman people, dedicated to Jupiter, sat atop the Capitoline Hill, and several other significant temples and structures dotted it.[19] The Capitoline was Rome's citadel, its center, and the city's ceremonial focal point. The Roman Forum had a remarkable concentration of important and historic temples and monuments, but it was also the beating heart of the city's civic and legal life. If the Capitoline was largely reserved for the most important religious occasions, the forum was dedicated to quotidian life as Rome's residents lived it. By the time of the Great Fire, the emperor's palace dominated the Palatine Hill, reason enough for it to be a priority for firefighters. But like the Capitoline and the Roman Forum, it also housed some of Rome's most historic temples and sites, particularly ones associated with Augustus and Romulus, Rome's founder. Augustus's house was there, as was a much-venerated hut thought to be the home of Romulus.

Units of the *Vigiles*, then, I am suggesting, likely made their stands in the forum and on the slopes of the Palatine and Capitoline, just as we would expect. When the eastern prong of the fire had reached and devastated what is known today as the Valley of the Colosseum, it turned left and surged up the forum towards the Capitoline. *Vigiles* fought back. The blazing column made it as far as the Temple of Vesta and the house of the Vestals and razed them, but it seems to have proceeded no farther than about halfway through the forum. The firefighters may have tried to keep the fire from entering the forum at all and been forced back, but they finally had some success just north of Vesta. Or they may have decided that the more southeasterly section of the forum was indefensible, or perhaps they simply arrived too late. In which case, they lost nearly half, but saved half as well, the half that was considered the heart of the Roman Forum. Did they demolish any structures to accomplish this victory, such as the house of the Vestals, to create firebreaks? We have no evidence, but it is not out of the question. By halting the fire's advance up the forum, they also protected the Capitoline's southeasterly flank.

Units deployed elsewhere around the Capitoline were having success of their own against the flames' incursions. The flames that were diverted from the forum continued to surge along the eastern slopes of the Palatine Hill, which skirted it. Meanwhile, the Great Fire's westerly prong, the one that had swept into the flatlands along the Tiber, was assaulting the Palatine from that side, as the fire at the western edge of the Circus Maximus had been doing from the south. This double onslaught may have reached the hill's heights, even if it did not "overwhelm" them.

A strong argument has been made that the flames climbed high enough on the Palatine to damage the portico of the Danaids that fronted the hill's Temple of Apollo or perhaps the temple itself, towards the southwest side of the hill.[20] The temple was a key element in what functioned essentially as Augustus's compound. Augustus himself had built the temple to Apollo, his patron deity, his home was right there, and he had renovated or built anew other structures in the vicinity, such as his own little temple to Vesta. Beyond the obvious importance the area would have had to any Roman, Nero associated himself most closely with Apollo of all deities and with Augustus of all emperors. For one thing, integral to both emperors' public relations was identification with Apollo and therefore with the god's attributes they wished to claim as their own.[21] It is easy to imagine the *vigiles* furiously defending these structures, sweaty and sooty, singed and at great peril to themselves, and even battling the flames in the portico that surrounded Apollo's temple, unable to avert the fire completely, but saving a great deal. They managed to protect Augustus's house, which in Suetonius's time apparently functioned as a museum where visitors could see the original tables and couches of Rome's first emperor.[22] It was an imperfect though highly significant victory.

The Campus Martius could not compete with the Palatine, Capitoline, and the Roman Forum for historic, religious, and political importance, and in Nero's day, it was not yet fully part of the city's core, as it is today. The Campus Martius was less densely populated than other parts of town—both with people and with venerated historic and religious buildings and sites. The key was that the Campus had two particular significances for Nero. First, its most southern quarter was essentially Rome's theater district. The Theater of Marcellus was right by the edge of the Campus, across from the Capitoline Hill; the Theater of Balbus was situated a bit farther north, as was the Theater of Pompey, slightly to the north and west of the Theater of Balbus. Nero's obsession with the theater and likely his intention to perform in Rome would have been known to the *Vigiles*' commanders, and when deciding where to deploy their units, above all they would have taken into account their willful and dangerous emperor's preferences. That is, they would know that among Nero's priorities would be saving the theaters, and so that is what they did.

Also in the area was the Amphitheater of Taurus, whose precise location is unknown, but it was certainly in the vicinity of the three theaters. The Great Fire destroyed this building, and both its fate and the contrasting preservation of the theaters make perfect sense. However much Nero may have enjoyed the gladiatorial combat, slaughter of animals, and grizzly executions, which were the usual fare of amphitheaters, he was no Commodus, eager to appear as a gladiator and to kill animals before crowds. His métiers were singing, acting, playing the lyre, and chariot-racing. Therefore the firefighting resources in the area were dedicated to the theaters, precious to the emperor, and not to the amphitheater. Second, like the Palatine Hill, the Campus Martius was particularly associated with Nero's great-great-grandfather Augustus, and it boasted quite a few important structures Augustus and his family—that is, Nero's family as well—had erected. Among them: the *horologium*, a sprawling calendar of seasons and much else; the predecessor of the Pantheon we see today; a grand public bathhouse; and Augustus's tomb. It would have made sense, then, for the *vigiles* to make a stand at this southern edge of the Campus Martius, simultaneously theater district and gateway to much of Augustus's architectural legacy. If this reading is correct, they saved the Campus and redirected the Great Fire towards the east, where it continued on its path.[23]

We today might expect the *vigiles* to focus on residential areas. What is more important than human life? That is not, however, how Rome's aristocrats saw things. They or their ancestors had built Rome's grand edifices, imposing and meaningful reminders of Rome's and their own families' greatness. Those structures had cost a fortune and were intended to last. Indeed, as long as they lasted, they conferred on their builders a measure of immortality. Of course, no one's family had contributed more to the cityscape than Nero's. As emperor, moreover, Nero was *the* inheritor and protector of Rome's heritage and grandeur, neither of which, in the view of Rome's leaders, was to be found in *insulae*. Besides, the *vigiles*, like all Rome's agents and authorities, were responsible to the emperor, not to Rome's denizens, and their commanders surely knew Nero's priorities, which outweighed all others.

As the *vigiles* made their heroic stands, the two prongs of the fire swept around the Palatine Hill and very likely united immediately to its north and then advanced around the Capitoline further to the northwest. The horseshoe had transformed into a slightly tilted figure 8 of flame and smoldering rubble, with the bottom loop surrounding the undamaged heights of the Palatine, and the top loop surrounding the largely intact Capitoline and heart of the Roman Forum at its base, although much of the area to the south, where the fire had started, may have been burned out by this point.[24] The Great Fire then began to spread eastward and northward, up the valleys that divided the city's other celebrated hills—the Caelian, Esquiline, Viminal, and finally Quirinal—working its way from south to north. As it had done before, it attempted to climb those hills, with mixed results. It must have seemed to Rome's terrified residents that the fire was laying traps for them, surrounding them in a classic military pincer movement, attempting to cut off avenues of escape, and when that failed, pursuing them along those avenues. The Great Fire seemed to have no limits—of time or place or ambition.

The Emperor

When the fire broke out, Nero was at his birthplace, Antium, a seaside town around thirty miles south of Rome along the coast.[25] In Tacitus's account, though, immediately before the story of the fire comes a description of the orgy to end all Roman orgies, and the orgy reads as leading to the fire. The Great Fire directly "follows" (in the sequence and in Tacitus's language) the culminating and most shocking element of the orgy, Nero playing the role of a woman in marrying a certain Pythagoras, a marriage that the emperor publicly consummated: "The bride's veil was put on the emperor; the usual witnessing was carried out, and the traditional dowry, nuptial bed, and torches were there; people watched everything that ensued, things that night normally hides, even when a woman is the bride. A disaster *followed*, whether accidental or through the machinations of the emperor."[26]

The "disaster" Tacitus speaks of is the Great Fire, and the "marriage" was only the culmination of a series of extravagances and "abominations":[27] a raft bedecked with gold and ivory manned by a crew with more sexual than nautical experience; women from Rome's most aristocratic families offered for sex on one bank while on the opposite bank naked prostitutes mimed and danced pornographically; Nero himself engaged in every vice imaginable; and when night fell, torches illuminating and music enhancing all the wickedness. Then the travesty of Roman marriage. Dio adds that slaves raped their mistresses in front of their masters, and gladiators raped noblemen's daughters right in front of their fathers. The alcohol-fueled license and disregard for any norms led to brawls, kidnappings, and deaths.[28] Nero's "marriage" and the prostitution of Rome's noblest women were tantamount to an assault on two pillars of Roman society, the family and the class systems—the evil and demented emperor was not just engaging in bizarre and immoral behavior, he was undermining the institutions and values that made Rome noble and great.

Although Nero had evidently decamped from Rome (and the orgy) to Anzio, Tacitus's telling creates the impression that he went directly from the subversive orgy cum wedding to the fire. It is almost as though news of the fire arrived in the midst of the debauchery, but the emperor was too preoccupied with the orgy's depravities to return immediately to supervise the firefight. Tacitus did not assert that, of course, but two weeks after reading his account, Tacitus's readers would likely recollect that the licentiousness initiated at Rome had moved to Anzio and that Nero dallied at an orgy while Rome burned. Tacitus's crafty juxtaposition of the great orgy and the Great Fire induces us to suspect as much.[29]

Nor did Nero return to the city until, Tacitus tells us, the "palace he had built to link the Gardens of Maecenas to the Palatine" was threatened. A subtle subjunctive verb in the Latin hints that it was only the threat to his own home that induced him to come to the rescue.[30] When Nero became emperor in 54, the core of the imperial palace was on the Palatine Hill, but he also inherited the splendid villa and gardens of Maecenas, an old confidant of Augustus, up on the Esquiline Hill, northeast of the Palatine and at the eastern edge of the city. Nero wanted to be able to go from one home to the other without having to go out into the filthy and unruly streets of Rome, so he devised a typically Neronian strategy to address this troubling situation—he planned and had started to build a very, very long and very, very elegant wing between the two so that he would not have to leave the palace in transit. It was this part of the palace, his Domus Transitoria (Passage Palace), that the fire endangered.[31]

Whatever the truth to Tacitus's intimation that Nero cared only about his own property, when he did arrive, he ordered sensible measures to assist Rome's population: the Campus Martius and its buildings were opened to refugees, as were the emperor's impressive array of gardens on the outskirts of the city; shelters were erected to accommodate the fire's homeless victims; provisions were shipped up the Tiber from Rome's port city, Ostia; grain prices were lowered. All of this was perfectly in line with what people expected of their aristocracy.

To a significant extent, noblesse oblige regulated relations between the wealthy and powerful, on the one side, and everyone else, on the other. When disasters struck a community, its privileged were expected to help alleviate pain and disruption, just as, when things were fine, those privileged few were expected to pay for festivals, shows, communal buildings, and other public goods. Once Augustus had killed the Republic, emperors became the ultimate benefactors for the entire empire, although local movers and shakers continued to pay for local projects and events and provide assistance to their communities when calamity fell upon them. For their own security's sake, at the very least, emperors tightly controlled the benefactions distributed in the city of Rome, making sure that almost everything positive flowed from or seemed to flow from them, thus assuring that the people's gratitude flowed back exclusively to the right person. Fulfilling the requirements of noblesse oblige justified the Roman world's highly stratified status quo, functioned to preserve it, and helped restore it when disaster imposed exceptional strains on society and good order. Nero's measures, then, provided evidence that Rome's residents needed him and could count on him to come through in even the direst circumstances.[32]

That emperors claimed to be "Father" to the Roman people heightened expectations. Starting with Augustus, the Senate customarily awarded emperors the title *Pater Patriae*, Father of His Country, and of Nero's predecessors only the cantankerous Tiberius had declined the honor. As *Pater Patriae*, then, Nero was father to the people of Rome, which suggested the intimacy, engagement, and devotion a father feels towards his children. Suetonius's description of the emperor Titus's response to disasters (Vesuvius's devastation, a terrible plague, and a three-day fire in Rome) provides an example of an emperor's ideal paternal behavior. While enumerating the excellent and costly measures Titus took to address the crises, alleviate suffering, and comfort his "children," Suetonius claimed, "amidst so many awful disasters, he showed not only the concern you would expect from an emperor but even the singular love you would expect from a father."[33] And if *pietas* was the moral glue of Roman society, being the Roman people's loving father intensified even further an emperor's obligations to his children. Such were the expectations Nero confronted upon returning to Rome, and for the most part, he met them.

Nero's return to Rome to address the catastrophe also occasioned one of the most notorious episodes in Roman history and endowed posterity with arguably the most compelling image of the Roman Empire—Nero fiddling while Rome burns. Despite their considerable visual and literary potential, not to mention their potential to encapsulate significant elements of the Roman experience, neither the grand city in flames nor even the Christians employed as human torches to light nocturnal festivities have rivaled fiddling Nero in the postclassical imagination. Indeed, fiddling Nero became and has endured as a visual shorthand for the Great Fire, Roman decadence, decline and fall anywhere and at any time, political cluelessness and irresponsibility, and madness. And no wonder. Grand fires and sadistic executions, however awful, are endemic to the human experience—disaster and cruelty thrive in our world as well. But few images or even notions are as bizarre and fascinating as an emperor in costume singing a song while the world's greatest city goes up in flames.

Here is the scene.[34] While the conflagration was devastating Rome, and its residents were desperately seeking to elude the flames, collapsing buildings, and stampeding hordes, Nero donned his personal theatrical costume and climbed the Tower of Maecenas on the Esquiline Hill, whose height and position allowed him to take in the vastness of the fire at a safe distance—essentially, the best seat in town from which to watch the calamity unfold. While gazing on the inferno and delighting, as he himself supposedly put it, in the "beauty of the flames," accompanying himself on the cithara he sang the poem, "The Sack of Troy," which told the tragic story of the Greeks' torching of Rome's mother city over a thousand years earlier. Nero himself wrote a poem or series of poems titled something like *Songs of Troy*,[35] and for all we know, he could have been performing a selection of his own composition from that work. Some of his courtiers presumably witnessed this performance (it was, after all, a performance), aghast and appalled, but we should assume they effusively complimented the young emperor on his apt and brilliant rendition. We can even imagine a tear or two shed, in part, they would assure Nero, because of the tragedy laying waste to Rome right before their eyes, but even more in response to his moving and flawless performance.

What are we to make of this? The most obvious explanation for Nero's shocking behavior is that he was mad. The next most obvious is to suggest that this story is just an anti-Nero fabrication. It is simply too weird to be true, even for Nero. Nero's behavior does make a certain sense, however, at least in Nero's funhouse world and in a Roman context.

First Nero. He was obsessed with the theater and keen to take the stage. His theatrical career did not come to full bloom until after the Great Fire, but his intention to become the Roman Empire's most accomplished and acclaimed star was evident earlier.[36] Nero was also, perhaps, already starting to conceive of his entire life as one grand performance in which there was no distinction between actor and character. Episodes in his life became, essentially, acts in a grand play. What transpired around him in what we would consider "the real world" provided the backdrop to this play, and he cast the people who witnessed his antics as bit players, or they served as the audience—sometimes both simultaneously. Of course, he was the star. For Nero the aspiring artiste, a man bent on erasing the distinction between theater and life, the fire provided a glorious once-in-a-lifetime opportunity, the grandest, most magnificent stage setting imaginable—indeed, the most thrilling sight the city had ever offered. The Romans loved special effects, but even their most creative stage managers, with unlimited resources, could never conjure up something so vast, awful, and majestic. The fire was not just stage setting and special effect, though. It is easy to imagine the emperor viewing the fire as audience, too, one worthy of his extraordinary talents. Perhaps Nero, with his extravagant ego and insatiable appetite to be the center of all attention, was even trying to upstage the fire, appropriate it, subsume it into *his* narrative. As grand as it was, the fire was, above all, material for the spectacle of *his* life. To put it differently, as great as the Great Fire may have been, it was not as great as Nero.

However excessive and peculiar his performance was, one aspect of it was quintessentially Roman: educated Romans tended to employ the past to make sense of the present to a degree and in ways we do not, and the clear distinction we modern people are confident we observe between history and myth did not exist in antiquity.[37] Because Romans employed mythological and poetical material in the serious endeavor of understanding their own experience and giving it meaning, for educated Romans contemplating and citing literature to make sense of catastrophe was not an affectation—it was a useful tool and part of their cultural DNA. In a letter to his brother Quintus describing the severity of the flood of 54 BCE, for example, Cicero put the event in perspective by quoting Homer, in the original Greek and without translation. He introduced the quotation with the observation that what Homer has to say on the subject "still has validity." Cicero was not pretentiously showing off his learning—he was writing to his brother, who knew perfectly well how learned Cicero was—but rather doing what Romans did with poetry and the past: clarifying the present.

When Tacitus described Nero as "assimilating the present ills to catastrophes of antiquity" by singing of the destruction of (already for them) ancient Troy while watching the destruction of (to them) modern Rome,[38] he pictured the emperor engaging in a perfectly familiar and normal Roman activity. Dio even has the Roman on the street—while the conflagration raged, with the horror so pressing that it drove some people mad enough to hurl themselves into the flames—processing the inferno around them in terms of Rome's last cataclysmic fire: the Gallic sack and burning of the city, an event that occurred more than four hundred years earlier, in 390 BCE.[39] We may wonder how many Romans were actually engaging in such comparisons as the disaster was unfolding, but for Dio and his readers, such behavior made perfect sense.

If Suetonius, Dio, and Tacitus were appalled at the notion of an emperor performing during so calamitous an event, it was the performance, not the evocation of the fall of Troy and the assimilation of the two events that so revolted them. Respectable Roman aristocrats *produce* shows; they do not star in them. As has been the case throughout much of the history of the West, theatrical people in Rome, however beloved, were a morally and socially suspect bunch.

Professional performers in Rome fell into a clearly defined low social and legal rank, *infamia*,[40] which entailed the forfeiture of full citizen status. Theatrical performers shared this degraded status with gladiators, pimps, slave-dealers, and the like—people whose professions were essential to Roman society, but like that of the equally essential *stercorarii* (the fellows who removed excrement from the city of Rome), something no respectable person, let alone an aristocrat, let alone an emperor, should engage in. Old-school Romans like our trio of sources considered Nero's theatrical inclinations both a symptom and an engine of the pernicious moral decay of Rome's governing classes. And so shortly after the Great Fire, one anti-Nero co-conspirator explained his detestation of the emperor: "I began to hate after you were revealed to be the murderer of your mother and your wife, a charioteer, an actor, and an arsonist."[41]

We might find it laughable that acting and chariot-racing find themselves alongside matricide, uxoricide, and arson as accusations, but traditional Romans took such breaches of the social code quite seriously. The fact that other aristocrats performed and that some people seemed to enjoy seeing their betters singing, dancing, and acting only made things worse—indications not of the natural evolution of social norms but of the spread of a wicked social corruption. And Nero's timing was all wrong. In the midst of any crisis, Rome's ruler and father should address the crisis. Afterwards, when we can deliberately examine what happened and what it meant, is when Romans should and, indeed, *need* to assimilate the current event to the past and to poetry. This is precisely what Tacitus does in his assessment of the consequences and meaning of the Great Fire—written, however, decades after the event. But Nero could not wait. The fire was raging, inviting his performance. It was now or never for him, a unique and transient and irresistible opportunity. Nero's performance makes Roman sense and Nero sense.

Complications in our sources' narratives of Nero's fiddling also contribute to the suspicion that the episode is an anti-Nero fabrication. This skepticism has become mainstream in much popular history. The History Channel's website, for example, asserts,

> In July of 64 A.D., a great fire ravaged Rome for six days, destroying 70 percent of the city and leaving half its population homeless. According to a well-known expression, Rome's emperor at the time, the decadent and unpopular Nero, "fiddled while Rome burned." The expression has a double meaning: Not only did Nero play music while his people suffered, but he was an ineffectual leader in a time of crisis. It's been pretty easy to cast blame on Nero, who had many enemies

and is remembered as one of history's most sadistic and cruelest leaders—but there are a couple of problems with this story.

For one thing, the fiddle didn't exist in ancient Rome. Music historians believe the viol class of instruments (to which the fiddle belongs) was not developed until the 11th century. If Nero played anything, it would probably have been the cithara, a heavy wooden instrument with four to seven strings—but there is still no solid evidence that he played one during the Great Fire. The Roman historian Tacitus wrote that Nero was rumored to have sung about the destruction of Troy while watching the city burn; however, he stated clearly that this was unconfirmed by eyewitness accounts.[42]

The problems in this statement should set off alarm bells: the fire lasted longer than "six days"; Tacitus did not state "clearly that this was unconfirmed by eyewitness accounts"; and no modern historian asserts that Nero played what we know as a fiddle—the anachronism was added to the tale centuries later and has no bearing on whether Nero performed or not. To make sense of this controversy, we need to examine our sources: Tacitus, Suetonius, and Dio.

This text's account of the episode relies mostly on Suetonius but includes an element or two from Tacitus's and Dio's accounts;[43] other sources are much later and derived from these three or from those later authors' imaginations. Although the three agree on the nature of the performance and the key elements—Nero sang or recited a verse narrative of the destruction of Troy in the palace while Rome was still burning—there are discrepancies among them. Suetonius has the performance take place on the Tower of Maecenas on the Esquiline Hill; Dio locates it "on the roof [*or* highest point] of the palace [*or* Palatine]." A location on the Palatine Hill does not make sense, since by the time Nero returned to Rome the fire had either already surrounded the Palatine or threatened to surround it. Too dangerous. But by Dio's day, the palace had engulfed the heights of the Palatine Hill, and so a reference to the "Palatine" could actually be a reference to the palace (meaning the emperor's home), which under Nero sprawled beyond the Palatine Hill and included the Esquiline.[44] By the time of the Great Fire, the Tower of Maecenas, along with the park that surrounded it, had become imperial property. And Nero's having earlier decided to link the Palatine Hill section of his palace with the Esquiline Hill section (including the Tower and surrounding park) through his Domus Transitoria indicates that he considered it all one, all his palace, however inconveniently those sections had been separated before the new construction. That is, the Tower was, for all practical purposes, part of the palace, though not on the Palatine

Hill. If we translate Dio's Greek as, "on the highest point [*not* 'roof'] of the palace [*not* 'Palatine']," the discrepancy is obviated, although we might wish that Dio had been more exact.

Tacitus locates the performance in Nero's "private theater," which is incompatible with Suetonius and Dio. There is no easy explanation for this discrepancy, but such variations in detail are not uncommon in our ancient sources, and as word of mouth spread the report of Nero's shocking behavior, details of the event would naturally have changed, even among Rome's well-educated elite. They relished scandal, wickedness, and gossip every bit as much as the folk in Rome's streets. Indeed, it would be surprising if details had not changed in the telling. Moreover, it is possible that Tacitus, who found Nero's theatrical aspirations so distasteful, may have chosen this language (*domesticam scaenam*— "private stage" or "the stage in his home") expressly to associate in his readers' minds Nero's performance with the, for Tacitus and his ilk, disreputable and vile stage[45]—and, perhaps, to anticipate one of the themes of the coming chapters of the *Annals*: Nero's complete abandonment of aristocratic restraint and dignity and his surrender to theatrical mania. As the discussion below suggests, Tacitus had perfected the art of employing association to suggest guilt.

Tacitus did not explicitly state that Nero had sung his notorious song, but only that rumor to that effect had spread throughout Rome. This assertion does not, however, amount to an expression of "a strong dose of disbelief," as one doubter of the historicity of the episode claims.[46] Indeed, Tacitus's inclusion of the rumor could just as plausibly suggest that he credited it as fact and expected his readers to do so as well, although he slyly declined to characterize it as such. The key things to note, however, are that Tacitus said nothing about his own view of whether Nero had actually sung, and the issue was irrelevant to the point Tacitus was making when he referred to the rumor. The context indicates that Tacitus brought the allegation up because it undermined the good public relations the emperor should have been getting for his sensible responses to the fire. Fact or fiction, the story had its impact. That is, in terms of public attitudes towards Nero, whether he sang or not was irrelevant, and so Tacitus did not assess its truth or lack thereof at all—nor did he need to. And yet the effect of the passage is vintage Tacitus—a crafty twofer for the master of innuendo. On the one hand, a week after reading Tacitus's account, most readers would simply remember Nero strumming the lyre. On the other hand, in relating the tale as rumor and in a passage ostensibly about something else, Tacitus afforded himself plausible deniability and preserved the affect of impartiality and objectivity. "I'm just reporting what folks were saying. What you take away from this is up to you." The modern claim, moreover, that "no one saw" Nero's performance and so we should doubt its historicity, puzzles.[47] Though they occasionally mentioned their sources, ancient historians were not, unfortunately for us modern historians, in the habit of listing their eyewitnesses or their other sources. If we apply the principle that when no eyewitnesses are cited for an ancient event it did not occur, most of ancient history would disappear.

A couple of final points. It is not entirely clear from our sources whether Nero sang or chanted. Most likely he sang, but it is very much the same either way—we should imagine a histrionic rendition in full costume. That is, a show. Dio had Nero donning his "cithara-playing garb."[48] Suetonius dressed him in less specific "theatrical garb" (*scaenico habitu*), which likely amounts to the same thing. In any event, Nero was not playing his famous "fiddle," an instrument that did not exist at the time, although the Romans did have an instrument called the *fidicula*, whose name evolved into the English *fiddle*. If he did play an instrument, it was his favorite and the one the costume Dio attributes to him suggests, the cithara.[49]

Could the whole story have been a fabrication? Absolutely. But the arguments against its historicity, I believe, are unconvincing. As I have already suggested, however callous and wacky singing amidst such a catastrophe seems to us, it makes a great deal of sense considering Nero's character and ambitions and the Roman practice of processing the present through the past.

Our only other description of Nero's behavior during the fire may suggest that he applied himself energetically to managing the response to the fire. Tacitus tells us that "while the palace was burning, [Nero] was rushing all over the place, unguarded, throughout the night."[50] Was the emperor everywhere, monitoring the efforts to fight the fire and help the fire's victims, working through the night? Or only concerned with his palace? Or was he running around in a directionless panic? Tacitus's language more strongly suggests this last, but as so often with Tacitus, it is difficult to pin down the difference between the facts he is relating and his coloring of those facts.

In any event, at someone's order, perhaps Nero's, a substantial number of buildings around the base of the Esquiline Hill were demolished to create a firebreak. The *vigiles* so thoroughly flattened so "vast . . . a tract of land" there that Tacitus described the formerly dense urban neighborhood as a "plain."[51] The *vigiles* almost certainly leveled whole city blocks, perhaps even entire neighborhoods, in other parts of the city as well, and the sections of the city the Great Fire had already ravaged now resembled a smoldering moonscape. Still, at that moment, the strategy *seemed* to have worked. The *vigiles*' victory near the Esquiline Hill appeared definitive, and the fire was felt to be spent in most sections of the city. Hope-filled rumor may have spread that the conflagration was over, a report everyone was desperate to believe. Many survivors would have been relieved to have escaped alive, found shelter and food, and heard that the fire had been halted. Nero was earning himself a high grade as emperor and Father of His Country. Things were looking up.[52]

Any relief Rome's inhabitants may have felt was short-lived, however, as the fire resurged and raged on for another three days. By this time, the more congested, populated parts of the city had been destroyed, and most surviving Romans would already have fled. In round two, then, fewer people were caught in or fleeing from their tenements. The further devastation to Rome's infrastructure was nonetheless considerable. Tacitus suggested that this second round of fire destroyed the city's temples and porticoes more widely than the first round had done. The survivors' senses also took another beating—more sickening smells, sounds, sights, and sensations. The psychological impact on the city's already exhausted and dispirited population must have been considerable—more evidence that everything and everyone was against them. It must have seemed interminable. Nine days of misery and loss that felt more like ninety. An extraordinary span of time for an urban fire: longer than the Great London Fire (1666), the Great Chicago Fire (1871), the Great San Francisco Earthquake and Fire (1906), and the Great Kanto Earthquake and Fire (1923). It was the longest-lasting major urban fire in history—for duration, at the very least, the greatest among the Great Fires.

Damage Done

When the flames finally died out, the largest, richest, most important city of the ancient world was a smoldering remnant of its former self. Of Rome's fourteen districts, according to Tacitus, who provides our only ancient estimate, four remained untouched; in seven, only a few structures remained, and even those were severely damaged and charred; three districts were completely obliterated (fig. 5). Tacitus declares, "it would not be easy to go into the number of homes and apartment houses and temples that were lost," and he does not even try. Nor does he provide even a guess at the number of casualties or a figure for the economic impact of the catastrophe. Suetonius offers no data either, and our third source for the Great Fire, Dio, reports vaguely that "countless" (literally) people perished in the fire.[53] This puzzles us. We expect assessments of

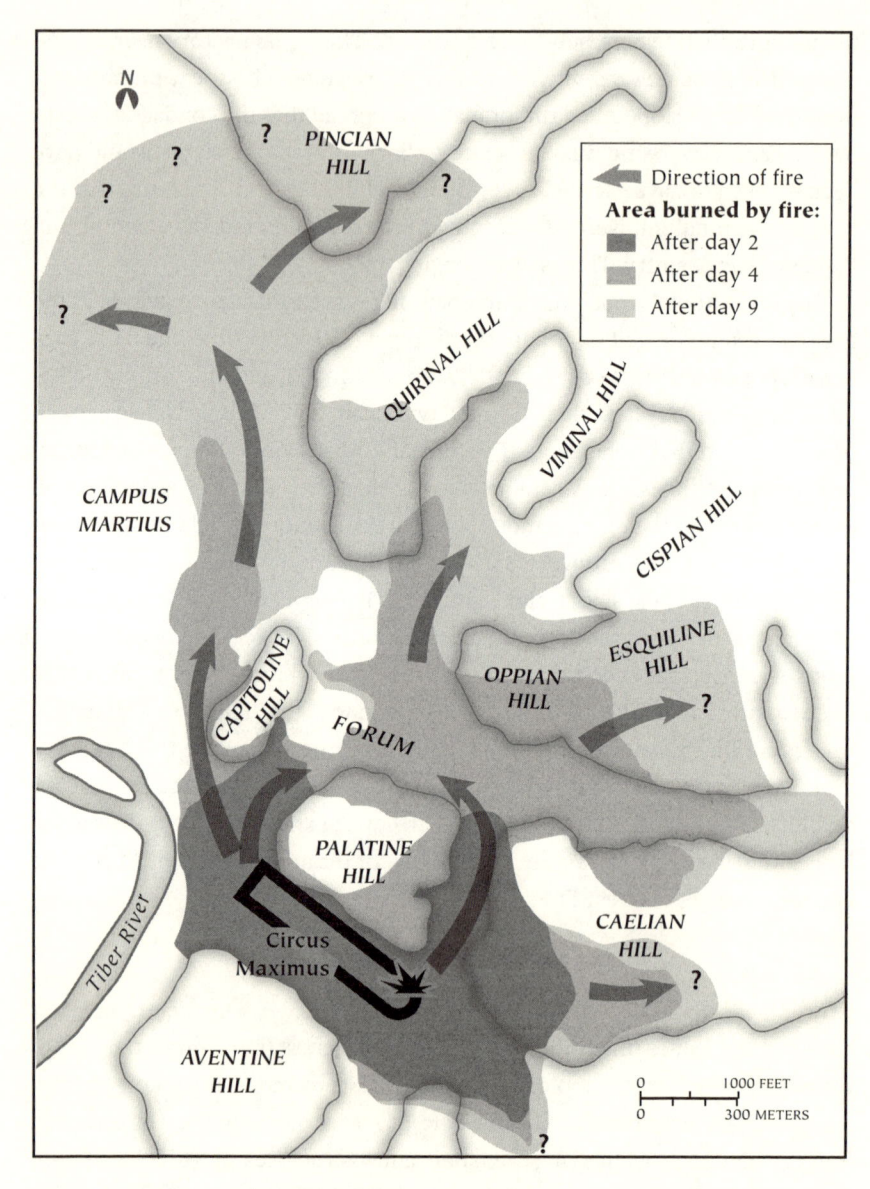

Figure 5. Map showing the extent of the Great Fire's destruction at the end of Day 9, when the fire went out. Lucidity Information Design, LLC

disasters above all to tell us two things: how many people died and the total value of the material and economic losses the disaster occasioned. Nothing is easier, for example, than finding online the number of deaths Hurricane Katrina caused (1,833, according to FEMA) or its economic impact ($108 billion; FEMA again). Both numbers can vary—we can debate whether some casualties should be attributed to an event,[54] for example, and the estimated financial impact is just an estimate—but there are always numbers. Indeed, an event's very meaning seems to depend on those numbers. But not for Tacitus.[55]

In a revealing expression of *Roman* values, when Tacitus summed up the damage Rome had suffered, he identified only five of Rome's structures as destroyed, and no others. These were already ancient buildings the Romans associated with the city's prehistoric founding and with the origins of the Roman people. Tacitus mentions, in order (I provide the modern name, Tacitus's Latin, and a translation of that Latin):[56]

- Temple of Luna (*[templum] quod Servius Tullius Lunae [sacraverat]*—"[the temple] that Servius Tullius [had dedicated] to the Moon")
- Ara Maxima (*magna ara fanumque quae praesenti Herculi Arcas Evander sacraverat*—"the great altar and shrine that Arcadian Evander had dedicated to Hercules in his presence")
- Temple of Jupiter Stator (*aedes Statoris Iovis vota Romulo*—"the Temple of Jupiter Stator vowed by Romulus")
- Regia (*Numae regia*—"the royal house of Numa")
- Temple of Vesta (*delubrum Vestae cum penatibus populi Romani*—"the Temple of Vesta with the patron deities of the Roman people")[57]

The most obvious characteristic all these buildings share is their religious function—even the Regia, whose name suggests a royal residence, was actually the headquarters of the Pontifex Maximus, Rome's chief priest, and the repository for some important records and religious artifacts. It thus makes perfect sense that Tacitus introduced this list of destroyed structures with the phrase *vetustissima religione* ("the most ancient religious veneration," or perhaps, in this context, "the most ancient objects of our religious veneration"). But it would be a mistake to suggest that by grouping buildings of religious purpose Tacitus intended to distinguish the religious from the secular or even the political. For the Romans, culture, politics, and history were inextricably interwoven with religion, as was virtually every facet of their lives. Theirs was a world full of deities who oversaw every aspect of life, both private and public, and the Romans attributed their unparalleled success in the acquisition and preservation of empire first and foremost to their religious scrupulosity, what they called the *pax deorum* (peace [or better: good relations] with the gods).[58] Separation of church and state would have struck them as irrational and dangerous. These buildings suggested even more, however, than the Romans' relationship with the gods.

They also suggested a checklist of Rome's most important and honored founders (here in chronological order)—and virtues:

- Ara Maxima: evoked Aeneas, the Trojan refugee who became the forefather of the Roman people and the one who set in motion the fulfillment of the divine plan to establish the Roman Empire. In Virgil's *Aeneid*,[59] Aeneas meets Evander, who becomes an ally and friend of the Trojan refugee, on the future site of Rome (ca. twelfth century BCE).
- Temple of Jupiter Stator: built by Romulus, founder of the city of Rome (as opposed to the Roman people—Aeneas gets credit for that) and the Romans' first king (eighth century).
- Regia and Temple of Vesta: both established by Numa Pompilius (eighth/seventh centuries), Rome's second king and the one credited with the creation of Roman religion (the Regia was originally his house, according to Roman lore). The phrase Tacitus employs here, moreover—*cum penatibus populi Romani* (with the patron deities [*penates*] of the Roman people)—again calls to mind Aeneas, who famously saved statuettes of the *penates* from destruction during the fall of Troy and brought them to Italy (again, ca. twelfth century).
- Temple of Luna: dedicated by their sixth king, Servius Tullius, who expanded the city by incorporating the Esquiline, Quirinal, and Viminal Hills, while enjoying significant military victories and a variety of religious and political accomplishments (sixth century).

Aeneas, Romulus, Numa Pompilius, Servius Tullius—a veritable *Who's Who* of greats from Rome's foundation and earliest days. The list evokes religion, politics, purpose, destiny, military victory—the very things the Romans considered essential to their success and character—and the origin of the Roman people and of the city of Rome. It's all there. Taken together, these buildings suggested Rome's heritage and even its identity. Rome was as much an idea as a place—an accumulation of traditions, values, and stories the physical city preserved and offered to Romans as reminders of who they were, or should be. This, Tacitus suggests by limiting his accounting of buildings to these five, is what the Great Fire destroyed. Not just buildings and infrastructure or even people, but Rome's character, purpose, and meaning. Along with the physical city, the Great Fire had gutted Rome's soul. On Nero's watch. Tacitus was noncommittal on the issue of whether Nero had started the Great Fire, and his description of the measures

Nero took to fight the fire and succor Rome's residents contains sensible and effective measures. Still, a kind of guilt by association damns Nero, and Tacitus's assessment of his behavior in the wake of the fire cements that association. If we extend the associations in the text back to the spectacular and transgressive orgy that immediately precedes the account of the fire, we have a suggestive narrative sequence: sexual depravity, Rome's most devastating conflagration, the city and its heritage demolished. The chain of events, as Tacitus presents them, may offer guilt by association only, by juxtaposition really, but guilt nonetheless, and links that would make perfect sense to Romans, with their tendency to read history through a moral lens: depravity leads to disaster, which in turn leads to catastrophic losses, even loss of who you are.

That the events this list of buildings evokes are mostly fictitious is irrelevant. The Romans viewed what we know to be fictional events as history, and even when skeptical of the tales' veracity, they could feel entitled to assert them—not because of their factual accuracy but for the greater truths the Romans felt they conveyed about Rome's character and significance. Tacitus's great predecessor in writing Roman history, Livy, put it this way in the preface to his grand history of Rome, from its inception to his own day:

> The things that have been passed down about events before or even when the city was being founded belong more to the lovely creations of poets than to the unembellished records of history. Therefore I do not intend to pass judgment on whether they are true or false. We simply need to indulge our most ancient accounts' tendency to make cities' origins more august by mixing the human with the divine. When you consider things, if any people have won the right to sanctify their origin and attribute them to the gods, it is the Roman people. Our reputation for success in war is such that when we claim even Mars as our father and the father of our founder, other peoples of the world just have to accept the claim with the same equanimity with which they endure our rule.

Essentially, Livy asserted, "OK, maybe we made this stuff up, but we earned it." In the same passage Livy went on to assert a principle disconcerting to modern historians:

> In any event, I think it is pointless to get into debates regarding these and related issues. Rather, I want each of my readers to focus intently on what sort of life our ancestors led, what their character was, through what men and what domestic and military practices they were able to acquire and extend their rule over others. The

reader should next follow how, as discipline was gradually slipping, their character began to sink, then slide more and more, and finally began to tumble headlong until this very day, when we have sunk so low we can bear neither our corruption nor any cure for it.[60]

Here Livy pretty much urged his readers not to concern themselves so much with what actually happened and instead focus on "the life and morals of the community; the men and the qualities by which . . . dominion was won and extended." Tacitus's (and Livy's) agenda, emphases, omissions, and looseness with the facts might strike modern historians as bordering on malpractice. From Tacitus's point of view, however, such tut-tutting would reveal a lack of sophistication, an inability to understand and to profit from what historical writing can and *should* do: present a true account of the moral significance of events and of the people who shaped them. He can do that and not lose credibility with his ancient readers because Roman historians were more concerned with truth than fact. Wisdom trumped accuracy, and moralizing superseded facts. Given these standards, Tacitus was not concerned to provide a precise tally of how many people had died, a comprehensive accounting of how many buildings had been destroyed (besides, as he notes, it would be impossible to give such an accounting), or an estimate of Rome's and the Romans' total financial losses—things *we* would expect. Readers simply needed to understand that the Great Fire's devastation was total. In addition to the physical city, it consumed everything that made Rome and the Roman people great and virtuous—their history and with it their very identity.

The rest of Tacitus's assessment of the destruction of the Great Fire evinces the same priorities. Among the losses "were the riches won through innumerable victories, splendid works of Greek art, and furthermore the ancient and genuine chronicles of brilliant men."[61] Tacitus did not provide any specifics about the innumerable temples, monuments, townhouses, fountains, apartment buildings, warehouses, and other structures the fire destroyed, but he made a point of mentioning Greek art and books. The Romans took immense pride in the richness of Rome's culture and beauty, both visual and literary, and the fire had delivered a substantial blow to the city's aesthetic and intellectual treasures. A Roman of Tacitus's wealth, status, and education would have been deeply interested in that lost art and particularly in the lost literature, and so he bemoaned the loss of culture.

There is, however, more going on here. The "riches" were, as Tacitus makes explicit, the result of Roman success, that is, indications and reminders of Rome's place as master of their world. The literature and art were reminders of Roman appropriation of the Greek peoples and their cultural accomplishments. Roman art was largely inspired by and derived from Greek art, and the Romans had plundered or purchased a vast number of Greek works, including many masterpieces by the Michelangelos and Picassos of antiquity. They did so without shame—we won, we should revel in that victory and its fruits, and our possession of your finest things should remind both you and us of who is in charge and who, obviously, the gods favor. This went for literature as well. Roman collections and libraries had both Greek and Latin texts, but the texts in both languages were reminders of the Roman appropriation of Greek culture. Educated Romans were steeped in the Greek classics in the original Greek, and Roman literature (including the writing of history!) was unabashedly derived from Greek models. Homer's *Iliad* and *Odyssey* inspired the *Aeneid*, Rome's national epic, and were a source for some of the "history" associated with the five destroyed buildings Tacitus names, for example, a fact of which Virgil expected his readers to be fully aware. Thus, when Tacitus lamented the loss of riches acquired through victory, of Greek works of art and of marvelous works of literature, he was also eulogizing the military accomplishments and the acquisition of empire that deservedly beautified the city of Rome and the minds of her conquering people. He was lamenting the devastation of a civilization—indeed, his civilization.

We have already seen how Aeneas's exemplary *pietas* amidst Troy's burning provided both a model and a challenge to Romans confronting their own moral dilemmas during the Great Fire. But in assessing the fire, Tacitus also brought up the second epochal fire in the Roman imagination. Any Roman reading an account of a cataclysmic fire laying waste to Rome would also think of the burning of Rome by the Gallic Senones in 390 BCE, the last time a foreign army had taken and torched the city. After routing a Roman army in the battle of Allia, the Senones marched on Rome, took the city, sacked it, and burned it to the ground. A few Romans had fortified themselves on the Capitoline Hill, however, where they held out for months and provided posterity with inspiring stories of heroism to dull the sting of defeat. Or, more likely, if these holdouts existed at all, posterity provided *them* with the heroic tales. Eventually, we are told, the two parties negotiated a surrender, and the Senones agreed to take a huge sum of gold in return for withdrawing. According to one Roman version, a Roman army then inflicted a major defeat on the departing Senones—a narrative sop to Roman pride.

The Senones' victory and burning of Rome is supposed to have served as a wakeup call. The Romans reconfigured their army and strengthened the city's defenses. That is, the response to the defeat moved the Romans farther along the path to becoming the military juggernaut that would conquer their world. They also attributed the jumbled and claustrophobic warren of alleys and tenements the Great Fire of 64 feasted upon to the hurried and haphazard rebuilding after the sack of 390, although archaeology has shown this belief to be exaggerated, if not erroneous. Tacitus explicitly associated the Great Fire with the Gallic sack and burning of Rome by noting that the Great Fire broke out on July 19, the anniversary of the Senones' destruction of the city, and he claimed, moreover, that some have calculated that "the interval between the two fires has an equal number of each of the following: years and months and days."[62] This would be an extraordinary coincidence, but extraordinary coincidences do in fact happen. Thomas Jefferson and John Adams died on the same day, July 4, 1826, which also marked the fiftieth anniversary of the Declaration of Independence's adoption, a confluence we would surely find suspicious if hard evidence did not confirm it. Whether the dates of the Gallic sack and the Great Fire do in fact coincide is of interest, of course, but discussion of the historicity of this assertion is as convoluted as the assertion itself—and the issue is most likely insoluble anyway.[63] For our purposes, the significant and revealing aspect of Tacitus including this in his account is that he wanted to make sure his readers would connect the two fires, and he assumed that the connection would strike them as natural and illuminating, not artificial or forced. Again, it is impossible to get a true reading of the present without considering its relationship to the past.[64]

Suetonius described the fire's damage to Rome slightly differently, but his account evinces the same priorities. He said that "an immense number of apartment houses" burned down, but he supplied no estimate of how many.[65] He singled out only the "houses of our venerable leaders of old, still decorated with trophies of their victories." He mentioned unnamed temples "vowed and dedicated by the kings, and then later during the Punic and Gallic wars"—kings and conquerors whose homes and temples evoked Rome's origins and rise to empire. Most revealingly, he lamented the loss of "whatever else was worth seeing and remembering that had survived from antiquity." The Great Fire had obliterated the architectural and artistic record of Rome's glorious origins and past, the city's clearest and most compelling expression of Roman values and identity. Suetonius did mention that some granaries were destroyed, but only to accuse Nero of having them torched so that he could appropriate the land they sat on for his palace. Apparently no losses, human or material, no matter how devastating, merited comment, unless they helped reveal the emperor's outrageous plundering and ruin of the city and its heritage.[66]

-III-
The Day After

THE CITY IN RUINS. Its people battered and miserable. What now?

First the city itself. Nero saw to the removal of the rubble and dead bodies at his own expense.[1] This must have been horrifying, grueling work for those assigned to do it. Tons and tons of material had to be moved without the help of bulldozers, backhoes, trucks, and the like, and amid that rubble were the remains of human and animal residents of the city who had not escaped the fire. The appearance of the charred, mangled, and even rotting bodies was shocking enough, but the smell must also have nauseated the workers. Some of the bodies had not only been burned but had been lying in the sweltering July heat day after day. The cleanup would have gone on for months. In addition to the workers assigned to this task were the thousands of Romans searching the debris for their missing family and friends and for any possessions that might have made it through the flames. Tacitus provides a heartbreaking description of relatives searching for those crushed in the collapse of the theater at the Roman town of Fidenae, combing desperately for remains of their loved ones: "As soon as removal of the debris had begun, people rushed to find and embrace and kiss their dead; arguments often broke out when the general configuration and the age of a corpse seemed familiar to different searchers, but the mangled face made identification impossible."[2] The bodies the Great Fire left behind—many not only crushed as at Fidenae but burned as well, and now putrefying—would have been even more difficult and excruciating to identify.

Just as at Fidenae, disputes over the identification of remains must have broken out in Rome. Grieving citizens and the emperor's removal crews also labored at cross purposes. Nero promised to pay for the removal of the bodies of the fire's victims, doubtless a considerable relief for many of Rome's poorest, but the workers were under instructions to get things cleared out as quickly as possible. The grieving were intent on finding the remains of their loved ones and treating them with respect. Suetonius suggested that Nero's cleanup crews were also engaged in appropriating for the emperor pretty much everything of value they could haul off. He even characterized those objects as spoils of war, suggesting that Nero was behaving not like the "Father of His Country" but like a conquering general taking possession of the property of the defeated, as was the practice in ancient warfare. Nero also blocked access to his own damaged property, reasonably concerned that the fire's survivors would loot his valuables as, at least Suetonius asserted, he was looting theirs.[3]

The cleanup also provided opportunities. The state of ancient technology was such that great public (or private, for that matter) projects demanded significant numbers of workers. As we have seen with Rome's fire department, the Roman way to effect something substantial was to throw bodies at the endeavor, and working-class Roman bodies were cheap and plentiful. Films and popular literature about the Romans give the impression that they employed slaves in their vast urban undertakings, and in fact slaves did take part. But contrary to our expectation, in such cases slaves and former slaves tended to furnish much of the highly skilled labor, not the backbreaking toil. This makes perfect sense. If you invest time and money in training free people, they can leave and take that training with them. Investment gone. If you train slaves, they must stay, and so you reap the benefits of your investment. Conversely, it makes little financial sense to keep lots of slaves when you do not have work for them. You have to feed, clothe, and shelter them whether they are being productive or not. Free workers, on the other hand, can simply be dismissed when no longer useful. Plantation owners would not keep the number of slaves required for planting and harvest but only the number they would need for the full year. They would hire free people for those exceptionally labor-intensive moments and then dismiss them when the task was done. Those familiar with the lives of modern migrant farmworkers will recognize the pattern.

The same was true for substantial governmental projects. Emperors did not keep a staff of slaves ready to build a Colosseum or a Pantheon, should the desire arise. Rather, they hired laborers from Rome's great mass of underemployed poor for occasional and exceptional undertakings and then let them go when the task was done.[4] Grand public projects not only beautified and ennobled the city and made it more livable but also provided employment to Rome's lower classes.[5] But only temporarily.

One such task was clearing the rubble from the Great Fire, and there were plenty of desperate people to engage in it. The Romans' trying way of life and their expectation of disaster made them particularly resilient. If you hoped to keep your sanity living in Rome or even to survive, you had to learn to endure and bounce back. We should assume that some refugees from the fire set up makeshift stands and ad hoc businesses relatively quickly after the catastrophe, most likely in the largely unaffected Campus Martius and on the west side of the Tiber, which the fire had completely spared and where so many Romans had taken refuge.

Our literary sources can give the impression that Rome's population consisted exclusively of great political men, libidinous women of leisure, a hungry and violent mob, and slaves. But many Romans had business in their blood, from tycoons engaged in grand enterprises that connected Italy with the provinces' bounty to small business owners and salespeople who owned or staffed shops making and selling everything imaginable to the city's vast and motley population. The Great Fire had probably destroyed the lion's share of those shops, and the possibility of establishing temporary stalls among the refugees would have been limited. In the wake of this unprecedented catastrophe, moreover, not all of those shopkeepers would have had the initiative and resources to make ends meet on their own. Along with their shops many had lost inventory, tools, and equipment.

The sum of economic losses individual Romans suffered must have been staggering, and there was no insurance to compensate them. For many, the losses meant financial ruin. Just as devastating would have been the loss of community and purpose, even identity, which for so many lower-class Romans was connected to their neighborhoods and professional guilds and communal sites of worship. These victims had to fight purposelessness and despondency. And, of course, a great many other poor Romans never had a shop, or a skill, or a profession; they had scrounged together a living from seasonal work, odd jobs, and the like. Their situation was trying before, but much more so after, the Great Fire. For most likely many thousands, then, employment clearing the city, however distasteful and difficult, would have provided a way to make ends meet until Rome (and they along with it) could get back on its feet. Of course, other businesses would have thrived in the postdisaster environment: specialists in construction are also specialists in demolition, removal, and leveling, for example. And wagon owners and drivers never had it so good.

The laborers clearing the city, however, would need to be paid, and when time came for the reconstruction of the city—bringing with it another round of vital employment for the city's poor and those the fire had dispossessed—outlays rose even higher. It was not just the cost of labor, which alone would have been enormous, but of the acquisition and transportation from afar of some materials (such as wood and stone) and of the manufacture and purchase of others (such as bricks). It is impossible to translate ancient money into modern equivalents—the worlds are just too different—but to get a sense of the scale of these expenses, we should think of billions and billions of dollars.[6] Moreover, the relief of the fire's numerous homeless and helpless victims in the days and weeks immediately after the fire added to the sum. To pay for all this, Nero turned to the rest of the Roman Empire, imposing onerous and, according to both Tacitus and Suetonius, even ruinous taxes.[7] Residents of other districts of Italy and provincials may have resented the exactions, which should not have come as a surprise. The center of an empire gets the first fruits—one of the points of having an empire, after all. But it seems that Nero also saw in the need to raise money to restore Rome an opportunity to satisfy his own priorities and desires.

To this end, he sent two agents, Acratus and Carrinas Secundus, to plunder the prosperous provinces of Achaea and Asia (essentially, southern Greece and western Turkey), provinces that were also veritable museums of acclaimed masterpieces. According to Tacitus, the two agents seized statues along with the more usual and easily convertible forms of wealth and shipped it all to Rome. How extensive were these confiscations, and how many of these sculptures wound up in Nero's private collection and not in the fund to restore Rome? The second-century Greek travel writer Pausanias asserts that Nero stole *five hundred* bronze statues just from Delphi![8] According to Dio Chrysostom, Acratus plundered across the entire empire, including villages.[9] We are surely, then, talking about thousands of sculptures, perhaps tens of thousands. And Pliny the Elder informs us that it was Nero who had brought to Rome the most famous of the works of art, paintings as well as sculptures, later displayed in the Temple of Peace. He had them confiscated, not to rebuild Rome, but to decorate the palace he built in the wake of the fire, his famous Domus Aurea (Golden House).[10] Indeed, the erection of that magnificent residence, undertaken simultaneously with the rebuilding of the sections of the city the Great Fire had destroyed, exacerbated the financial pressure. Even ravaged Rome was not spared, as Nero requisitioned gold dedications from some of the city's temples.

Tacitus characterized this requisitioning as plundering, of course, and noted that the looted gold consisted of works that had been dedicated to the gods as expressions of gratitude or in the hope of winning their good will. That is, these were works dedicated on behalf of the Roman people throughout their history, records and symbols of their centuries-long ascent to rule over the Mediterranean world and beyond, expressions of the relationship with the gods that underpinned the Romans' success and that were integral to their identity. For Tacitus, the obliteration of the Romans' heritage did not end when the fire went out. And, of course, appropriating the property of the gods was a dubious and risky thing to do, though not unprecedented.[11]

Otherwise, Nero appeased the gods scrupulously. The Sibylline books were consulted.[12] They offered advice on the steps needed to restore the gods' goodwill, the *pax deorum*, which, for most Romans, was the prerequisite to the future preservation of the physical city. The consultations recommended prayers and propitiations to Vulcan, Ceres, Proserpina, and Juno, and these were made. Banquets in the gods' honor and nocturnal vigils were carried out, and presumably other rituals as well. These actions were indispensable. Regardless of what ancient leaders themselves thought of divine agency, or even existence, it was in their interest to appease the gods scrupulously, given that their subjects were prone to see disasters as manifestations of divine discontent with leadership. In response to a famine and some troubling omens, a crowd in the forum even roughed up the emperor Claudius because Rome's residents attributed their woes to divine displeasure with him.[13]

This mode of thinking is not entirely dead, even among modern monotheists. To give just one example: the spectrum of people who expressed the view that God sent Hurricane Katrina (2005) as a form of punishment is remarkable and telling. Just a brief sample: some conservative American Christian ministers claimed that God had sent the hurricane to punish Americans for toleration of homosexuality and/or abortion; at the same time, Louis Farrakhan, of the Nation of Islam, read the disaster as God's punishment for racism in America; al-Qaeda rejoiced that God had punished the Americans for their oppression; while an ultra-Orthodox Israeli rabbi attributed the catastrophe to insufficient American support for the Jewish settlement of the Gaza strip and to American blacks' insufficient study of the Torah. For all our science, some (though exceptional) religious leaders are still finding the hand of an angry God in disasters of all sorts.[14]

None of our three principal ancient sources for the Great Fire, Tacitus, Suetonius, or Dio, attributed the Great Fire to divine wrath. Tacitus does talk about *religion*—we know about the steps Nero took to propitiate the gods—but not about the *gods* as actors or players of any sort in the catastrophe. Many other Romans as well thought the cause was to be found in the human sphere—indeed, with one particular human. Tacitus said, "But no human aid, no distributions from the emperor, or even the appeasement of the gods could stop people from believing the pernicious rumor that the fire had been ordered."[15] "Ordered," that is, by Nero. The accusation raises two questions: (1) Did Nero in fact set the fire? (2) What did he do to address the rumor?

Whodunit

Suetonius baldly asserted that Nero started the Great Fire:

> But he spared neither his people nor the very walls of his capital. When someone or other cited a line of Greek poetry in a general conversation, "When I am dead, let the earth be consumed by fire!," he corrected the speaker, again in Greek, "No—while I still live!" And that's just what he made happen. For pretending that he was appalled by the ugliness of the city's ancient buildings and by its narrow, winding streets, he set fire to the city so openly that several former consuls avoided interfering with members of Nero's personal staff, even though they had been caught red-handed on the former consuls' property with tow and torches. And there were certain granaries near his Golden House whose plot of land he particularly wanted. Since they had been sturdily constructed with stone walls, he had them knocked down with siege engines and then set afire.[16]

This is a remarkable passage, as complicated and difficult to pin down as Nero himself. The opening sentence seems to suggest that Nero was hoping to witness, and presumably revel in, some sort of apocalyptic Götterdämmerung. As strange as this seems, one can imagine Nero's extravagant, theatrical, and troubled imagination finding the prospect of a spectacular Roman Armageddon alluring. To a degree, this Nero is consistent with the fiddling Nero. Suetonius then says, "And that's just what he made happen." That is, he torched Rome. So far, so (weirdly) good. But in the next sentence Suetonius suggests that Nero started the fire under the *pretense* of being disgusted at the hideousness of the city's old buildings and higgledy-piggledy layout, as if finding a city ugly, old-fashioned, and inconvenient would be a reasonable excuse or pretense for committing a terrible atrocity, a pretense devised to hide some truer and even darker motivation. Are we to imagine Nero gleefully awaiting the thrilling sight of the city and its inhabitants going up in flames, while telling people—because this would be acceptable to the dull and tiny minds that surrounded him—that he was going to destroy the city and murder its people as an act of urban renewal?

Once Suetonius starts to describe the fire, we get a suggestion of yet another motive: Nero wanted particular granaries destroyed so that he could appropriate the land for his own purposes. Those purposes are not stated in the passage, but Suetonius must be thinking of Nero's intention to upgrade and expand his palace, for which he had his eye on certain suitably located tracts of land. What are we to make of these different motivations? Was Suetonius a bit confused in his effort to attribute motives to Roman (and likely all) history's greatest arsonist? Was he intentionally offering all these motives in something of a jumble to leave it to his readers to sort them out? Or did he intend the reader to attribute *all* these motives to Nero, a kind of triple whammy of melodramatic craziness, cruel aestheticism, and greed? Or was Nero just too much for Suetonius to wrap his head around?

In any event, with the sole exception of Tacitus, our extant ancient sources agreed that Nero started the fire. Tacitus said it is unclear whether the fire started by chance or through Nero's machinations. He also asserted that some authors believed Nero was behind the Great Fire, but others considered it an accident.[17] That is, Nero did have his defenders, though Tacitus did not supply us with names, and no passage defending Nero against the charge of arson survives.

Most modern scholars think that the Great Fire was an accident. In that metropolis of daily fires, as much a vast heap of wood, wool, and combustible waste as a city, an accidental conflagration of even this grand scale was no surprise, and perhaps even inevitable. The limitations of Roman firefighting technology, resources, and strategy explain why even at the top of their game Roman firefighters could easily be overwhelmed. Furthermore, what the modern world has discovered about the behavior of fires explains much of what puzzled the ancient Romans about how the Great Fire spread, and actions that seemed like attempts to abet the fire can be read as the time-tested and still employed strategy of creating firebreaks. Dio's accusatory account of these attempts is incompatible with Tacitus's in some significant respects, but both are compatible with people misunderstanding what the *vigiles* were up to. We also now know that eyewitness testimony, once considered conclusive, is highly unreliable.[18] After the chaos and terror the Great Fire had inflicted on Rome's residents—consider just the sensory overload!—how likely is it that its victims provided accurate accounts of what had actually happened? That they even *understood* what had actually happened?

How do victims make sense of a catastrophe of this scale, anyway? The Great Fire would have been the most significant event in most of their lives. Though inured to discomfort, danger, and disaster, they had never experienced such vast and crushing devastation, as their world was reduced to rubble and confusion. Friends and family lost; injuries whose pain and scars would serve as lifelong reminders of the trauma; property and possessions incinerated; your sense of security and of the normal in life, however much it entailed acknowledgment of Rome's endemic discomforts and perils, shattered; firsthand experience of a previously unimaginable catastrophe; your entire neighborhood, the very context for your life, your world, literally gone up in smoke. People need to account for an event so unaccountable and overwhelming in its character, scale, and impact, and for many, "Sometimes terrible things happen in Rome" would not have offered sufficient consolation or explanation. Perhaps an event so extraordinary and shocking calls for an explanation just as extraordinary and shocking. And that explanation can be devoid of evidence or logic, as long as it speaks to something visceral in how we view the world.

This makes perfect psychological sense, and history provides many examples. Here is one. In 1923, an immense earthquake, the Great Kanto Earthquake and Fire, devastated Tokyo, Yokohama, and their entire region. Estimates place the casualties at well over 100,000, and photographs of the aftermath show entire communities leveled. Fires broke out in the cities—like ancient Rome, mostly constructed of and furnished with highly flammable materials—and a particularly vicious fire tornado killed tens of thousands. Rumors soon spread that Korean immigrants were exploiting the earthquake to start fires, poison wells, undermine Japan's government, and, so frequent an accusation in such cases, rape Japanese women. Vigilantes, often with the support of officials, killed thousands of Koreans. The battered residents of the Kanto region did not, of course, blame the Koreans for the earthquake itself, but rather for much of its awful wake, including, of particular interest to us, fires. Again, "Terrible things happen" was not an adequate explanation or consolation for frustrated, bewildered, and angry victims of the quake and the fires it caused. Someone, something needed to be found to help explain the disaster but also to shoulder blame for it and offer their rage an attainable target. The alien Koreans filled the bill and suffered for it.[19]

Scholars who think the Great Fire of Rome was an accident, then, attribute the accusations leveled at Nero to the human need to process disasters and through that processing to assert some control, however illusory, over them. This need is a powerful and essential element of the story of many disasters, and certainly that of the Great Fire, but it tells us nothing about the actual cause of the disaster. In this interpretation, Rome's vulnerability to fire is guilty, and Nero is innocent.

The explanation for Rome's Great Fire just sketched out has not settled the case. There is another school—or schools, since there are variations—of thought that maintains that Nero did it, torched his own city with the intention of razing it to the ground, or at least sizeable sections of it, and therefore was guilty of one of history's most heinous crimes. The case is still open, and it remains one of history's most compelling murder mysteries, up there with the identity of Jack the Ripper, the culpability for the murder of the princes in the tower, and the identity of the Zodiac Killer, but for its body count and historical ramifications, it is in a league of its own.

Here are some of the arguments and counterarguments of the cases for the prosecution and the defense.[20]

Prosecution: Save Tacitus, all the ancient sources that survive agree that Nero started the fire.[21]

Defense: None of our surviving sources were eyewitnesses, none of them specify *their* sources, and everything about Nero and what he stood for so appalled them that they were eager to embrace any story that helped them express their disgust. Also, to what extent were these writers eager to ingratiate themselves with the anti-Nero regimes under which they were writing? That is, we have accusations and slander, but no hard evidence. Besides, Tacitus tells us that other sources, ones that unfortunately happen not to have survived, thought him innocent. We have no idea how many ancients were on each side, and the surviving authors who assume Nero was guilty number not even a handful. They are a tiny sample. Regardless, we do not determine the truth by voting.

Prosecution: Nero's intention to burn Rome is the only explanation for a series of "truly extraordinary ... events" and "remarkable actions" Nero took before the Great Fire. In Tacitus's telling, Nero made his theatrical debut in Naples and had decided to travel to Greece to perform but kept changing his mind: head off to Greece; nope, trip canceled and return to Rome; head off to Egypt and elsewhere in the East; nope, trip canceled; remain in Rome and enjoy the depraved orgy and "marriage" Tacitus describes right before he tells the story of the Great Fire; then, the Great Fire occurs (apparently after Nero had headed to Anzio). Nero also declared that, because his people could not bear his long absence, he decided not to take his show on the road, which suggests that he knew Rome's residents would soon be enduring a catastrophe. Only his knowledge of the impending, indeed *planned*, catastrophe can explain this strange, "abrupt and inexplicable abandonment of foreign travel." The Great Fire was in the works.[22]

Defense: Too much is made of a mere couple of canceled or postponed trips and of Nero's changes of mind and hesitation as he was about to embark on his performance tour of the Greek east—where the most discriminating and intimidating audiences were to be found. The tour meant, essentially, hitting the boards on Broadway or in London's West End. Nero's vacillation should not surprise considering his insecure, changeable, emotional nature. Additionally, a couple of events during his period of wavering would have unsettled even a more stable temperament: right after he performed in Naples (opening out of town, essentially), the theater collapsed—that is, Nero barely escaped death; and he suffered a panic attack in the Temple of Vesta back in Rome.[23] If Nero's changes of mind and action were the result of his plan to burn Rome, the sequence is just as puzzling: I will go to Greece; no, stay here and burn the city; maybe head to Egypt after all; oh, right, I am burning the city and so had best stay.

Prosecution: Our sources reported that Nero's agents started the Great Fire by (1) setting fires at different spots throughout the city (Dio), or (2) openly and menacingly setting fires on aristocrats' property, clearly here and there throughout the city (as in Dio), and then demolishing and torching buildings (Suetonius). Tacitus claimed that unidentified people prevented bystanders from fighting the fire, while other villains started more fires, on someone's authority, they claimed, and there can be little doubt who that someone was.[24] So, there is much testimony that Nero's agents started and then assisted the fire.

Defense: The agents who seemed to be starting or abetting the fire were actually fighting it. Eyewitnesses to their actions misinterpreted the time-honored firefighting strategy of creating firebreaks through controlled burning and demolition. Besides, Tacitus, whose account has the greatest authority, asserted that the fire started in the Circus Maximus, not here and there throughout the city. The idea that the Great Fire originated in different places most likely reflects people's experience of seeing that immense and relentless blaze spreading throughout the city and so appearing in different places at the same time. This tells us nothing of the fire's origin.

Prosecution: Tacitus informed us that after the fire had apparently been extinguished, it reignited on the property of Tigellinus, Nero's Praetorian Prefect, unscrupulous henchman, and impresario of imperial orgies.[25] Tacitus explicitly connected this fact to the suspicion that Nero had set the fire in order to rebuild the city to his liking. This is hardly a coincidence. Clearly, the fire had not yet razed all the sections of the city Nero had targeted for obliteration, and so he ordered Tigellinus to get it going again to finish the job.
Defense: There is no need to see human agency in the resurgence of the fire. Seemingly extinguished fires often flare up again from their smoldering embers, and there is no reason why that would not have happened during the Great Fire and why it could not have happened on Tigellinus's property. Besides, it is likely that the fire had *not* been extinguished at all—the *vigiles*' success in halting the fire's assault on the Esquiline Hill, some waning in the fire's intensity, and optimism generated by desperation created this false impression. Besides, Nero and Tigellinus would have been fools to reignite the fire on Tigellinus's property, when they had the authority and manpower to restart the fire in a less incriminating location—unless, in a display of civic leadership in the midst of a crisis, Tigellinus had expressly started *controlled burns* on his own property in an effort to contain the Great Fire, fires that were later misread as arson.[26]

Prosecution: After the fire, Nero rebuilt Rome to his taste, and, particularly suspicious, built his sprawling and lavish Golden House largely on land the fire had cleared. This suggests that he started the fire to open up space for his coveted expansion and embellishment of the palace. He did not intend to burn the better part of the city, but the fires his agents started got out of control, as fires are wont to do.
Defense: The building of the Golden House is evidence that Nero took advantage of the land the fire made available, however shameless that might have been, but not evidence that he set the fire. This accusation is a perfect example of *post hoc propter hoc* fallacious reasoning.

Prosecution: According to Tacitus, Nero returned to the city *only* when parts of his palace were threatened. That must have been because it was his plan to raze all the structures on the land he desired to appropriate *but not* on the land on which his own home stood.

Defense: Nero's slow response to the fire does not indicate that he started it. Besides, Tacitus's assertion that Nero returned only to save his palace is really a crafty slur based on no actual evidence—that is, Tacitus attributed to Nero motivation based on his reading of Nero, not on any actual testimony or evidence.

Prosecution: Rome endured and managed fires all the time, but nothing remotely of this scale; this fire became so exceptionally widespread, *the* Great Fire, because the authorities, acting on Nero's orders, were protecting and assisting the fire instead of doing what they normally did—fighting the flames.

Defense: The real surprise is not that a fire of this magnitude accidentally occurred, but that it had not occurred earlier. Conditions in Rome were such that "the big one" was inevitable.

Prosecution: That batty "fiddling" was more exultation in the fire than lamentation of it. It makes most sense (granted, of that peculiar Neronian sort) as the celebration of the successful implementation of a plan. This fits perfectly with Suetonius's assertion that when someone said (at some point before the Great Fire), "When I am dead, let the earth be consumed by fire!" he corrected the speaker, "No, while I still live,"[27] virtually a declaration of the desire to create a Götterdämmerung.

Defense: Nero need not have started the most spectacular sight he would see in his life to marvel at it and embrace it as an opportunity for performance. Besides, the story of Nero's "fiddling" could just be anti-Nero propaganda. As for his proclaiming his desire to experience the apocalyptic destruction of Rome—there is a gap between expressing such a desire (perhaps at a well-oiled event) and bringing it about. Tiberius "often" expressed the same sentiment in virtually the same language.[28] It is likely that the quotation was attributed to Nero *after* the fire in the imaginations and resentments of those convinced that Nero had started it, perhaps transferred from Tiberius, who really had said such a thing, to Nero, under whom such a twilight of the gods just happened to occur.[29]

Prosecution: Almost a year later, in 65, a conspiracy against Nero was hatched and failed,[30] and one of the conspirators, a tribune named Subrius Flavus, who was an officer in the emperor's guard, when Nero asked him why he had participated, responded, "I began to hate after you were revealed to be the murderer of your mother and your wife, a charioteer, an actor, and an arsonist."[31] One scholar argues that this is reliable and virtually eyewitness testimony: "Subrius Flavus was not a man to act on popular rumor . . . and he was actually with Nero when Rome was burning. The accusations of Subrius Flavus might be explained away by those who would prefer to believe in Nero's innocence, as just the sort of thing that a conspirator would say, but it still looks very much like a lone fact in a debate based on opinions about probabilities."[32]
Defense: Well, it *is* just the sort of thing a man about to be executed by someone he loathed would say. Throw at the villain every plausible accusation, the more shocking the better, most or all of which conspirators would naturally be inclined to credit anyway. Also, Tacitus suggested Subrius was with the emperor when he returned to Rome *after* the fire was well under way and was involved in the emperor's *response* to the fire, but these facts tell us nothing about Subrius's knowledge of the Great Fire's *origin* or *cause*. If Subrius was such an upright fellow, he was precisely the sort of person the emperor would have kept out of the loop while planning and undertaking such a monstrous crime.

Prosecution: This is just the sort of thing the deranged and narcissistic Nero would do.
Defense: Nero may have indeed been deranged and narcissistic, but he did nothing else quite like this; besides, "It's the sort of thing X would do" is just argument by insinuation.

The prosecution and defense rest. For now, however, no judgment can be made, and the court cannot be adjourned.

Scapegoats

Whether Nero was responsible for the fire or not, some people believed he was, and that was a problem. He needed to divert suspicion away from himself and at someone or something else. This is not as easy as it seems. The best scapegoats are relatively powerless, without influential advocates and sympathizers, unpopular, already suspected (of what? that does not really matter much), and plausible candidates for the part. Particularly useful, when scapegoats will be facing the cruelest punishments, they must be perceived to be outsiders, like the Koreans in the wake of the Great Kanto Earthquake and Fire. The Romans considered themselves to be civilized, but like most ancient peoples, they had refined the skill of recategorizing certain fellow human beings as über outsiders—as a virtually different and separate species of humans, a species not entitled to (or one that had forfeited) the consideration and sympathy civilized people accord others.[33] That skill enabled the Romans to treat conquered peoples, slaves, and gladiators, to give the most infamous examples, in ways we might consider inhumane and even savage, but the Romans considered just.

The earliest Christians checked every box for scapegoat candidature, and then some:

- A Roman governor had executed their founder—they were, then, followers of a criminal and so plausibly viewed as something of a criminal organization.
- Their sect was new and foreign—despite their habit of adapting foreign customs and beliefs, the Romans' initial reaction to the new and the foreign tended to be suspicion.
- They were antisocial—the Roman world's grand, community-defining gatherings were almost all religious in some respect or other: the celebration of military victories, chariot races, the Olympics, public banquets, parades, theater, just to name a few such occasions; some, likely most, Christians would avoid such events.[34]
- Rumors of cannibalism and incest may have already been dogging them—in the Roman world, accusations of ritual atrocities and particularly of human sacrifice and cannibalism were standard operating procedure in slandering unpopular outsiders,[35] but that does not mean no one believed the rumors.
- In that the Christians tended to keep to themselves and were not terribly numerous, sympathizers among the general population were few; many residents of Rome did not care what happened to this antisocial and tiny minority, and many more likely had never met a Christian or perhaps even heard of the sect; to judge from later Christian rhetoric, when some Christians engaged with the world outside

their faith, they may have employed insulting and belligerent language that was unlikely to win friends.
- Anyone aware of Christian beliefs would have known that Christians were expecting the world to end soon—not in the coming centuries or decades but perhaps even in the coming weeks. Would it be surprising if these apocalyptic fanatics were hastening and abetting this end by setting Rome ablaze? And, for all we know, a Christian or two might have misread the moment and shouted a few injudicious Hallelujahs amidst the flames.

And so, Tacitus tells us, Nero selected the Christians to take the fall for the Great Fire. The price they paid is shocking. Tacitus's account of their fate immediately follows his description of Nero's measures to help the fire's victims, rebuild the city, and placate the gods, and it is one of the greatest and most notorious set pieces of ancient literature, *the* account of all ancient accounts of persecution.

> But no human aid, no distributions from the emperor, or even appeasement of gods could stop people from believing the appalling rumor that the fire had been ordered. Consequently, to quash the rumor, Nero scapegoated and afflicted with the most inventive punishments people the crowd had begun to dub "Christians" and hated for their abominations. The origin of this name was a certain Christus, whom the governor Pontius Pilate had executed when Tiberius was emperor. The pernicious superstition was temporarily suppressed but broke out again, not only throughout Judea, its place of origin, but even throughout Rome itself, where everything heinous and disgraceful from every place imaginable gathers and thrives. And so at first, whoever admitted to being a Christian was arrested. Next, on the basis of the information they provided, a huge crowd was convicted, not really as a consequence of the crime of arson but rather because of their misanthropy. The methods of execution were selected to mock them: some were covered in the hides of wild animals and torn apart by dogs; others were fastened to crosses and set aflame, and so when daylight faded their burning was used to illuminate the night. Nero offered his own gardens for his show, and he produced such entertainment in the circus during which, dressed like a charioteer or actually standing in a chariot, he mixed with the common folk. The result, though, was that pity for the victims arose, even though they were guilty and deserved the most extreme punishment. That was because people felt that they were being killed not for the public good, but to satisfy one man's cruelty.[36]

This account is so powerful and horrifying and efficient that it seems to require no further elucidation. Could the images or could Nero's motives be any clearer or more disturbing? Still, Tacitus's crafty and indirect Latin prose, ambiguities in his word choice, and even textual complications in the original Latin raise quite a few significant questions to which scholars have dedicated innumerable pages. Alas, definitive answers to these questions are few and far between.[37] This is not the place to address—let alone answer—all of them, but here are some of the most significant and controversial and, for some of them, a best-guess answer.

- Who believed the rumor that Nero started the fire? How many people and of what sort? Had this become the consensus on the street, among Rome's elite, everywhere? Or was this a minority but nonetheless potentially destabilizing explanation for the fire? Some among Rome's elite were convinced that Nero had started the fire, but others were not. Unfortunately we have no evidence for how widespread the suspicion was among the rest of Rome's population.[38]
- Why did Tacitus characterize Christianity as a "pernicious superstition" (*exitiabilis superstitio*) and its adherents as worthy of "the most severe punishment" (*novissima exempla*)? What were the Christians' "abominations" (*flagitia*)? The most obvious explanation for the abominations is the rumors that the Christians participated in depraved and criminal orgies highlighted by incest and cannibalism. Later sources attest to these charges, but sources close in time to 64 do not.[39] These earlier sources on the Christians are meager, however, and none of them offers the pagan perspective. Was Tacitus retrojecting the later charges? Or was he using the usual defamatory language Romans tended to apply to the new, foreign, and suspected? Since Tacitus characterized Rome as a cesspool into which everything dreadful and disgraceful flows, he may have simply been lumping the Christians in with all the other foreign filth and depravity that, of course, found its way to the filthy and depraved capital.[40] Or the charges may have been circulating in Rome. We do not know for certain. In any event, Tacitus's language suggests that it was not arson the Christians were guilty of—scapegoats are not the actual culprits—but unspecified abominations unrelated to the fire.
- Of what were the Christians "convicted" (*convicti sunt*)? Of being Christians? Of arson? To what did they confess (*fatebantur*)? Again, to being Christians or arsonists or something else? The most sensible solution is that they were charged with and convicted of arson. Did they confess to being

arsonists? Under torture, that is certainly possible. But it may make more sense to assume that the authorities simply equated Christians with arsonists, or pretended to. That is, at least in the official rhetoric, Christian conspirators torched Rome, and so the authorities found it reasonable to treat all who confessed to membership in that criminal and fanatical cult as members of the arsonist gang.

- What did Tacitus mean when he said the Christians were convicted, "not really as a consequence of the crime of arson but rather because of their misanthropy"? Scholars have agonized over these lines. Reading them rhetorically rather than legally offers the best solution. Tacitus did not mean that their misanthropy was in any way the legal charge, but that the underlying cause for their selection as scapegoats was their perceived hatred of others that made *them* in turn hated by some of those others. This also made executing them relatively painless (for the authorities and the public, that is) and uncontroversial, or at least that is what Nero anticipated in selecting them.

- Was Tacitus actually talking about Christians?[41] The manuscript evidence is unclear whether Tacitus originally wrote Christians (*Christianos*) or Chrestians (*Chrestianos*). Tacitus's contemporary and friend Suetonius said that the emperor Claudius, Nero's predecessor, "expelled the Jews from Rome, since Chrestos was constantly inciting them to cause trouble."[42] So, were these folks we assume to be Christians actually an entirely different Jewish group, the Chrestians, led by a provocateur named Chrestus? Maybe. A better guess, though, if Tacitus did in fact write *Chrestianos,* is that the spelling of the name of this new group was not entirely clear to Tacitus and Suetonius or, more likely, to their sources. *Chrestus* was not an uncommon Greek name, and the word was a common adjective meaning, essentially, "good." *Christus*, in contrast, was a more unusual word in ancient Greek, and only became a name, as far as we can tell, when it was used to translate the Hebrew "messiah."[43] An *e* in place of an *i*, moreover, would have been a relatively minor error, and spelling in the ancients' largely oral society was more flexible and varied than in our world anyway.

In addition: the name *Chrestus* meant "Mr. Good Guy" in Greek, the name's original language. It is not out of the question that the early Christians' critics ironically referred to Jesus as "Mr. Good Guy" and his followers as "Mr. Good Guy's Guys"; in some Roman circles that bit of snark may have been a running joke that found its way into Suetonius's and Tacitus's texts. And Suetonius's reference to Rome's Jews causing disturbance because of a certain "Chrestos" would make perfect sense, if Chrestos refers to Christos/Christ. The earliest Christians were almost all Jews, and it would be some time before Jewish/Christian conflicts would be anything more than one kind or sect of Jews feuding with other kinds or sects of Jews, at the very least in the eyes of pagan observers. In any event, Tacitus's comments on the origin of the arsonists make it clear that he was referring to Christians.

- The manuscript tradition of Tacitus's Latin text raises another vexing issue. It is uncertain whether he meant to say, "others were fastened to crosses *and* set aflame," as I have translated his Latin above, or "others were fastened to crosses *or* were set aflame." As my translation indicates, I incline towards the former reading of the Latin.[44] If the former is correct, it would mean that Nero's Christians were not crucified in the traditional sense, that is, affixed to crosses on which they were to die of asphyxiation, but rather that they were affixed to crosses in order to be burned alive and so supply Nero's nocturnal show with ghastly illumination. Another option, however, preserves the most likely reading of the Latin text and makes perfect sense in terms of the event: Nero's victims were crucified in the traditional sense, and so the audience could relish their protracted suffering through some of the late afternoon and early evening; but instead of allowing the crucifixions to run their course to death, as night fell the crucified, still alive, were set afire to light the festivities. Crucified by day, then lit up at night—a twofer, though of an awful sort. The third-century Christian martyr Pionius likewise endured a mixed-methodology execution: he was tortured, nailed to a cross, and then burned alive.[45]
- Tacitus claimed that "a huge crowd" (*multitudo ingens*) was convicted—and so, ultimately, executed. Was he exaggerating to emphasize the scale of Nero's cruelty? When it comes to a mass execution, particularly a public and gruesome one, how many victims do you need to have a "huge crowd"? A hundred? Two hundred? Thirty? Seventy? There is no way of knowing. In any event, Rome at the time could not have had a large community of Christians—they were only just getting started. Did two hundred Christians live in Rome? Five hundred? A thousand? We can only guess.
- Why were the Christians crucified, burned, and torn apart by dogs? The Romans particularly prized two principles in the punishment of their worst criminals: at best, the punishment should evoke and match the crime, and it should entail public humiliation. Burning is obvious—an appropriate and conventional punishment for arsonists (the Romans even had a word for it:

vivicomburium—"burning alive"). There may have been an additional bit of poetic justice tossed in, too, if the Great Fire had destroyed or damaged the temple of Luna Noctiluca (Luna, Illuminator of the Night) on the Palatine Hill, so called because it was illuminated nocturnally, a rare bright spot amidst Rome's nightly gloom: "You villains will now supply the light you deprived us of!"[46] Crucifixion was a standard Roman method of execution in the most severe cases, and Roman authorities were aware that the founder of this cult of arsonists had died on a cross. Crucifying and then burning these victims offered spectators a witty and satisfying nexus of allusions and ironies and a fitting one-two punch to those who would overturn the Roman order. Was there a logic to dressing the Christians in animal hides and siccing dogs on them? It suggested that the arsonists were no more than animals deserving of this savage demise, of course, and the theatrical appeal of such a sight must have been considerable.

In Rome, executions were entertainment as much as justice; indeed, it is difficult to disentangle the two in the Roman worldview and sensibility. Nero's faux hunt added variety to the proceedings, something the Romans prized in entertainment: tableaux of protracted agony that crucifixion presented, the dazzle and crackle of human torches, and the frenzied action of canine beasts tearing human beasts apart. Something for everyone, and enough variation to keep the cruelty from descending into tedium.[47]

There might, however, have been more to the dogs than their show-business appeal. The Christians' fate evoked that of Actaeon, a mythological hunter who saw the goddess Artemis bathing, a violation the virgin hunter-goddess punished by transforming him into a stag whose own hunting dogs then tore to shreds. Such was a suitable end as well for those who had employed fire to violate the images and homes of the gods. The Romans' love for nasty reenactments of violent myths and historical events, what Kathleen Coleman aptly dubbed "fatal charades,"[48] adds credibility to this reading of the dogs. Suetonius recorded two unsettling examples of Nero having a transgressive and a perilous myth performed before a live audience, the first portraying the Minoan queen Pasiphae's sex with a bull, and the latter depicting Icarus's failed attempt to fly: "A bull penetrated a woman portraying Pasiphae, who was hidden in a wooden effigy of a heifer; at least that's what many in the audience thought they saw. At his first attempt to fly, Icarus immediately crashed close to Nero's couch and splattered him with blood."[49] In the first instance, Suetonius seemed to think (or hope?) that the horrifying bestiality presented was not real—perhaps a bit too

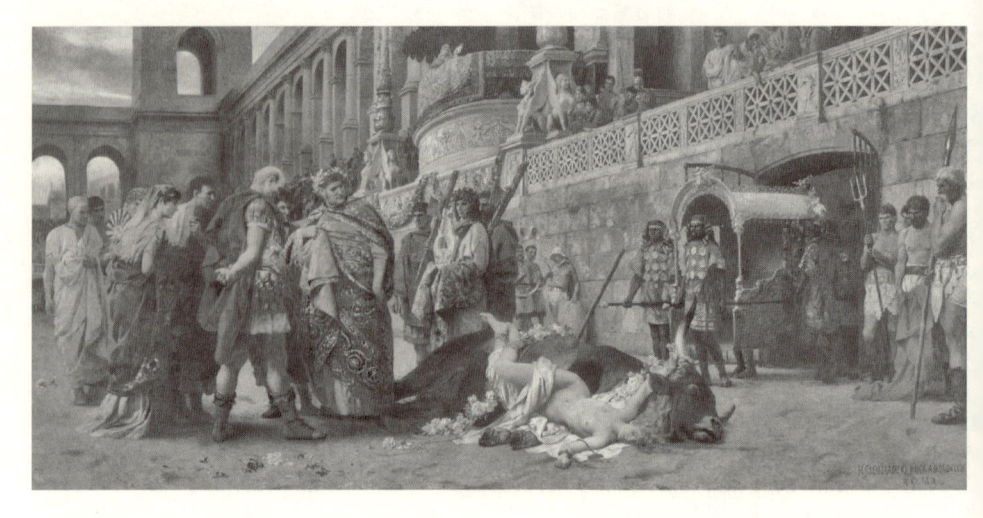

Figure 6. Henryk Siemiradski's *Christian Dirce* (1897). The painting depicts one of the Christian martyrs Nero scapegoated for the Great Fire. She has managed to find a lovely pose in death, and her beauty remains unspoiled. Nero does not fare so well in the painting. National Museum, Warsaw; courtesy of Wikimedia Commons

warped even for Suetonius, a connoisseur (though a censorious one) of aberrant excess. Roman special effects? Either way, the audience enjoyed the frisson of witnessing the most outrageous depravity. Suetonius's description leaves no doubt as to the lethal and messy outcome of the Icarus performance.

Another source suggests that two further methods of execution likely offered even more variety to Nero's proceedings.[50] Writing towards the end of the first century, just a few decades after the Great Fire, Clement of Rome mentioned Christian "Danaids and Dirces" having suffered ghastly deaths.[51] The most plausible interpretation of Clement's assertion is that these were women the Romans dressed up as Danaids or Dirces and executed in enactments of other Greek myths, and the only plausible context for these enactments is Nero's notorious scapegoating executions.[52]

In their tale, forty-nine Danaids murdered their bridegrooms on their wedding night and so, in one version, were condemned to an eternity of pouring water from jugs into a bottomless tub. Did Nero stage some sort of watery death for the Christian "Danaids"?[53] He might have had them drowned before the crowd, for example, possibly in some unexpected way. The Romans were, after all, antiquity's masters of all things hydraulic, as their aqueducts, bathhouses, and fountains testify,[54] and their ingenuity was boundless when it came to staging executions. In a different myth, a stepmother worthy of the grimmest fairy tales, Dirce tried to get her stepsons to kill their mother; instead, they tied Dirce to the horns of a bull, which dragged and gored her to death. Did Nero present bulls savaging Christian "Dirces" (fig. 6)? The use of animals in executions was standard operating procedure among the Romans—think of those dogs again—and around 130 years later a heifer was used to dispatch the Christian women martyrs Perpetua and Felicity in a Roman arena in Africa.[55]

Tacitus did not mention Danaids or Dirces, but we should not assume that in his brief account of the Christians' sufferings he was enumerating every act in Nero's production. If the martyrs Clement mentioned were part of Nero's spectacle, there may have been an additional point to their inclusion. The only building Dio named as destroyed in the Great Fire was the Amphitheater of Taurus, named after the general who erected the amphitheater and whose name translates as "Bull." The myth of Dirce might have offered a bit of vicious poetic justice to the putative destroyers of Bull's Amphitheater. The Great Fire may also have approached, reached, or even damaged or destroyed the colonnade of Danaids that mostly fronted the Temple of Apollo on the Palatine, and the temple and colonnade may have been the site of one of the *vigiles*' most successful defenses of Rome's architectural and religious heritage.[56]

If so, then how satisfying must it have been to dress these impious arsonists as the Danaids they had threatened or even harmed and to extinguish their lives with fire's primary adversary, water? The Romans relished this sort of nasty wit. Besides, one of the functions of the fatal charades was to restore what the Romans deemed to be the proper order of things and among people. A definitive restoration of order required that the villains be deprived of their dignity and even their humanity. Moreover, if *vigiles* did save the Temple of Apollo and its colonnade, this performance could have doubled as a celebration of a Roman victory over the purveyors of murder, devastation, and subversion at a moment when the city's exhausted and dispirited population had little to celebrate.

- The context indicates that the show in the circus consisted, at least in part, of another round of public executions of Christians.[57] But why was Nero prancing around in a charioteer's kit and posing and mingling with the crowd from a chariot? What could be more bizarre and less dignified than an emperor, or any human being, wearing a costume and preening on a chariot amidst the sights, sounds, and even smells of excruciating death? There is always the "Nero was nasty and mad" explanation, which is not without merit, but Nero's madness was rarely arbitrary, and even his most outlandish behavior had its own Neronian logic, as we have seen with his fiddling.

First, the costume and chariot fitted the setting. Next, Nero was not only a fan of chariot-racing but determined to actually race. Just a few years after the Great Fire, he competed in chariot-racing at the Olympic Games. Unsurprisingly, the judges declared him the winner even though he fell from his chariot, which had ten instead of the usual pedestrian four horses.[58] Nero had also started publically identifying himself with the god Apollo as early as 59, an identification that was to intensify after the Great Fire. By Nero's day, Apollo had become associated with the sun god Sol and was imagined as bringing day and light to the world by riding the chariot of the sun across the sky. By dressing as a charioteer and riding a chariot, then, Nero was suggesting a variety of telling and bold equivalencies: Nero = Apollo, Nero = *the* charioteer, Nero = bringer of light and a new dawn after the misery of the Great Fire, and Nero/Apollo = righteous avenger of the sacrilegious attempt to destroy his temple on the Palatine Hill.[59]

A portion of Rome's population loved Nero's public antics, the more outrageous the better. In a world with very little social mobility, where most people were trapped in a life full of discomfort, insecurity, and danger, and where the lower classes were subject to the whims and coercion of Rome's elites, some would be amused by a bit of subversion from the emperor—another delightful element of the entertainment. One can imagine Romans who attended telling those who had not, "You won't believe what the emperor was wearing at the executions," and all having a good laugh about it.

Nero's performance at the executions—and it *was* a performance, replete with costumes, props, scenery, and even stage lighting of a ghoulish sort—was another act in the grand and exquisite work of performance art his life was becoming, starring himself, surrounded by a cast of thousands, an audience of tens of thousands, the most impressive theatrical settings the world had ever seen, and, of course, conducted with an unlimited budget. As actors (however unwilling) in Nero's drama, the Christians were not really themselves, but bit players dressed to play the part the emperor had scripted for them. The Christians affixed to crosses were almost certainly wearing the *tunica molesta* (the irritating tunic), a robe daubed with pitch to facilitate burning; as night fell, this costume was then transformed into a second, more startling costume—one of fire. Others wore animal skins or outfits that evoked the myths of the Danaids and Dirce. Nero was resplendent in the guise of Apollo, the transcendent charioteer, the Sun, the god of musical performance, of performance itself. He must have been ecstatic.

Like all Roman spectacles—indeed, like all life in ancient Rome—the executions engaged all the senses. The audience heard the victims' screams and groans, almost certainly mixed in with exclamations to the strange cult's strange deity; the dogs' growling and barking as they savaged and fed upon their victims; the crackling of the fires from the human torches; and perhaps the splashing and mechanical grinding of death-dealing waterworks. And, of course, the gasps and cries and cheers from the crowd. The odor of burning flesh likely mixed with that of the spectators' bodies—since the Great Fire opportunities for bathing must have been limited—and if perfume was added to the proceedings, as was often the case, it may have less masked the stench than endowed it with a cloying accent. The executions must have been a heady and thrilling multisensory experience, enhanced by the satisfaction of seeing, or at least of pretending to see, Rome's most vicious enemies brought to justice. And yet Tacitus suggested that pity arose for the victims "because people felt that they were being killed not for the public good, but to satisfy one man's cruelty." A Roman spectacle was a complex transaction between the show's sponsor and the audience, and miscalculation on a sponsor's part could lose the audience. In a show he gave in 55 BCE, Julius Caesar's great rival Pompey lost the spectators when they started to pity the elephants whose slaughter he was staging for their amusement. He garnered curses instead of the anticipated gratitude.[60]

In the case of the Christians, Tacitus suggested that Nero lost some in the crowd because they saw through his scapegoating and read the emperor's personal cruelty, not the public good, as the impetus for the executions. If so, the executions' "inventiveness" and Nero's performance at them likely aggravated the audience's disaffection. It is certainly possible that Tacitus was projecting his own later reaction to the spectacle back onto the crowd. Yet the audience reaction, so integral to the meaning and success or failure of any Roman show, but particularly to such an important one, may have been remembered. Another consideration: It is not out of the question that much of the executions' engagement of the spectators' senses may have evoked sensations they had experienced during the Great Fire and so prompted memories of their recent and still raw sufferings and losses. Perhaps they even triggered flashbacks to the conflagration. The executions' evocations of the Great Fire may have been too close in time and subject for a still traumatized people.

-IV-
Neropolis

Reconstruction

Devastated Rome became one of the great construction sites of human history. The city's energy and manpower and the empire's resources and know-how turned Rome into a beehive of activity. Rather than leveling all the rubble from the Great Fire, Nero decided to have the lion's share of it hauled away, and he implemented an efficient plan to effect this and to supply the fire's victims with food: barges that hauled the wreckage away were required to bring grain back to the city when returning to pick up another load.[1] This twofer strategy may have contributed to the decision to dump the debris in the marshes near Ostia, Rome's port city, where seagoing ships would bring grain designated for Rome to be unloaded and then loaded onto barges for transport up the Tiber to the capital. Once the rubble had been cleared away and the ground leveled, or at least some portions of the city had been sufficiently cleared and prepped, the actual construction commenced. As in a real beehive, the activity was furious but not haphazard, for Nero was determined that the old muddled mess of narrow twisting roads and overcrowded combustible buildings not rise again.[2] Rather, a new sort of Rome should emerge—a planned, more orderly and rational city, a salubrious and beautiful one, and one less prone to another grand conflagration. Tacitus described the principles on which the new Rome was built.

First, the layout. The lines of the streets were planned and regularized, and broad boulevards were created. Nero paid for the addition of porticoes or porches to the fronts of both townhouses and apartment buildings, "a new form of urban architecture that Nero himself came up with," according to Suetonius.[3] Tacitus asserted that the porches' purpose was to protect the fronts of the buildings, presumably from fire; Suetonius said that they provided roofs that could be mounted to fight fires.[4] These suggestions are not mutually exclusive, and the porticoes served other purposes as well. Among them: to provide shade against Rome's relentless summer sun and shelter from its occasional drenching rains. By day, Romans lived their lives mostly outdoors, as we have seen, and porticoes providing shade were a standard amenity of the most prosperous and sophisticated Mediterranean cities. Nero mandated open spaces, which made the new city airier and less claustrophobic and made it harder for fire to spread—anticipatory firebreaks, essentially, and the broad boulevards would serve the same function. He limited the height of buildings, which also made for a more open city, reduced the concentration of tinder for future fires, reduced the likelihood of collapse, and increased the likelihood of escape when fire did strike. And the walls of buildings could no longer abut the walls of other buildings. This mandated separation also created space intended to retard the spread of fire.

Next, Nero transformed the very fabric of the city. By regulation, the new buildings consisted primarily of relatively fire-resistant stone, and the employment of timber beams was reduced. It is virtually certain that brick and concrete also became favored materials, although Tacitus does not mention them.[5] The sturdier buildings that resulted would offer future fires less flammable material and would be less prone to collapse. The shift from timber beams to stone, concrete, and brick inaugurated a shift in the very shape of much Roman domestic and commercial architecture. Before the fire, wooden beams very likely supported most of the ceilings and roofs in those buildings—the standard post-and-lintel configuration employed in most homes in the United States, for example. Replacing the beams with stone and concrete (and perhaps other less flammable materials that Tacitus does not specify) meant that the new structures would be employing vaults rather than post-and-lintel supports. The Romans employed concrete and vaults earlier, of course, but not in domestic architecture on the revolutionary scale now under way.[6]

Lastly, Nero took measures to enhance the ability of the city to fight fires. Residents of Rome were now required to keep firefighting equipment easily accessible, which would facilitate the prevailing and most effective Roman strategy for fighting fires—nip them in the bud. Guards were posted to secure the water supply. Well-to-do Romans, farmers, shop owners, and even owners of houses of prostitution had felt entitled to siphon off water from the public aqueduct system for their own use, an illegal practice that reduced the flow of water to the city, which in turn meant less water available to extinguish fires.[7]

All these reforms and policies together constituted a revolution. Even Tacitus had to admit that Nero's innovations were useful and had made Rome more attractive, although he notes that some residents grumbled that the more open city had robbed the population of salubrious shade. Innovations always bump up against the cranky champions of "the good old days"—or was Tacitus incapable of praising Nero without reservation? Perhaps both.[8]

Nero also employed strategies to push private property owners and contractors to focus on completing their reconstruction projects as quickly as possible. He put the emperor's resources and clout behind clearing the rubble even on private property and then urged the property owners to tackle the reconstruction. He offered bonuses to those who completed their reconstruction projects expeditiously, and developers and builders who could not meet specified deadlines forfeited the rewards. For those building the new Rome, time was indeed money. The way these rewards were distributed was a perfect reflection of Roman values and of how the rich are better able than everyone else to navigate and even profit from disasters. Rank and wealth determined the level of reward you could expect.[9] To encourage Italians without full Roman citizenship to help in the rebuilding, Nero offered citizenship to those who had more than 200,000 sesterces if they would invest 100,000 sesterces in construction in the city.[10] Presumably, Nero took other measures to accelerate the reconstruction of the city that are not reflected in our sources.

The jury is out on the efficacy of Nero's urban innovations. There is no doubt that fires continued to plague Rome. Writing around a century after the Great Fire, Aullus Gellius describes himself observing a blaze as he and some acquaintances climbed the Cispian Hill: "We . . . saw a lofty, multistoried *insula* engulfed in flames, and all the neighboring buildings were already burning in a grand conflagration." In response to that fire, one of the speaker's group said, "The profits from urban property are considerable, but the dangers are far greater. If some solution could be found to prevent houses in Rome from constantly burning, I swear I'd sell my country property and buy real estate in the city."[11] Indeed, we have evidence for several major fires in the century and a half or so after the great one. So, problem apparently not solved.

On the other hand, the record of evidence for the post-64 fires seems to suggest that for quite some time after the reconstruction, the sections of the city where domestic architecture had been rebuilt according to Nero's specifications for the most part avoided conflagration. It was not until 191 CE, nearly 130 years after the Great Fire, that we have unambiguous evidence for a significant fire devastating sections of the city that the Great Fire had previously destroyed.[12] The quotations from Aullus Gellius, for example, do not specify where that fire broke out. Since the passage describes the interlocutors as ascending the Cispian Hill, it may make sense to assume that the fire described was on that hill, which, as far as we know, was beyond the Great Fire's reach. That is, a major fire devastated a neighborhood the Great Fire had not touched and so one that likely consisted principally of pre-Neronian buildings or buildings constructed much later, when the Neronian regulations may have been enforced less scrupulously.

In sum, then, our very limited record may suggest that for some time, major fires, at any rate, largely bypassed the sections of the city rebuilt according to the new standards. Nero's innovations may deserve a decent grade for fire prevention after all. As for the innumerable smaller fires that beset the city—they may have been reduced but were never to be eliminated. Even if the Neronian principles of construction helped avert conflagrations, the city remained full of tinder, its residents' way of life invited fires, much of the city's construction remained fire-friendly, corruption, corner-cutting, and code violations remained endemic to the Roman construction industry (like the rest of Roman life), and it is unclear how long after Nero's death the regulations retained their full force. The rebuilding and reconfiguring of Rome in the wake of the Great Fire certainly lasted decades after Nero was gone.

The additional air and space that new configuration produced may have made the city somewhat healthier, and the lighter, more open city may have reduced the opportunities for crime. The *insulae* built with Neronian materials and on the new principles should have been less prone to collapse, although the rush to resurrect the city likely resulted in some slapdash construction and cursory inspections. Moreover, the more spacious, rationally designed urban landscape allowed for the easier and more efficient movement of people and materials. Living in and moving about Rome became somewhat less of an ordeal. Tacitus experienced and lived in this new Rome, and since sections of the old city had survived the Great Fire, he was able to compare the two Romes. Despite his contempt for Nero, he had to admit that Nero's Rome functioned better and looked better than the old city had.[13] But how much better? We just do not have enough evidence to know for certain, unfortunately, but the slender evidence we do have suggests that any impact the new city had on Rome's many perils was limited. For one thing, much of the city—the parts the Great Fire had not razed—remained tangled warrens of narrow snaking streets that retained some of the old combustible construction. Rome also remained an unprecedentedly overcrowded and complex preindustrial city whose inhabitants were inured to discomfort and risk and lived lives that contributed to that discomfort and risk. Nero's innovations reduced certain hazards to some degree, but Rome continued to be just the place to drown, get food poisoning, contract some dreadful disease, suffer from sleep deprivation, get your throat cut, or yes, be burned to death. Rome was still Rome.

In any event, for years to come the actual clearing, reconfiguration, and reconstruction of the city provided Rome's residents with a new set of nightmares while exacerbating some of the old ones. The constant shipping of materials into and out of the city made sleep even more difficult, and the construction itself increased the insufferable din. The urgency with which all these efforts were undertaken likely guaranteed that the racket, like the work, went on around the clock. Building in ancient Rome was always dangerous—the city lacked regulations to protect workers or even passersby and gawkers, and workers compensation did not exist—but the scale and haste of reconstruction after the fire must have turned huge swathes of the city into mazes of materials and objects poised to crush your feet or skull or, that recurrent nightmare of life in ancient Rome, to bury you alive. Huge beams could fall off wagons, walls put up in haste could come down, crane cables toting tons of material could snap and pour their loads earthward, piles of bricks could tumble—all on you. Juvenal expressed precisely this fear of the dangers of construction in Rome: "An immense fir-tree beam wobbles along on an approaching wagon, and other freight wagons are conveying a tree. These loads sway high above and threaten the bystanders. And if the axle that supports blocks of marble gives way and pours its mountain of stone down on the crowd, what will be left of their bodies?"[14]

With so much of the city undergoing clearing and reconstruction, navigating Rome was even more trying than usual, perhaps particularly so for those anxious to avoid the ubiquitous and perilous construction sites. Years after Nero was gone, but still in the wake of the Great Fire, Martial even complained of getting stuck behind a traffic jam of blocks of marble being dragged to a construction site,[15] an inconvenience Rome's residents doubtless endured again and again. The thousands of workers on the job or out and about might have reduced crime, but the gangs of workers might have provided cover for other sorts of gangs. Always unhygienic and insalubrious, the state of Rome immediately after the fire and the overcrowded and makeshift conditions so many Romans were reduced to increased the likelihood of illness and even disease. It must have been disheartening, but not entirely surprising, that plague struck Rome the year after the Great Fire, a horrifying disaster in its own right that cost thirty thousand or so Romans their lives, according to Suetonius.[16]

Unfortunately, our sources tell us very little about the short-term economic and social impact of the city's reconstruction on new lines, but we can imagine some of the problems the transformation would have caused.[17] First, broader streets, mandated open spaces, and porch/portico fronts would have changed property lines, and in many cases these reforms occasioned loss of property—the boulevards and spaces meant a net gain in public property, which largely came at the expense of private property. The regularization and realignment of streets also wrought havoc with the pre-Fire property lines. Some of the newly laid-out streets, for all their rationality, must have run right through where the walls and rooms of destroyed buildings had been. Lawsuits regarding property rights and lines must have proliferated, unless Nero made clear that they would not be tolerated in light of the emergency. In any event, Romans could not sue the government or the emperor. The net loss of private and particularly private residential property in the city center would have driven up real estate values and rents, and the rents of the first *insulae* completed and ready for occupation must have been astronomical. Tens of thousands of people were eager to move back into the center of things, and the new layout and airier, more salubrious, pleasant, and attractive Rome that was starting to emerge would have had great appeal to those who could afford to live there. The transfer of so much private property to Rome's byways may also have resulted in smaller apartments for most tenants. As Rome outdoors became more spacious and open, Rome indoors likely became even more cramped. The plague that followed the Great Fire may have ameliorated the housing crisis somewhat by reducing the city's population, but at an appalling cost.

Compensation following disaster was not unprecedented in ancient Rome. Decades before the Great Fire, when another fire destroyed some *insulae* on the Caelian Hill, Tiberius made up the owners' losses; apparently Caligula occasionally did so as well.[18] But such imperial munificence was not the norm, and we have no evidence that Nero compensated the Great Fire's victims for their losses. Indeed, it is very likely that he could not have afforded to. The initial relief to Rome's population, food subsidies, the clearing of the rubble, the shipping of food and other materials, the imposition of the new network of streets and open spaces, the rebuilding or restoration of the abundant public buildings the fire had destroyed or damaged (from temples to markets to warehouses—even firehouses!), and his extravagant plans for the upgrade and expansion of the palace, among other expenses, would have already cost a fortune. Even with the exorbitant exactions on the rest of the empire, the imperial coffers had their limits. Nero's measures immediately after the Great Fire supported and comforted the inferno's victims and refugees, but they soon found themselves largely on their own.

At the same time, for many Romans the construction must have been exciting and even exhilarating. Residents of the city were witnessing and many even participating in one of history's greatest urban regeneration projects. They had seen nothing comparable in their own lives, and they could find nothing comparable in their history books and lore. With the Great Fire, Rome's residents had endured destruction on an unparalleled scale, and in its aftermath they were experiencing creation on an equally unparalleled scale—surely a heady experience, particularly after such a dismaying one. Opportunities abounded, although as usual the rich and powerful were in a better position to capitalize on them.

No one was richer and more powerful than the emperor, of course, and he seized this irresistible opportunity to do something unprecedentedly magnificent and narcissistic, even for a Roman emperor. He appropriated a vast swath of the land the Great Fire had ravaged, added it to his already considerable holdings in the city, mixed in evocations of the rural countryside, and garnished it all with the most sophisticated and costly design, decoration, materials, and refinements. The resulting concoction was a sprawling country estate, but one he embellished with urbane elegance and situated in the most crowded urban environment in the ancient world. He dubbed this very best of both worlds the Domus Aurea, his Golden House, and it was to be the centerpiece of the new Rome, Nero's Rome, a city he intended to rename Neropolis.[19]

A Golden House

According to Tacitus, Nero returned to Rome to address the Great Fire only when it threatened his Domus Transitoria (Passage Palace), the new wing of the palace that would make it possible for Nero to go back and forth between his Palatine and Esquiline estates without having to leave home.[20] It was not that Nero shunned appearing in public. In fact, quite the opposite. No emperor, indeed no performer, reveled more in the adulation of an audience, and at the time Nero was approaching full-time performance mode. But he was no fan of improv. He prepared meticulously, even fanatically, for his theatrical appearances, and like many a star/producer, he needed to be in complete control of the setting and the script and particularly the audience. But not even the emperor was in complete control of Rome's rowdy streets and the city's feisty residents. In any event, the construction of the Domus Transitoria was largely in vain, since the better part of it was destroyed in the fire.

Instead of rebuilding the Domus Transitoria along the old lines, however grand and elegant those lines might have been, Nero built his spectacular Domus Aurea. Suetonius's description, rather spectacular in its own right, is worth reading:

> Still, Nero was more fiscally ruinous in his building than in anything else. He made his palace stretch all the way from the Palatine to the Esquiline. At first he called it his Passage Palace, but after it was soon burned down in the fire and rebuilt, he called it his golden house [*domus aurea*]. What follows will give you a pretty good idea of its dimensions and splendor. It had a forecourt of a scale to accommodate a 120-foot statue with the emperor's face. It was so vast that it had a triple portico a mile long. It also had a lake that resembled a sea, surrounded by buildings that looked like cities. Not enough, it offered rural expanses that went from farmland to vineyards to pastures to forests—all populated with a multitude of every sort of farm and wild animal. In the rest of the palace, everything was overlaid with gold and adorned with jewels and mother-of-pearl. It had dining rooms with movable panels of ivory so that flowers and perfume could be showered down from above through pipes. The principal dining room was circular and revolved without pause, day and night alike, just like the sky. Both salt and sulfur water flowed in the complex's bathing facilities. When the palace I just described was completed and dedicated, all he said by way of approval was that he could finally start living like a human being.[21]

Tacitus's description, though briefer, is very much along the same lines: "Meanwhile, Nero exploited his country's ruin and erected for himself a palace in which jewels and gold, luxuries our extravagance had long since made pedestrian, were not so remarkable as the fields and lakes, along with deserted backwoods over here and open spaces affording panoramic views over there; the complex's architects and engineers were Severus and Celer, whose talent and audacity were up to defying nature through art, and to foolishly squandering the emperor's resources."[22]

It all sounds rather marvelous. No extravagance was spared, and who would not love to have a sprawling country estate smack dab in the middle of a city, particularly, *the* city? Especially a country estate with all the amenities and refinements urban sophistication can contrive? Travel in the ancient world was something of an ordeal, even for emperors, and now Nero would be spared that unpleasantness when he needed to escape the city for the beauty, salubriousness, and respite nature affords. The Domus Aurea included just about every kind of natural landscape Italy had to offer, replete with the appropriate creatures to enrich the authenticity of the setting and the charm of experiencing it. And yet the estate also included "buildings that looked like cities," gold and jewels everywhere, and every technological marvel of that age—trick ceilings, a rotating room, your choice of flowing water. Could those "buildings that looked like cities" have been evocations of specific cities under Roman sway? A bit of Egyptian Alexandria here, a set of buildings reminiscent of Syrian Antioch there, architectural recreation of something quintessentially Athenian on an opposite slope, and so on? Possibly, although the sparse archaeological evidence unearthed so far suggests that an immense rectangular building may have surrounded the showpiece pond. Could that have been the "buildings that looked like cities"? Or could they have dotted the grounds around that building? After all, Suetonius uses the plural for both "buildings" and "cities."

And that statue! There is much controversy over whether it was completed while Nero was still alive—no, seems to be the *opinio communis* of the moment—and if it indeed had Nero's features and what that would mean. In any event, the Elder Pliny indicates that the sculptor was Zenodorus and that Pliny *used to* visit the workshop and "marvel at" (*mirabamur*) clay models and sketches for the statue. Pliny could not have been a regular visitor to the workshop with access to Zenodorus's models and sketches unless he was on good and at least somewhat familiar terms with the sculptor, which makes sense, because at the time Pliny was an accomplished scholar and writer in his forties who had already had a distinguished military career. He was already *somebody*, that is, and his curiosity was unbounded. So when Pliny states that "the colossus was intended to portray that emperor [sc. Nero]," he surely got that information from Zenodorus, at the very least from his apprentices, and so we know that is what Nero commissioned him to do. Suetonius's 120 Roman feet in the passage above translate to around 35 meters; the Elder Pliny's estimate is a bit over 30 meters, astonishingly lofty either way, particularly for its designated location in the heart of the city.[23] Nero's Colossus would have rivaled the famous Colossus of Rhodes, one of antiquity's Seven Wonders of World, which Pliny tells us was around 33 meters tall, had that statue not tumbled in an earthquake in 226 BCE.[24] By way of modern reference: New York's Statue of Liberty is approximately 34 meters from its heel to the top of its head, and Michelangelo's majestic David comes in at a paltry 5.7 meters, if one excludes the pedestal. On top of all this, plundered or purchased masterpieces of Greek art adorned the interiors of the complex, and, likely, its gardens. In a sense, the Domus Aurea placed before Nero and at his disposal the entire Roman Empire, or, perhaps, the entire world: all of nature and humankind's most magnificent creations to boot.

The literary evidence for such an absurdly extravagant and sprawling estate strains credulity. Was *everything* really overlaid with gold, as Suetonius asserts? Had *all* of Rome really become just one house, as the poet Martial grouses?[25] Did downtown Rome actually accommodate a vast lake that resembled the sea and was surrounded by minicities and expansive landscapes representing nature's diversity and bounty? The limited archaeological record and common sense caution us not to take the ancient descriptions at face value: the lake was a large artificial pond, and the "cities," if in fact evocations of cities in the empire, could only have been pastiches of limited scale; a considerable portion of Rome's real estate had fallen into imperial hands well before Nero became emperor, and most of the city's land was still available to accommodate dwellings, markets, shops, shrines, and the like; the *entire* complex was not gilt and bejeweled.

Surprising, however, is the extent to which the archaeological record has confirmed that the Domus Aurea was, by any estimation, enormous, extravagant, spectacular, and architecturally adventurous—a stunner. Its grounds had not gobbled up the entire city, but they were indeed vast, shockingly and unprecedentedly so, and Nero did appropriate an inexcusably extensive swath of central Rome for it, land the Great Fire had cleared for him. Most noteworthy today is the lengthy pavilion, one of the principal buildings of the estate, uncovered in the Oppian Hill, an outcrop of the Esquiline. In building a massive bathhouse over the pavilion at the beginning of the second century, the later emperor Trajan employed it for his baths' foundations, and so in burying the pavilion ironically preserved much of it. Approximately one hundred fifty rooms have been discovered so far, and the design of what has been revealed suggests that dozens more lie hidden. The remains indicate, moreover, that much if not most of the building had a second floor, which was removed when Trajan built his bathhouse. Archaeologists have so far confirmed a length of approximately two and a half football fields, and it is likely that the structure extended another field's length. If one adds to the number of confirmed rooms estimates of the number of rooms in the as yet uncovered section of the pavilion, and the number of rooms on the second floor, this pavilion alone—just one component of the Domus Aurea—may have had well over three hundred rooms. Trajan's crews sensibly removed as much of the gold, gems, marble, and other costly materials as possible before packing the pavilion's rooms with rubble to make the foundation for the bathhouse, but even the stripped remains of the building suggest that Nero was indeed lavish in his employment of those materials.

To get an idea of the elegance and ingenuity of the architecture and decoration, let us consider just one of the Oppian pavilion's excavated rooms, the fountain room of the Cyclops Polyphemus and the Greek hero Odysseus. The room was designed to evoke Homer's famous description of the cave in which the Cyclops trapped Odysseus and his men and ate some of them—raw. The vaulted ceiling was a lofty 10.5 meters or so above the floor and was decorated with faux stalactites to create the illusion of a natural cave. To make the connection to the Cyclops' cave explicit, placed in the center of the vault was a mosaic depicting Odysseus giving the Cyclops the heady wine that enabled the hero and some of his men to escape. Despite the fragmentary state of the mosaic today, the artistry of the depiction, which included some gilded tesserae for highlights—appropriately enough for a "golden house"—is evident. Where the base of the vault met the walls of the room or, in keeping with the room's illusion, where the cave's ceiling met its walls, bands of mosaics decorated with shells extended around the space, and below the bands the walls were revetted with marble, which also covered the floor. The defining feature of the room, however, was the water cascading down the rear wall and then flowing into a basin. This was just one of the numerous dining rooms the Domus Aurea offered Nero and his guests. More than just a dining room, however, it served as a fanciful and theatrical setting for feasting and drinking, evoking the mythology and literature the emperor and his guests were steeped in, and as a witty allusion to the activities that would take place there: the special wine of the story (and of the mosaic above) had befuddled the mind of the Cyclops and thus liberated Odysseus from the danger the Cyclops represented, just as the best of Nero's cellar would liberate his senses and those of his guests; and as they ate, the setting might remind them of the Cyclops' cannibalism, an association we might find an appetite-killer but one that would appeal to the Romans' occasionally grisly sense of humor.

The Oppian pavilion has come to stand for the entire Domus Aurea. One of the great thrills in visiting Rome today is taking a tour of the rooms excavated so far. Since the whole edifice is now underground and in a somewhat fragile state, visitors are required to wear construction helmets as they descend into a vast warren of rooms that now feel like caverns, which adds an Indiana Jones flavor to the tour. There is nothing quite like it. These tours are legitimately advertised as tours of the Domus Aurea, but we should keep in mind that the Oppian pavilion, however extensive and splendidly appointed, was only one element of the vast estate. Nero undertook construction and renovation throughout the Valley of the Colosseum,[26] stretching south and west up onto the Palatine's slopes, westward into the edges of the Roman Forum, and over to the immense base that had been intended for the Temple of Claudius at some distance to the south, abutting the Caelian Hill. For an ancient visitor to notice or experience the estate's vastness alone, however, would have been to miss a key aspect of the complex. Nero had all the elements of the estate situated and oriented to offer a web of sensational sightlines that unified the whole.[27]

Let us imagine the views just from the Oppian pavilion. It was oriented towards the south, and the rooms on its southern flank were mostly open and provided Nero and his entourage with a spectacular panorama of the varied natural landscapes below, the creatures populating them, and the grounds' ponds and architectural features. From the terraces in front of the pavilion, if the emperor turned his gaze to the right, westward, he would enjoy the city's most breathtaking vista: the vast showpiece pond and the buildings that surrounded it; beyond that the immense forecourt with its towering statue, Nero bestriding the city; next, lengthy porticoes; then beyond the grounds of the Domus Aurea, the Roman Forum with its impressive and historic assemblage of temples, arches, basilicas, and monuments; and finally, rising as a backdrop to the series, the Capitoline Hill, Rome's citadel, capped by the Roman people's principal temple to their principal god, Jupiter—all together, a breathtaking visual feast of grandeur, beauty, and heritage, lined up for the emperor's delectation. Directing his eyes slightly back to the left, southward and eastward, he would see the grand pre-Neronian and Neronian structures of the Palatine rising beyond the forum and now integrated into his magnificent villa complex. Turning further to the left and gazing across the pond, Nero could see in the distance, at the base of the Caelian Hill, the majestic fountain he had built and engineered into a massive flank of the platform that had been constructed for a temple to the Emperor Claudius. Around two football fields in length, the fountain's façade stretched from approximately 300 to 400 meters from the pavilion, rising roughly 15 meters on one of the loftiest positions in the city. The fountain marked the extent of the Golden House to the southeast, but beyond it the outskirts of the city and the countryside were visible. Then the emperor's eyes could return to the panoramic microcosm of the world that lay sprawled below. All while dining.

However delighted Nero was that he could, as he put it, finally start living like a human being, others were not so thrilled with the Domus Aurea. Suetonius and Tacitus clearly considered Nero's extravagance vain, fiscally irresponsible, and, one senses, immoral. Without stating so explicitly, their descriptions seem to suggest that they considered the whole complex vulgar, a defect that all the gilding in the world could not conceal. Indeed, all that gilding was part of the problem. A glittering, megalomaniacal Disney World cum Madurodam and petting zoo would be tackier than a subdued, matte one, and scattering the Louvre's art collection about the place would only accentuate the absurdity of the whole endeavor.[28] The Domus Aurea was a fitting abode for someone whose narcissism trumped his taste. The very idea of the estate so irked them that Tacitus described it before addressing the reconstruction of the city, and Suetonius dedicated almost as much space to his description of the Domus Aurea as he did to his account of the Great Fire.

The crass audacity of the whole project may have riled Rome's aristocracy, but for most Romans, although they were inured to the excesses, greed, and bullying of their betters, the bitterest pill must have been the outrageous appropriation of all that prime real estate, formerly the locus of many shrines, shops, apartment houses, gathering places, and other structures among which so many of Rome's residents used to live, work, worship, and socialize. One can imagine how disheartening it must have been for people who had lived in what we now know as the Valley of the Colosseum, for example. First the Great Fire had incinerated the context for their day-to-day lives, disabled and scarred many, and cost some of them family and friends. Now their old neighborhood was being converted into a private pond. We do not know if the Roman on the street had access to the pond and fields of the Golden House. If so, admission would surely have been limited to times and occasions that fit the emperor's whims, and it is difficult to imagine the emperor considering visitors more than an audience for the ongoing Nero Show, or perhaps merely props for it. Still, some Romans, perhaps many, may have enjoyed playing bit parts in that show, which gave them access, however rare or circumscribed, to the splendors and beauty of the high life, opportunities to luxuriate in a setting they otherwise could barely imagine.

This must have been weak consolation, however, for those who had lost a neighborhood, a livelihood, and a home, and the scale of the appropriations was shocking. It is no surprise that the Elder Pliny characterized the Domus Aurea as "enveloping the city" and that resentful witticisms ridiculing the emperor's voraciousness circulated in Rome. One example survives: "All of Rome will wind up as just one house. Flee to Veii, Romans, unless that damned house has seized Veii as well!"[29] Veii was a town around ten miles from Rome.

It was one thing for an emperor to leave his subjects to fend for themselves after a disaster, but it was quite another for the "Father of the Country" to exploit public tragedy for private gain—a reverse exercise in noblesse oblige and *pietas*, where instead of seizing an opportunity to help your subjects, your children, you seize an opportunity to despoil them. Whether Nero had started the Great Fire or not, in snatching so much land in its wake, he certainly seemed to be behaving like a general who had subdued and taken possession of an enemy city. Nor was the loss of homes, however painful for so many, the only adverse impact of Nero's extraordinary appropriation of property. We have already seen how the reconfiguration of the city, in demanding the seizure of much private land, had wrought havoc on housing availability and prices. The Domus Aurea's consumption of so much prime real estate made the crunch considerably worse. In referring to the Domus Aurea years later, Martial made clear who the particular victims of Nero's appropriations were when he observed, "an arrogant country villa had robbed the poor of their homes."[30] Combining the notion that Nero had acted as an invading general with the observation that he had victimized Rome's common folk in particular, the anti-Nero conspirator Piso described the Domus Aurea as "that hated palace, erected through the plundering of Rome's citizens."[31]

The outrage the Domus Aurea provoked and the satirical edge of so much of the commentary help explain some of the critics' implausible exaggeration. No one actually thought the Domus Aurea might extend over ten miles to Veii, and people knew that the showcase pond, however outrageous and outsized for an urban setting, did not resemble the sea. But the wags' and censors' portrayals were not so much concerned with providing an accurate picture as with conveying how the Domus Aurea *seemed* or even *felt* to the people of Rome, and what it *meant*. Readers need to understand more than they need to know. Truth over factual accuracy yet again.

Still, one must be cautious not to underestimate Nero's audacity. Archaeologists believe they may have found that extraordinary rotating dining room on the slopes of the Palatine.[32] According to Martial, the Domus Aurea "used to glisten."[33] And Nero was the man who, after all, had the Theater of Marcellus, a facility with a seating capacity in the fifteen-thousand range, gilded for a single day to welcome a visiting dignitary,[34] and had a 120-foot-high portrait of himself, something the Elder Pliny characterized as unprecedented, painted and displayed in a garden.[35] The vast majority of the Domus Aurea's landscape, architecture, and artistic features are lost or lie undiscovered. Who knows what wonders may yet come to light?

The Great Fire provided Nero with three splendid opportunities to fulfill his aspiration to live his life as theater. The first was the fire itself, which gifted him with the most spectacular background and special effect the city of Rome could offer. Nero made the most of it by seizing the starring role with his notorious rendition of "The Fall of Troy," in attire to match the performance. The second opportunity was the execution of the Christians. Those spectacles were not so grand as the fire itself—what could be?—but Nero made the most of it: costumes, special effects, lighting, sounds, smells, cast and audience of thousands, tragedy and comedy (of that gruesome Roman sort), and, of course, with himself at the center of all. One cannot count on a steady flow of cataclysms to provide setting, plot, and effects for performances, however, and so Nero would have to supply his own. The Great Fire made this possible as well by allowing him to finally erect a permanent stage befitting his genius. The city and palace he built out of the ashes of the fire were to serve as a fittingly extraordinary theater for the world's most extraordinary performer.

When he said upon moving into the Domus Aurea that he could finally start living like a human being, he might more accurately have said, like a star. Although traditional Romans might grumble about the narcissism and profligacy of Nero's Domus Aurea, they should have recognized as quintessentially Roman one aspect of the project: the desire, almost compulsion, to control. This enormous new theater cum pleasure palace was constructed according to his own specifications, asserted for him control over the city and even nature, and incorporated every delight and indulgence an artistic and cosseted soul like Nero could desire. It was so vast and comprehensive that he would scarcely need to exit this stage of his own creation, unlike lesser actors, who, at the end of a performance, must return to their mundane lives and true selves. For Nero, however, performance *was* his truest self. His new Rome would allow him to stay in character without intermission.

Nero's vast estate and the extensive swaths of Rome rebuilt or being rebuilt according to his specifications now dominated the city. The Rome that would emerge would not only be to his liking—it would be his creation, an expression of his vision, indeed, *his* Rome. The destruction of Troy had impelled Aeneas, Nero's ancestor, according to his family's and now official Roman genealogy, to lead Troy's survivors to Italy to intermarry with the natives and to give birth to the Roman people. The Romans and their greatness had been born out of the fiery destruction of a grand city. The founder of the city of Rome itself and another ancestor of Nero, Romulus, had endowed it with its original name. The first emperor and Nero's great-great-grandfather Augustus had substantially remade, beautified, and modernized the city. Under his guidance, a new and better Rome arose. Progenitor, Founder, and Refounder, and all Nero's ancestors. As author of Rome 3.0, Nero had planned and given its residents the city they would henceforth inhabit.[36] A family tradition. It is hardly surprising that Nero may have intended to change the city's name to Neropolis, an aspiration that Suetonius, who provided us with this information, clearly considered an outlandish manifestation of his insatiable craving for renown and immortality.[37] When one considers the impact the Great Fire had allowed him to have on the city, this is not quite as presumptuous or mad as it seems. It was no longer Romulus's city, nor Augustus's city—it was Nero's.

Tacitus deemed the Great Fire Rome's Great Destroyer—so much of the physical city, so many of its inhabitants, and, of course, the Romans' heritage, traditions, and values were all casualties of the conflagration. Since Tacitus so closely associated Nero with the fire, perhaps even as its perpetrator, his Nero shared culpability for the devastation. Tacitean moral logic entwined the emperor's depravity, profligacy, narcissism, and artistic pursuits with the Great Fire in the project of destroying Rome and the Roman people. Through his juxtaposition of the orgy and the conflagration, his selective and pointed inventory of buildings the fire destroyed, and his intimations of Nero's self-absorption and indifference to his people's fate, Tacitus also suggested that Nero was a kind of anti-Aeneas, the undoer of what Aeneas had accomplished and stood for. A descendant of the Roman people's progenitor had ironically become their annihilator.[38] Nero, on the other hand, thought of himself as the Great Creator. For him the fire was not so much a destroyer as a means for the fulfillment of his inventive vision. It cleared the field for his brilliant acts of creation. In their own lore, after all, the Roman people had been born to greatness out of the ashes of Troy, and now they and their city would again be born out of conflagration, but to yet greater things.

The approximately four years Nero lived between the Great Fire and his suicide were not remotely sufficient for him to realize his vision. He did not survive to complete the project. But the creation—and destruction as well—was to continue for decades after his death in unanticipated and extraordinary ways that were to transform Rome and a good deal more.

-V-
Legacy

A FULL ANALYSIS of the long-term impact of the Great Fire of Rome would require yet another book. It should not surprise anyone that the most devastating blow to the largest and most powerful city of its era and, up to that moment, of any era, would have substantial and enduring consequences. The *nature* of some of those consequences, however, does surprise, and the impact of the fire is visible even today. What follows is a brief look at just five of the fire's long-term aftereffects. All are significant, and all are, in some respects at least, unanticipated. The Great Fire mattered. Indeed, we shall see that the legacy of the Great Fire turned out to be colossal.

Rome's Superstar Bad Boy

A statue of Nero adorns the cover of *National Geographic*'s September 2014 issue. It emerges from and towers over a red-tinted Rome, from which embers and ashes rise—appropriately enough, since the cover's caption reads, "Rome's Bad Boy—Nero Rises from the Ashes." A subtler, but equally telling element of the cover is the burning match Nero's extended and muscular arm holds aloft over the city. The cover captures precisely what has made Nero *the* emperor for posterity—the Great Fire.

There are, essentially, three principal Romes of the modern imagination.[1] First is the republic, which managed to conquer the Mediterranean world and beyond, the model of successful and sensible government that the United States' Founding Fathers considered closely when trying to figure out what sort of

Figure 7. Poster for Enrico Guazzoni's 1913 *Quo Vadis*, one of many films that tell the tale of the Great Fire and the persecution of the Christians it occasioned. The prospect of seeing the fire and Nero "fiddling" was clearly expected to attract moviegoers. Courtesy of the Library of Congress

government they should create for their new country. Just as instructive: after thriving for centuries, the Roman Republic devolved into a monarchy, offering a cautionary tale as well for contemplators or creators of modern republics.[2] The second is the imperialist, totalitarian bully that figured in so many movies after World War II and during the Cold War.[3] Rome stood in for the Nazis, the Italian Fascists, the communist Soviet Union, or the capitalist United States, depending on your point of view. (Rome was certainly imperialist, and unapologetically so, but hardly totalitarian.) The third, of course, is the Rome of sex, drugs, and rock n' roll, the decadent Rome engaged in an ongoing orgy, a hothouse of unrestrained cruelty and absolute power corrupted absolutely in the service of fulfilling every dark, depraved desire. For maximum effect—and appeal—a dollop of the bizarre needs to be added to the mix. We prefer our Roman decadence to be inventive, shocking, and weird.[4] This Rome fascinates us, appalls us, or titillates us—sometimes all three at the same time. In any event, it is difficult to look away from it, whether we are disgusted or want to join the party.

All three Romes reflect genuine aspects of the Roman empire and experience, but they are also reflections distorted by what subsequent generations, including our own, have wanted or even needed ancient Rome to be. Rome No. 3 is constantly falling these days in opinion pieces, since modern contemplators of this fall and connoisseurs of civilizational decline have found among the causes the very decadence they deplore and fear in our own world.[5] Ancient Rome can help us make sense of our own world and process our frustrations with it, although in this endeavor we may wind up reimagining—even recreating—Rome in our own image.[6] Certainly, if one is looking for decadence, political as well as personal, Nero's Rome, the Rome of the Great Fire, fills the bill perfectly (fig. 7).

Nero can shock, appall, and titillate with the best of them, even in the age of *Game of Thrones*. He strutted the stage in female roles and even wore a mask with the features of his wife Poppaea, who was not only dead but whom Nero was rumored to have kicked to death. He would wear a disguise and prowl Rome's bars and streets looking for trouble. In a long list of debaucheries and cruelties is the claim that Nero castrated a boy, "tried to make a woman of him" (what precisely that means for certain is unclear), married him, and then treated him as his wife. According to Tacitus, Nero attempted to assassinate his mother, Agrippina, using a collapsible boat. The attempt was unsuccessful (Tacitus's narrative of the fiasco is a comic masterpiece), and so Nero had her put to the sword. Rumor had it that Nero then inspected and assessed her naked and dead body, which might have elicited a particularly knowing smirk from those who accepted the gossip that he had had an incestuous relationship with her in better times. These, among a great many other scandals, feature in Nero's story.

Yet Nero has considerable competition for the designation Rome's Most Outrageous Emperor. Caligula, for example, is supposed to have murdered his predecessor, Tiberius; apparently considered himself a god and so established a temple to himself, complete with priests and ceremonies previously reserved for the gods; was heard to converse and even argue with Jupiter; murdered his brother (among many others); slept with all of his sisters, and initiated the sexual relationship with his favorite sister, Drusilla, when she was still a child; and when Drusilla died, he made it a capital crime for anyone to laugh, bathe, or eat with one's parents, spouse, or children. He turned part of the palace into a brothel and offered respectable women and young men for a price. When a man tossed to the beasts to die protested his innocence, Caligula had the man brought to him, cut out his tongue, then tossed him back to meet his fate. This is but a small sample, for Suetonius dedicated pages and pages to Caligula's extravagance, viciousness, and madness, and our other ancient sources chime in, whether the stories are reliable or not.[7]

Nor was Nero the most consequential emperor. Augustus, the first emperor, brilliantly transformed the ailing Republic into a monarchy, brought an end to a destabilizing and harrowing series of civil wars, transformed the city of Rome, and oversaw an astonishing expansion of Roman territory and power. He is one of history's most important figures. And a fascinating one as well, in that he was as much a ruthless scoundrel as a political genius, and his hands were thoroughly stained with the blood of the numerous political enemies he had killed. Yet Nero is the emperor we know best (or presume we know). It is Nero above all who mesmerizes.[8] That is above all because, I would suggest, however much Augustus may have transformed the world, and however lengthy and riveting Caligula's list of atrocities and depravities may be, Nero owns the Great Fire and its consequences. It is the Great Fire that made Nero *National Geographic*'s Bad Boy, a superstar of film, and the subject of a major exhibition in Rome and of numerous other scholarly and popular reassessments and rehabilitations.[9] Nero's youth, creative aspirations, and theatrical performances, which the traditionalists among his contemporaries of course considered pathological, add to his allure as an unstable but sensitive and artistic soul born into an uncomprehending world in which his position nonetheless enabled him to realize his theatrical ambitions so theatrically—and so bizarrely.[10]

The artistic expressions that still make the greatest impression, however, are those connected with the Great Fire: a costumed Nero producing, directing, and starring in the spectacular execution of Christians; the Domus Aurea, the extraordinary stage he constructed for his anticipated life of performance. Above all, that fiddling while an inferno engulfed his subjects. Innumerable politicians have since been depicted as fiddling while their city, country, or the entire world for that matter, burns.[11]

Beyond his ubiquitous and immortal fiddling, Nero is enjoying a heyday in contemporary political punditry. Editor of the *New Yorker*, David Remnick, to give but one recent example, in 2018 compared President Trump's love of gold to Nero's and the president's club Mar-a-Lago to the Domus Aurea, to make sense of the president's character. Nero is also still finding his way into literature. Salman Rushdie's 2017 novel, *The Golden House* (a title that is, of course, a literal translation of Domus Aurea), a meditation on contemporary and shifting mores and anxieties, stars a character named Nero Golden, who, like Rome's Nero, fashions a new identity for himself through wealth and real estate. When contemporary commentators evoke Nero to interpret the present, the Great Fire and its aftermath play their part.[12]

Irwin Allen's 1957 movie *The Story of Mankind* slyly expresses the Great Fire's role in making Nero "Nero."[13] The devil and the "Spirit of Mankind" present to a celestial jury the cases for and against humankind. The Spirit and the devil, played by Vincent Price with his usual hearty serving of ham, visit a PG-rated Roman orgy presided over by Nero (Peter Lorre, looking thirty years too old for the part). Although he is amused by a dance that would have been more appropriate to a 1957 beach party than a 64 CE bacchanal, this Nero seems mostly bored with the festivities. It is only when it is announced that the fire is under way and he grabs his lyre to provide it with his notorious musical accompaniment that he truly comes to life and expresses delight. His moment has arrived. Hollywood's most ridiculous Nero recognized that it was the fire that got him the part in this movie.[14]

A Colossus Rises from the Ashes

Rome had always been a massive construction site, and through grand building projects its nabobs had for centuries left their mark (and names, of course) on the city's topography. When the Great Fire cleared vast swaths of the city and put them at his disposal, however, Nero had an unparalleled opportunity to remake the physical city, and he seized it. The Domus Aurea gobbled up a considerable area, and elsewhere in the city the fire enabled Nero to realize much of the more open, rational Rome that Tacitus and his contemporaries experienced, a sturdier city built largely of stone, concrete, and brick. It is difficult to assess the extent to which the innovations of his town planning and of the Domus Aurea influenced subsequent Roman architecture and the construction and configuration of urban spaces and structures, but their impact seems to have been considerable. "Neropolis" most likely accelerated a revolution in the employment of durable and adaptable materials such as brick and concrete, and forms such as the vault and the dome.[15]

There is no doubt, in any event, that Nero put Rome's culture of construction on steroids. The boom continued for years, even decades, after Nero's suicide in 68 CE. For one thing, even with the Romans' considerable experience and expertise at building and with the resources of the empire applied to the task, the Great Fire's devastation needed decades to address. Suetonius told us that once Vespasian in 69 had won the civil war that arose in the wake of Nero's death, he was confronted with a Rome still in desperate need of reconstruction: "Since the city was still ugly from earlier fires and collapsed buildings, he allowed people to seize vacant plots and build on them, if their owners had not."[16] This passage provides evidence of the scale of the Great Fire—even five years or so of construction and incentives to rebuild had been insufficient to fully address the damage it had caused. It offers evidence, too, that the Flavians, Vespasian and his sons Titus and Domitian, would also be overseeing and promoting a great deal of reconstruction.[17]

They had more in mind than restoration, however; they also planned grand imperial projects that would leave *their* mark on the city. Elements of their building and urban reconstruction projects can be viewed as anti-Neronian. The Colosseum provides a telling example. When Vespasian came to power in 69, the Domus Aurea's notorious artificial pond stood at the center of today's Valley of the Colosseum. In building the Colosseum on that very spot, the Flavians were saying, essentially, "The land Nero took for himself is now returned to the Roman people," or as Martial characterized it, "With you in charge, Caesar, Rome has been restored to itself, and the master's delights now belong to the people."[18] At the same time, however, the Flavians had actually assumed the building frenzy that Nero had initiated, the frenzy that the Great Fire had made possible and necessary. They, too, accepted and embraced the opportunity the Great Fire offered to remake the city in the emperor's image and to his glory. In a sense, they were emulating Nero.[19]

The Colosseum, then, one of the two emblematic buildings in today's Rome and one of the most recognizable images and influential buildings in history, is a grandchild of the Great Fire. The conflagration cleared a huge plot of densely urbanized land in Rome's overcrowded cityscape; Nero took and converted the plot into his pond, which left the land essentially undeveloped for his successors; and the Flavians in their turn built the Colosseum there, in part as a repudiation of Nero's response to the Great Fire, but in its scale, grandeur, inventiveness, and exploitation of the city's greatest disaster, quintessentially Neronian.

The Great Fire and its aftermath fathered other grand imperial projects, of which only fragments have survived. The Flavians also built the Temple of Peace, which, as we have seen above, doubled as one of Rome's preeminent art museums.[20] The temple celebrated the Flavians' suppression of the Jewish revolt and the restoration of calm after the civil war they had won. But it was built on land that had been occupied by businesses, residences, and a major market that the Great Fire had destroyed, and so the temple also suggested a restoration of the stability that Nero's turbulent reign had shaken, turbulence the Great Fire epitomized. There they put on public display masterpieces of art that Nero had appropriated to finance the reconstruction of Rome after the fire but had instead hoarded in the Domus Aurea for his own pleasure. Another example: in the first decade of the second century CE, the emperor Trajan (reign: 98–117) built a vast, unprecedentedly grand bathhouse on the Oppian Hill, largely on top of the remains of the Oppian wing of the Domus Aurea. Again, land cleared by the fire was left available for the Domus Aurea and then returned to the Roman people. Both buildings remained in service for centuries.

Superstars of a Different Sort

One of the greatest unsolved mysteries of the ancient world—up there with the sexier, "Did Nero start the Great Fire?," but more consequential—is why persecution of the Christians occurred in the Roman Empire. More specifically, scholars have dedicated innumerable pages to trying to figure out the legal basis of the persecutions. It is clear that starting around 250 CE the Roman authorities were going after the Christians, using a variety of strategies bolstered by laws targeting them. Search and search though they might, however, historians have failed to find any law prohibiting the religion for the first two hundred years or so of Christianity's existence. Contributing to the puzzle, for those first two hundred years or so, persecution was sporadic and relatively uncommon. This is not to say that the outbreaks could not be savage and lethal—they certainly could be—but until the middle of the third century most Christians lived their lives in peace, although with the anxiety that that peace could be broken at any time and with horrific consequences. The central government in Rome had no policy of pursuing Christians and apparently no law that would require or even encourage them to do so. Provincials with provincial concerns generally initiated the occasional persecutions, and all they needed to get things going was a governor willing to hear the charges and punish with death those who refused to renounce their faith. Again, no law.

This makes no sense to the modern legal mind and even less to modern common sense. Enshrined in modern Western law are the principles *nullum crimen, sine lege* ("without a law [violated], there is no crime"),[21] and *nulla poena, sine lege* ("without a law [violated], there can be no punishment"). Obviously, these days, we take it for granted that you just cannot accuse and punish people unless they have broken a specific law. But the Romans could and did.[22] A provincial could bring charges against anyone for anything, and it was up to the governor, who alone under normal circumstances could impose the death penalty, to decide whether to hear the case and whether to impose the penalty. One way to look at this is that in the Roman view you had to occasionally break a few eggs to make the proverbial omelet, and for them the omelet was an orderly empire. The authorities would, therefore, hear cases in which no specific law had been violated. Still, it would be most useful for the accusers—perhaps essential for their prospects for success—and for governors inclined to hear cases and inflict punishments, if there was some precedent for punishing a particular behavior or even identity, that is, if the governor had a sense that "this is what we do with these people, whether a specific law concerning them exists or not, and we have a record of treating them this way. Besides, their interactions with us up to now suggest that they are *mali homines* (bad people), whom the empire, and the world for that matter, might be better without."[23] This is where the Great Fire enters the picture.

So much is unclear and controversial about Tacitus's account of the Neronian persecution of the Christians, which is the only surviving explicit testimony of the event.[24] It has even been argued, among other things, that (1) the passage is an interpolation, inserted by later Christians; (2) Tacitus did write the account, but he was retrojecting later pagan attitudes about and experience of the Christians into it, essentially rewriting history; and (3) the Christians got what they deserved, since they did in fact start the Great Fire.[25] I do not find these arguments credible, and they are minority views, but they cannot be entirely dismissed. The nature and limitations of the sources, and the fact that just about everything concerning early Christianity is contested, make it unlikely that everyone will ever agree on what happened, or even *whether* certain things happened at all.

This is the problem of trying to make sense of a world long gone and from which very little evidence has survived—and the very little *written* evidence, at any rate, reflects the ancients' way of making sense of their history and experience, a way very different from our own. But our inability to agree about even the most basic of facts—Who or what started the Great Fire? Did Nero really persecute the Christians?—let alone their meaning, should not surprise. If two thousand years from now clips of the American 2015 primary debates survive, historians will be tempted to assume that the Republicans and Democrats were inhabiting two different countries, so different were the realities and even facts of the two parties' narratives. Today's Israelis and Palestinians not only disagree about how to interpret their recent past—they have entirely different, factually irreconcilable narratives of the history of their conflicts and of the region they both inhabit. Like all human pursuits, history is messy.

Still, there is something of a scholarly consensus that the Neronian persecution was likely *the* precedent for subsequent persecution of the earliest Christians. As I suggested above, *officially* Nero's Christian victims were punished as arsonists, not for their religious convictions, behavior, or identity, but their association with this devastating catastrophe (however contrived) would have been sufficient to tarnish them as *mali homines*. Add to that the malevolent buzz that accompanied the accusation and persecution, and it is not surprising that both the Romans on the street and the ones in the corridors of privilege and power would have had a strong sense that there was something troubling about these peculiar and antisocial fanatics. Not strong enough for the Roman government to go after them, however. One somewhat common but false stereotype of the Romans is that they were totalitarians, knocking down doors and tossing to the beasts all their subjects not entirely on board with their beliefs and way of life—Maoist China, but with spears and togas. The notion that the Roman authorities saw the earliest Christians as a threat, moreover, is a fantasy. Still, the sense that there was something wrong with the Christians, coupled with and confirmed by the Neronian precedent, was strong enough to encourage the occasional pagan to accuse and the occasional governor to hear the accusation. For the earliest Christians, the Great Fire was a huge PR disaster, and like many PR disasters, it had ramifications beyond public opinion.[26] As a precedent, it made subsequent prosecution and persecution possible.[27]

If this reading of the role the Great Fire played in the persecution of early Christians is correct, it would be difficult to overestimate the impact of the disaster on the history and development of Christianity.[28] First, of course, would be the impact of the fire on those Christians Nero executed so cruelly. Next would be its impact on the experience of post-Neronian Christians for the two centuries following. Some perished in the sporadic persecutions that broke out here and there throughout the empire, but even those who were spared would have lived lives of insecurity and apprehension. The peace they generally enjoyed with their pagan neighbors was fragile. Later, around 250 CE, the Roman authorities decided to go after the Christians. Would this have happened without the preceding years of intermittent persecution, which had perpetuated and validated the sense that Christians were suspect undesirables who had occasionally faced the justifiable wrath of their pagan neighbors and the Roman authorities?

Most significant, however, martyrdom became intrinsic to the early Christians' sense of themselves, of their place in the world, and of their relationship to God—part of their DNA, one might say—and the vast majority of the A-list saints from Christianity's earliest centuries were martyrs or came to be considered so. Martyrs, above all Christians, were to be admired, venerated, and emulated—their uncompromising and (from a Christian point of view) triumphant reliance on God made them what popular culture today might characterize as the ultimate role models.[29] It makes perfect sense that all twelve Apostles (including Matthias, Judas's replacement) wound up with martyr stories, some of which were clearly invented, others most likely invented, and the rest of which accrued at least some apocryphal material.

It would be a mistake, however, to view these later creations and embellishments as purposeful deceptions, attempts to fool readers. Rather, for their originators, they were understandable and reasonable additions to the existing record. It was perfectly natural for early Christians of postapostolic generations to assume that saints of the Apostles' stature must have been martyrs, so compelling and intrinsic had martyrdom become to Christian identity. Nor did the role martyrdom and the earliest Christians' sufferings played in the lives and thought of Christianity cease with the Christianization of the Roman Empire. In telling the story of the Christian religion from its origin to its triumph through the Emperor Constantine (rule: 306–337), the great church historian Eusebius announced the travails of Christian martyrs as among his principal themes,[30] and he dedicated considerable space to their stories. For Christians of Late Antiquity and the early Middle Ages, the story of the birth and victory of the Church was inextricably entwined with that of the faith's martyrs, and most martyr stories situated in the Roman Empire originated in the fourth century CE or later.

Long after the Roman Empire was consigned to the history books, martyrdom continued to be a powerful and even defining idea and ideal for Christians. Examples are myriad, but one of the most revealing is how British Protestants and Catholics identified as martyrs—not merely as victims or even heroes—those whom the other side had killed, since the word *martyr* and what it stood for retained their power and magic. Each side claimed its own as the true martyrs (and considered the other side's martyrs heretics), and essential to these claims was the assertion that our side's martyrs are the inheritors, the modern equivalents, really, of the earliest Christian martyrs. This British debate about martyrdom was more than part of the public relations campaign each side was waging against the other. It was also a tool to put the contemporary conflict into historical and theological context, to make sense of the conflict and its victims, and to confer legitimacy on one's own side.[31] And martyrdom has maintained its hold on the Christian imagination into the twenty-first century. It is no surprise that in 2016 Pope Francis characterized contemporary martyrs as "the lifeblood of the Church," a telling evocation of Tertullian's characterization of martyrs' blood as the "seed" for the spread of Christianity.[32] Another legacy of the Great Fire.

St. Peter and the World's Biggest Church

By the early third century at the latest, Christians had come to believe that Nero had martyred Saints Peter and Paul, and where they located Peter's tomb indicates that the persecution they were thinking of, even if they did not say so explicitly and even if some apocryphal material offered inconsistent wrinkles to the narrative, was the one that occurred in the wake of the Great Fire. Writing in the second half of the second century CE, Dionysius, Bishop of Corinth, stated that Peter and Paul taught in Italy "and endured martyrdom at the same time," a formulation that suggests they also died in Italy. A certain Gaius, writing in the first quarter of the third century, said that he can show his readers the "trophies" of Peter and Paul, if those readers are willing to go to the Vatican for Peter, and to the Ostian Way, the grand road leading west to Rome's port city Ostia, for Paul. Citing those two (and other) earlier writers, Eusebius explicitly asserted that Nero had Peter crucified and Paul beheaded in Rome.[33] Towards the end of the fourth century, Jerome not only placed Peter's tomb in the Vatican area but asserted that crowds from the entire world flocked to the site.[34]

From very early on, then, and right up until this day, the belief has persisted that it was during the Neronian persecution that Peter was martyred and buried, and that both events occurred in the vicinity of where St. Peter's Basilica now stands.[35] This belief was and is based on the assumption that the gardens and circus that Tacitus mentioned as the locations for the executions are the ones in the vicinity of the Vatican Hill. It is possible that the Christian community of Rome accurately remembered and passed down through the generations the Vatican Hill area as the site of their fellows' Neronian martyrdom, including Peter's, but this is difficult to prove. Some scholars consider this belief mistaken, and the debate about where and under what circumstances Peter died remains lively and keen.

Attitudes towards Christianity and particularly towards the Roman Catholic Church unavoidably lurk in the background of the discussion, and so the issue matters to a great many people beyond the academy.[36] A fascinating debate, to be sure, but for our purposes the crucial and undeniable fact is that some Christians early on *believed* Peter was among Nero's victims, and this had consequences. They were convinced that Peter had been caught in the fateful net Nero cast when he scapegoated Christians in Rome for the Great Fire.

Nonetheless, other Christians fashioned different explanations for Peter's death, explanations that disassociated the martyrs from the fire and so exculpated them from suspicion that they may in fact have been guilty of arson. The late second-century Acts of Peter, to give one colorful example, universally acknowledged to be invention, claimed that fury at the sexual alienation of converted wives and mistresses from their pagan husbands and lovers caused Peter's death, and upon hearing of his demise, Nero was irritated that he had not had the opportunity to torture Peter at great length, for Peter had alienated a great many of the emperor's own associates, as well! A talking dog also plays a significant part in these Acts, and Peter resurrects a dead fish hanging in a shop window, among other oddities.[37] Still, it is highly significant that some early Christians located Peter's martyrdom in the Circus of Caligula, the remains of which have been identified on the grounds of today's Vatican City, and that fact indicates that whatever new explanations and contexts early Christians invented for Peter's martyrdom, the link between Peter's death and the Great Fire endured and mattered.[38] Peter's death leads to the next significant part of the story, his burial, but to understand that we need first to understand a bit more about the ancient Vatican's topography.

In ancient Rome, the land where St. Peter's Basilica and Vatican City now stand was occupied by gardens, the Circus of Caligula, an important road out of town (Via Cornelia), tombs, and the slopes of the Vatican Hill, which was to give its name to the area (fig. 8).[39] The Vatican Hill overlooked the Via Cornelia, which ran, essentially, east to west from the city, lengthwise right through the center of what is today St. Peter's Square and then through the center of St. Peter's Basilica, although neither existed, of course, at that time. Like most

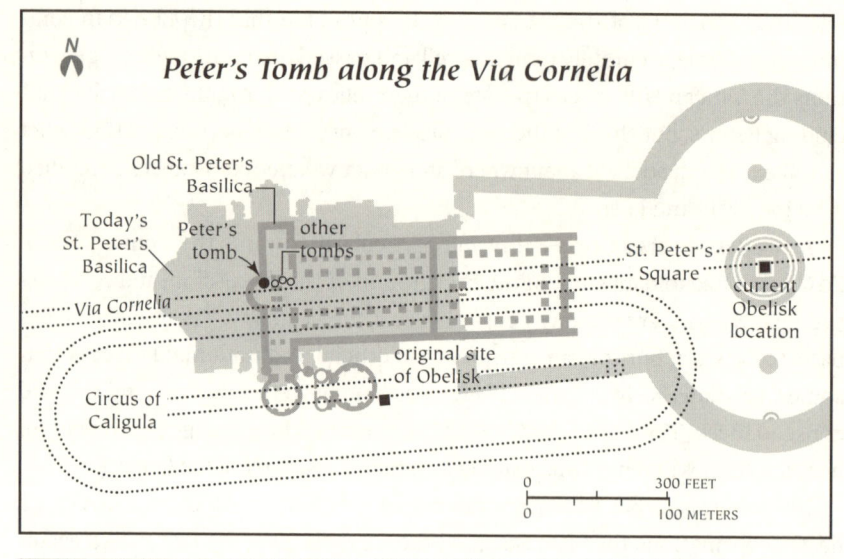

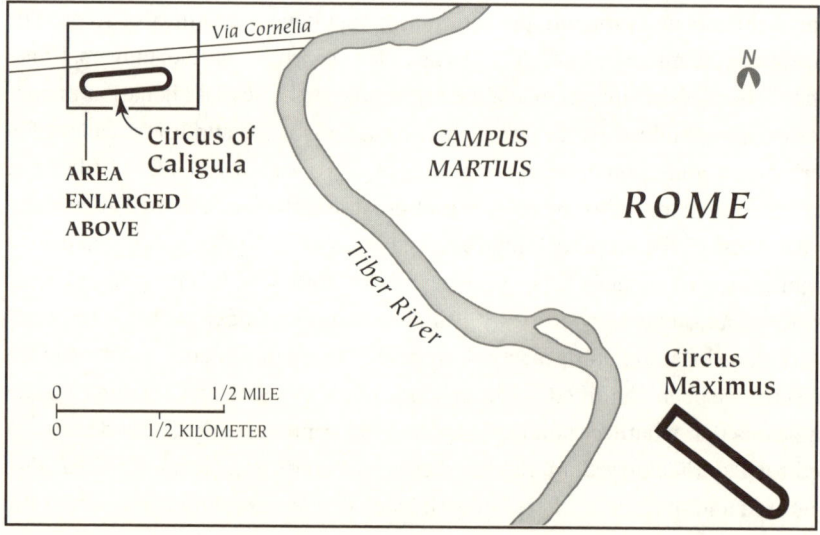

Figure 8. Map of St. Peter's Tomb along the Via Cornelia. Lucidity Information Design, LLC

of the grand highways leading out of Rome, the roads along which many of the Great Fire's survivors took refuge during the catastrophe, sections of the Cornelia were lined with burials of various sorts.[40] Along the southern side of the Cornelia, perhaps on the fringes of or within ancient Rome's Vatican gardens, stood the Circus of Caligula, which stretched east to west along the road.[41] The burial area nearest to the Circus, then, was along or near the Cornelia, just to the north of the Circus. After Peter's death, according to this narrative, his fellow Christians took his remains to the nearby Cornelia and buried him there, on the spot above which today the center of St. Peter's massive dome soars.

Christians naturally remembered and venerated that spot, although not ostentatiously, considering their precarious position with their pagan neighbors and the Roman authorities. Eventually, the emperor Constantine took the first steps towards the Christianization of the Roman Empire and with it, of course, towards the Christianization of the city of Rome. When Romans wanted to mark something as significant, to send a message to the world and to themselves, buildings were usually part of program, particularly in the city that had for centuries aggressively presented itself as center and master of all things. So, to mark and honor the spot where the apostle/martyr Peter was buried, and to provide Christians with a place to worship associated with one of Christianity's most important figures and martyrs, in the early fourth century Constantine built the first St. Peter's Basilica. An Egyptian obelisk that stood in the Circus of Caligula was left in its original location, to serve as a nearby marker of the spot "in the centre of Caligula's Circus, where Saint Peter was martyred."[42]

In the sixteenth century, the project of replacing Constantine's somewhat dilapidated St. Peter's with the one we see today began.[43] In 1586 Pope Sixtus V had the obelisk moved from its original site in the Circus to the middle of St. Peter's Square, where it still stands, a "silent witness of the martyrdom of St. Peter and of many other Christians," according to an unofficial but Roman Catholic site,[44] although the obelisk actually did its witnessing in its original location, in the center of the Circus of Caligula.

The sequence of events is remarkable. The conviction that Peter had been martyred in the Circus of Caligula in the wake of the Great Fire of Rome and so buried near the site of his death led to the marking of the spots of martyrdom and burial in Christian memory; this led to the building of the first St. Peter's Basilica when the Christians came to power, which led to the building and adornment of today's St. Peter's, to which a *Who's Who* of Renaissance and Baroque architects and artists, including Michelangelo and Bernini, contributed significantly.[45] Michelangelo's magnificent dome over today's St. Peter's serves as a sort of canopy that both shields and proclaims the tomb directly below, and Bernini's colonnade, two arms extending out from the Basilica, embraces not only worshippers as they head towards St. Peter's façade but also Peter's martyrdom itself, symbolized by the obelisk that thrusts heavenward at the center of the arms. Like the Colosseum, St. Peter's Basilica is a grandchild of the Great Fire. Indeed, without the belief that as a result of the fire Peter had been martyred and buried where Vatican City now stands, would the Roman Catholic Church's headquarters have been situated on that spot, or even in Rome? The Great Fire's substantial impact on the modern city of Rome goes beyond its skyline and its most iconic buildings, however momentous they are, to the city's very identity and character.[46]

Monsters Lost and Found

Extent of artistic and architectural influence is always difficult to assess, but this is particularly true when we have little testimony from architects and artists on their inspirations and models—unfortunately, almost always the case with ancient artists and architects. Undisputed, in any event, and most surprising is one particular impact the legacy of the Great Fire had on art in the Renaissance and beyond, and the surprising way in which that legacy came about.

In the Middle Ages and early Renaissance, Nero's Domus Aurea had become the stuff of legend—only legend. The literate few who knew Latin and could get access to the texts could read Suetonius and Tacitus and talk and wonder about it, but there was nothing to see. That vast estate had been dismantled, plundered, and built over. The Colosseum and Trajan's bath complex are but two examples of the ancient structures that were built on and over the sprawling estate, although they are particularly significant ones. Ultimately, vines and gardens wound up claiming the Oppian Hill above the now-famous and accessible pavilion, and what was below was forgotten.[47] Then chance intervened. Around 1480, the story goes, a boy fell through a gap on the Oppian Hill and found himself in a most curious cavern, a *grotta*, in Italian. He had rediscovered the Oppian wing of the Domus Aurea, which had been covered over and largely filled in to serve as the foundation for Trajan's enormous baths.[48] As we have seen, Trajan had the works of art and valuable materials, including the gold that made the Golden House golden, stripped before burying the building, but the frescoes and stucco reliefs that lined the walls and ceilings of so many of the building's rooms and halls were left behind. The Romans had no archaeological or art historical interest in preserving walls painted with frescoes or adorned with stucco, as we have today, with Pompeian and other ancient frescoes that are presented so lovingly in museums.

The find created a sensation. Visitors, many of them artists, lowered themselves down into the caverns and inspected the now-subterranean frescoes by torchlight. Since the rooms had been largely filled in when the Domus Aurea was converted into a foundation for Trajan's baths, the explorers mostly stood or kneeled on infill and viewed the frescoes and stucco reliefs on or near the ceilings. Eventually, they cut through walls into new rooms, and gradually more and more of the frescoes were exposed. During these forays, they would sketch the mysterious images they saw, which offered them the rare thrill of seeing, touching, and copying actual paintings from antiquity and the shock of viewing ancient images of unbridled and possibly demented imagination.

They saw freakish hybrid creatures that blended one animal's features with another's, or with vegetation, or even with architecture—an unnatural world seemingly without rules and without boundaries, which enchanted and inspired many and unsettled others.[49] The flickering torchlight that illuminated the frescoes in the dark and dirt of the low chambers, often accessed only by crawling through the shadows, made the experience of the images uncanny, if not downright eerie. The explorers' thrill was heightened when they identified the un- or even antinatural images they saw with the frescoed images the Roman architectural writer Vitruvius (first century BCE) had lamented as *monstra*—abnormalities or, yes, monsters or monstrosities.[50] The artists might not have shared Vitruvius's scorn, but they always experienced an additional frisson of excitement when they could identify some ancient artifact with passages in ancient writers, and Vitruvius had reached near oracular status among Renaissance artists and architects. Since the fantastic creatures were found and experienced in what the early Renaissance visitors called caves or grottoes, they were thought of and eventually designated "things from the caves/grottoes," that is, "grotesques," which is the origin of the English word.

Among the visitors to the mysterious chambers were stars such as Raphael, and they appropriated what they had seen and so revived ancient forms and images, which became a significant and widespread feature of Renaissance painting and decoration.[51] Gothic art and architecture already had their share of bizarre creatures, of course; just think of all those gargoyles. But it was the Neronian frescoes that set in motion a fashion for the grotesque, and one that featured the specifically Roman creatures, architecture, composition, and decorative elements that the Domus Aurea's ruins had brought back to light. Grotesques colonized the grand homes and public buildings of Rome, then the rest of Italy, and ultimately the rest of Europe. The Vatican and the Villa Farnesina in Rome provide spectacular examples, to name just two. The Domus Aurea's bizarre ornamentation wound up decorating books, housewares, weapons, and a great many other artifacts. Eventually, Roman grotesques reached other shores, and today the grand Thomas Jefferson Building of Washington's Library of Congress sports Neronian-style grotesques in its galleries, corridors, and other rooms, to give just one of many examples.[52] The Great Fire's grandchildren could not be confined to only one continent.

The Great Fire was transformative in so many ways. It devastated the unprecedentedly grand and complex capital of a vast empire, a city that has served as precursor to and frequent inspiration for the capitals of later empires. The destruction and its aftershocks and impact have reverberated down through the centuries, leaving their mark on art, architecture, religion, and the ways later generations have tried to make sense of their own political, social, and moral experience. Some of those marks are even tangible and visible to this very day.

Examining this cataclysmic event provides insight into the ancient Romans' ways of thinking and living and into the environment that both shaped that thinking and living and was in turn shaped by them. While much of what one learns is particular to Roman civilization and to the city of Rome, the study of the Great Fire also addresses concerns that did not lose their significance when the Roman Empire ceased to exist. Prominent among those concerns are the nature and challenges of urban life and our experience of disaster—how we anticipate, confront, respond to, and make sense of catastrophes, including the ways and extent to which our level of preparedness and our manner of thinking help create them. In other words, how different peoples anticipate, experience, respond to, and make sense of disasters essentially *creates* different disasters and endows them with different meanings. To a considerable extent, as we have seen, we are the agents of our own disasters. It is no accident that the Romans made only limited efforts to forestall the calamities that plagued their greatest city—they considered those calamities an inescapable feature of life, just as they did the lesser but unrelenting day-to-day perils of life in the city, and the authorities and the city's well-heeled residents had a very circumscribed notion of their responsibility to Rome's less fortunate.

The Romans remain important and fascinating because they utterly transformed the world. Another aspect of the abiding fascination with them—and one of the things that makes study of them so valuable—is that they are simultaneously so familiar to us and yet so utterly alien. We see ourselves in their lives and culture, and yet we see a people and a culture that in so many respects do not conform to our expectations. Studying the Great Fire helps to illustrate the lives of these ancient forebears of our culture and history, a people with whom we share so much and from whom we also so greatly differ. Such examination reveals, as well, how much we can reconstruct of their lives and how much remains, like aspects of the Great Fire, a tantalizing mystery.

APPENDIX A
Sources

Only three ancient accounts of the Great Fire survive—those of Tacitus (full name: Publius Cornelius Tacitus), Suetonius (Gaius Suetonius Tranquillus), and Cassius Dio (Cassius Dio Cocceianus). Tacitus's account is by far the most important. His is the most detailed, and for an ancient historian he comes closest to our expectations for accuracy and impartiality (however distant that nonetheless is). Suetonius's account is the next most important. It is not quite a narrative, but Suetonius does provide information that fills in some of the blanks in Tacitus.[1] Dio is the last chronologically and the least helpful. These writers' accounts diverge on some key points, and when they do diverge, it is impossible to ascertain with certainty whom to trust. (One example I discuss in this text is their accounts of Nero's notorious "fiddling" episode.)

By modern standards, all three accounts are frustratingly sparse and short on data and even facts. They reflect the Roman emphasis on rhetoric and style, and ancient writers' consciousness of their literary tradition; Roman historians like Tacitus and Dio (Suetonius's material on the fire is in a biographical work) were as much in dialogue with their predecessors as with the events they were recounting. Additional help in making sense of the fire comes from (1) a few other ancient writers who allude to the fire or its aftermath, (2) what we know about fires and firefighting in ancient Rome, (3) the sparse (and frustrating) archaeological and epigraphical record, and (4) what the modern world has learned about the behavior of fires. Our three principal authors require a closer look.

Dio

Most of what we know about Dio comes from his *Roman History*, which also contains his account of the Great Fire. His family came from Bithynia in modern-day Turkey, and his father was a Roman senator who also served as a governor. Dio was born sometime around 165 CE, came to Rome probably around 180, and died after 229. The chronology is uncertain. Dio was a Roman senator, but he is best known for his depiction of his contemporary Commodus, the gladiator-mad emperor of the late second century whom Joaquin Phoenix played in the movie *Gladiator*.

There are several reasons why Dio's account of the Great Fire is of less use than Tacitus's and Suetonius's: (1) he was writing some 140 years or more after the fire; (2) his account of the fire survives only in an epitome by an eleventh-century monk, Xiphilinus, and we cannot know for certain the extent to which Xiphilinus may have altered Dio's text—that is, the Dio-through-Xiphilinus text that we have can be viewed as about a millennium later than the fire; and (3) Dio's narrative is short on details and long on rhetorical flourishes—the whole thing strikes the reader as more an exercise in how one *might* write about a fire, any fire, than a narrative based on actual human experience of a specific fire. All ancient writers had this rhetorical tendency, to be sure, but Dio was particularly subject to it.

Suetonius

Suetonius's account is of considerably greater value. He was born six years or so after the Great Fire and by the '90s CE was in Rome, where he was fortunate to find a powerful patron in the Younger Pliny. Suetonius became, essentially, a professor/bureaucrat. He wrote many books, most of which are lost, including ones on famous prostitutes and on the language of insult. He served in the Roman government *a studiis* and *a bibliothecis*. We are not sure exactly what those jobs entailed, but our best guess is that he was some sort of researcher (*studiis* = studies) and librarian (*bibliothecis* = libraries), though surely not the reshelving-the-books sort. He rose to the position of overseer of the emperor's correspondence (*ab epistulis*; *epistulis* = letters) under the Emperor Hadrian (117–138), though he eventually fell out of favor and lost that position. While serving Hadrian, he most likely wrote the key work for our purposes, *The Twelve Caesars*, a series of biographies of Julius Caesar and Rome's first emperors, among them Nero, number five. They are, however, odd biographies by our standards. Suetonius does not provide a continuous and chronological narrative of each emperor's life, but rather describes—*assesses* might be a better word—each emperor by topic.

In the case of Nero, Suetonius presented the good aspects of his rule (a relatively short account) and then offered the bad aspects (a quite extensive account, of course). Again in his *Nero*, Suetonius treated Nero's theatrical and athletic performances all together, and in a separate section treated his scandalous sex life. Chronology gets jumbled, cause-and-effect obscured, and events closely associated or even elements of a single event are scattered and isolated in the biographies—and, most vexing, Suetonius did not feel obliged to say, "Oh, by the way, the context for this action was what I was talking about ten pages ago." And so Suetonius described the Great Fire among Nero's evil deeds (chapter 38), his persecution of the Christians among his good deeds (16; with no reference to the fire, although Nero went after the Christians as scapegoats for the fire), the regulations for Roman architecture among his good deeds (16; again, with no reference to the fire, although these regulations were in response to the fire), and the Domus Aurea among his excesses (31; yet again, with no reference to the Great Fire, although it was the fire that made its construction possible). A reader with no other information, taking these events in the order Suetonius presented them, might assume that the transformation of the city's architecture came first, the persecution of the Christians second, the construction of the Domus Aurea third, and the Great Fire last! And that reader would have no idea that these events were interrelated, that the fire either directly bought about or provided the context and impetus for the others.

In some ways, Suetonius was more of an encyclopedist than a biographer, more intent on tossing in all sorts of material than providing readers with context. On the other hand, Suetonius's information tends to be relatively accurate, and his positions in the Roman government gave him access to all sorts of records and documents. His description of the Domus Aurea is easily the most detailed, though one must allow for a certain degree of exaggeration.

Tacitus

Still, it all comes back (and down) to Tacitus's exciting, moving, and brilliant narrative. His is the most complete and detailed account, and he was describing events that occurred during his own lifetime. The account of the Great Fire I offer in chapter 2 owes more to Tacitus than to any other source.

Tacitus's narrative survives in his *Annals*, a chronological (unlike Suetonius's biographies) history of the reigns of Rome's first series of emperors—Augustus, Tiberius, Caligula, Claudius, and Nero, a dynasty we designate collectively the Julio-Claudians and who were all related to each other in various ways and loosely descended from Julius Caesar. Like most Roman historians, Tacitus relied principally on written sources for his information, but there is much to suggest that there is more to his description of the Great Fire than what he found in books.

Tacitus was approximately eight when the Great Fire devastated Rome in 64 CE, although, alas, we have no idea of where he was at that crucial moment; he was born in the provinces but settled in Rome at some unknown point, at least by around 75 or so. Whether he had visited or even resided in the city at some point or points earlier, we do not know. Nor do we know when Tacitus started assembling materials for the *Annals*. Our best guess is that the work was published shortly before his death, around 120, but it is a lengthy and complicated work that would have taken years to research and write. In any event, the generation that as adults had endured the Great Fire and known pre-Fire Rome had not entirely died out, nor had residents of Rome who were children at the time of the fire and who doubtless had vivid memories of the event. That is, there were still eyewitnesses around to consult, and we know from a famous example—and one related to another notable disaster—that Tacitus would consult eyewitnesses in researching his historical works. Tacitus's fellow senator the Younger Pliny was a teenager and in the Bay of Naples when Vesuvius erupted and destroyed Pompeii and a good deal more in the bay. Tacitus asked Pliny to describe his and his uncle's experiences during the eruption, and Pliny wrote two letters in response. Although we do not know how Tacitus employed those letters—unfortunately, much of Tacitus's work is lost, like that of most ancient writers—Pliny's letters survive. As a member of Rome's senatorial elite, moreover, Tacitus had at his disposal the archives and libraries of Rome, not to mention the city's enormous and fertile rumor mill.

Nonetheless, as was the usual practice, Tacitus rarely named his sources, at times referring to unnamed *scriptores* (writers) or the like, as he did to our immense frustration when he claimed that views on Nero's culpability for the Great Fire were divided.[2] The most interesting source we know he did use is the Elder Pliny, the Younger Pliny's uncle, whose death during the eruption of Vesuvius the Younger described vividly in one of the letters to Tacitus. The Elder Pliny most likely was in Rome for the Great Fire, and he may be among the eyewitnesses Tacitus interviewed.

Two other considerations concerning Tacitus as a source are worth keeping in mind. First, when the Great Fire occurred, it must have had an enormous impact on Romans living elsewhere, particularly members of or aspirants to Rome's elite, like Tacitus's family. One of those "Where were you when you heard about . . ." moments—like 9/11, the death of Princess Diana, or the assassination of John F. Kennedy. The eight-year-old Tacitus must have been hungry for news about the disaster. Second, the Rome Tacitus wound up in, most likely starting while still in his teens, was full of visual reminders of the Great Fire and of its aftermath and legacy—sections of the Domus Aurea, Vespasian's and Titus's architectural and urban planning responses to it (among them, the Colosseum), Domitian's projects, devastated property still undeveloped, and above all, the Neronian streets and residential architecture. Indeed, it is hard to imagine Tacitus and his contemporaries strolling around Rome much *without* noticing and commenting on the Great Fire and its consequences. And we cannot rule out that he had visited the city earlier, when much of the destruction and Romans' first responses to it were still visible.

However much Tacitus had access to firsthand accounts and reasonably accurate information (for antiquity), readers must keep in mind that he was principally concerned to convey his broader truth about Rome under the emperors—that the Roman people and their capital city had experienced crushing moral degeneracy, which started at the top of the political and social hierarchy and wound up soiling and subverting everything. As this book suggests, Tacitus could be a slippery character in conveying this message, which is one of the characteristics that place him among ancient Rome's most fascinating writers.

A couple of final notes about our sources.

First, unfortunately the Romans wrote no scholarly examination of life in their city, or at least no such text has survived. We have to piece together a sense of life in the city from a great variety of sources, none of which were intended to provide posterity with a comprehensive overview of the perils and pleasures of life in Rome. Nor does any ancient textbook on fires and firefighting survive. Many of the sources modern scholars must employ to describe life in ancient Rome, moreover, are tendentious or even satirical. This is particularly true of Juvenal and Martial, who pop up in this book again and again. The consequence is that modern scholars must fill in a great many blanks and employ sources whose interpretation is thorny.

Second, the archaeological record for the Great Fire and even for the architecture and layout of pre-Neronian Rome is sparse and vexed. Among the reasons: (1) most of the structures destroyed (particularly *domus* and *insulae*) consisted of perishable materials and were completely obliterated in the fire; (2) the ancients often rebuilt subsequent layers of a city on top of the destroyed layers, which can be of immense help to archaeologists trying to understand the earlier city and the scale and nature of the destruction, but Tacitus tells us that Nero had most of the Great Fire's wreckage removed to the swamps near Ostia; that is, most of the physical evidence of the destruction was removed already in antiquity—the scene of the crime wiped (relatively) free of evidence; (3) the ancient city has largely been built over, and the greater part of it has not been excavated, despite the impression the Roman Forum and Palatine Hill give of a completely unearthed archaeological site; (4) the Neronian and subsequent ancient reconstructions obliterated most traces of the fire and of the pre-Fire city that the removal of wreckage had left behind. Archaeologists have uncovered a few indications of the Great Fire, but those precious traces are few and insufficient to help us determine the extent of the fire with certainty. This means that in depicting the course and extent of the fire, and even the city's pre-Neronian architecture, we are often reduced to speculation.

APPENDIX B
Proposed Timeline of the Great Fire

Our sources do not provide a day-to-day chronology of the sequence of the Great Fire's spread, and we can attach only two events in the fire's story to specific days: (1) it *appeared* to have spent itself on the sixth day at the foot of the Esquiline but reignited on the Aemilian estate of Tigellinus; and (2) it ended on the ninth day. Otherwise, we are reduced to speculation. Tacitus claimed that Nero returned from Anzio to Rome when he got word that the flames were threatening his Domus Transitoria, for example, but he did not indicate what day that was, or how extensively the fire had spread in other directions when Nero made his decision to return.[1]

The archaeological record is of limited help regarding the extent of the fire, but of no help at all in clarifying its chronology. The sequence outlined below, then, is largely speculative. It for the most part follows Clementina Panella's analysis (with accompanying simulation) of the spread of the fire, the most ambitious, detailed, and credible attempt at a geographical chronology of the conflagration's progress.[2] Little is certain, unfortunately. Most of the events outlined below, moreover, could be moved up or back a day or so.

- **Day 1** (see fig. 3): starts at the northeastern corner of the Circus Maximus; travels the length of the Circus, westward towards the Tiber, and engulfs most of the edifice; threatens the Aventine Hill on the Circus's southern flank but does not climb very high; when the fire reaches the western end of the Circus and the Aventine, it destroys the Temple of Luna on the hill's lower slopes;[3] meanwhile, flames are starting to spread northward toward the Palatine Hill.

- **Day 2** (see fig. 3): begins curling around Palatine, starting to form a horseshoe around the hill and executing something resembling a pincer movement; the left/westerly prong sweeps into and devastates the lowlands by the Tiber, destroying the Ara Maxima along the way, and heads towards the Campus Martius and the Capitoline Hill to the north; the *vigiles* successfully divert the fire from its path into the Campus, saving the theaters at the Campus's southern edge, but fail to save the Amphitheater of Taurus; the right/eastern prong starts heading northward up the valley between the Palatine and the Caelian Hills towards what is now known as the Valley of the Colosseum; the fire attacks the slopes of the Palatine from the south, west, and east; as it becomes clear that this fire is becoming something extraordinary, all the units of *vigiles* are deployed or preparing to deploy—from this point until the fire dies out, they are moved about as need dictates, and they receive little rest; the battle to defend the Palatine is now under way, and Nero's Domus Transitoria, which linked his Palatine and Esquiline estates, is now in the Great Fire's sights.

- **Day 3** (see figs. 3 and 4): surrounds (or almost surrounds) the Palatine Hill and surges further up its slopes; fire threatens and perhaps even damages the Temple of Apollo that overlooks the Circus towards the southwest corner of the Palatine;[4] for the most part, however, the Augustan compound, including Augustus's historic home, is saved; perhaps the Temple of Luna Noctiluca on the Palatine is damaged or destroyed; the eastern prong reaches the Valley of the Colosseum to the north and then turns towards the forum;[5] the fire reaches sections of the Domus Transitoria; the battle to save the forum commences; as the day goes on, the fire threatens the northern flank of the Palatine from the forum—the hill is virtually surrounded; Nero returns to Rome and, intoxicated at the sight of the conflagration, sings his infamous song from a relatively safe distance (at that moment) on the Esquiline Hill.[6]

- **Day 4** (see fig. 4): heights of the Palatine saved, in part due the *vigiles*' efforts, and in part because the hill's lower slopes to the south, east, and west are now largely burned out; units of the *Vigiles* focus on saving what they can of the forum as the fire surges westward towards the Capitoline Hill—the eastern half of the forum is lost, including the Temple of Jupiter Stator,[7] the Temple of Vesta, and the Regia, but the fire's advance is halted, and the western half of the forum and the Capitoline beyond it are saved; fire continues to move north into the valley between the Capitoline and Palatine Hills (to the west) and the Esquiline Hill (to the east), and to spread eastward, into the saddle between the Esquiline and the Caelian Hills; Campus Martius, imperial gardens, and the like opened to refugees, and shelters constructed.[8]

- **Day 5** (see figs. 4 and 5): by now the fire has completed or nearly completed a figure 8 maneuver and so surrounds or nearly surrounds both the Palatine and Capitoline Hills, although the flames in much of the 8 are waning or burned out; as the threat to the Esquiline Hill mounts, the *vigiles* likely work throughout the day and into the night to execute the massive destruction of neighborhoods to the west and south of the hill, in the hope of preventing the fire from reaching Nero's Esquiline holdings and of retarding the fire's spread towards the east and north; fingers of the fire are now moving northward through the lowlands between the Campus Martius to the west and the eastern slopes of the Viminal and perhaps even Quirinal Hills to the east, a densely populated area with one of Rome's highest concentrations of *insulae*.

- **Day 6** (see fig. 5): the firebreak on the fringes of the Esquiline is completed and apparently works; for the moment, the fire appears extinguished; either this day or on Day 7 fire breaks out again, possibly starting on Tigellinus's "Aemilian property";[9] it is likely, however, that the success around the Esquiline and the satisfaction and relief that success occasioned created the impression that the fire had been entirely extinguished; in fact, localized and smaller fires may have been burning here and there throughout the sections of the city that had not been utterly burned out.

- **Day 7** (fig. 5): flames spread even further eastward towards the Quirinal Hill and there resuscitate the fire, or, more likely, join low-burning pockets of the fire that were never actually extinguished; the reinvigorated fire spreads northwards while attacking the western/left slopes of the Quirinal and Viminal Hills.

- **Day 8** (see fig. 5): the fire continues to burn out much of what was left standing in the area west of the slopes of the Quirinal and Viminal, continues to attack the westward slopes of those hills, and surges northward, in some places perhaps as far as the imperial gardens at the fringes of the city.[10]

- **Day 9** (see fig. 5): at long last, the flames go out.

NOTES

Prologue

1. Jerry Toner (*Roman Disasters* [Polity, 2013—hereafter in this text, *Disasters*]), characterizes Roman culture as "A Culture of Risk," as he titles one chapter in *Disasters*. That chapter's analysis of how and why that was so is exceedingly useful (87–107).

2. Despite many if not most Romans' perception, the second outbreak of the Great Fire was more likely the intensification of some relatively small pockets of fire that had never gone out than the resuscitation of an extinguished fire.

3. Assessment of severity of fire: *gravior et actrocior* (*Annals* 15.38.1).

4. A major earthquake may not occasion a disaster at all. The 8.7 Rat Islands earthquake of 1965, for example, was a massive geological event, many times greater than the Bay Area or Bam earthquakes, but it caused no casualties, and neither its shocks nor its tsunami triggered a disaster. It occurred off the tip of the Aleutian Islands of Alaska, far from any population centers—an undeniably immense natural event, but no disaster.

5. Toner (*Disasters*, 1–16) offers an accessible introduction to contemporary thinking and scholarship about disasters and vulnerability, with particular application to the ancient Romans (87–93); the text also offers a comprehensive bibliography (204–215).

6. On Tacitus, see appendix A.

7. On which a great deal has been and is being written. A concise introduction to the post-fact trend: Francis Fukuyama, "The Emergence of a Post-Fact World" (*Project Syndicate*, 12 January 2017; https://www.project-syndicate.org/onpoint/the-emergence-of-a-post-fact-world-by-francis-fukuyama-2017-01).

8. Giuseppe Pucci's study of Nero's many appearances in films and television is titled "Nerone Superstar," in *Nerone*, ed. Maria Antonietta Tomei and E. Rossella Rea (Electa, 2011), 62–75.

Chapter 1: Perils of Life in Rome

1. This chapter prioritizes sources from the first century CE, that is, the century in which the Great Fire took place, but the nature of the sources makes it necessary to range beyond that century for evidence about life in Rome. The vast majority of the sources employed come from the period stretching from the first century BCE to the middle of the second century CE. The idea is not to give a snapshot of life in Rome on the eve of the Great Fire, but to convey a sense of what life was like in Rome in its heyday, which spanned centuries. Throughout those two and a half centuries, the perils in particular of life in the city did vary in degree over time, but they remained essentially unchanged.

2. Alexandre Grandazzi, in *The Cambridge Companion to Ancient Rome*, ed. Paul Erdkamp (Cambridge UP, 2013—hereafter cited as *AR*), 8–32, offers a useful and efficient survey of Rome's early development.

3. Livy (c. 59 BCE–c. 17 CE) 5.55, Diodorus Siculus (first century BCE) 14.116.8–9, among others.

4. 1.86.1–2.

5. 7.61.

6. *On the Agrarian Law* 2.96.

7. Archaeological evidence on residences in Rome itself is sparse. For *domus*, then, we rely to a significant extent on the evidence from Pompeii and Herculaneum, although those places were very different from Rome. For apartment houses, we supplement the meager evidence with that from Ostia, Rome's port city, which, though urban, was also a different sort of place. Evidence is particularly thin for Rome before the Great Fire, that is, for the Rome that burned, and the archaeological remains of Ostia we visit today are for the most part post-Fire. The only ancient apartment house in Rome remotely near our period that provides substantial remains is the Ara Coeli *insula* at the base of the Capitoline Hill; it is post-Fire and may not be typical. *Insula* can mean different things, depending on the context (G. R. Storey, "The Meaning of *insula* in Roman Residential Terminology," *Memoirs of the American Academy at Rome* 49 [2004]: 47–84). *Taberna*, which does give us the English word *tavern*, can be a shop or humble residence—for our purposes, often the same place.

8. The Regionary Catalogues (the *Curiosum* and the *Notitia*), fourth-century CE tabulations of the physical city district by district, suggest that at that time *insulae* outnumbered *domus* something like 46,500 to around 1,800. We cannot be sure what precisely they mean by *insulae* (apartment houses, apartment units, floors in apartment houses, or something else?), the statistics in the catalogues may be imprecise, and their information comes considerably later than our period. Still, the basics of the distribution of types of residences almost certainly apply to our period as well. The texts are in Arvast Nordh, *Libellus de Regionibus Urbis Romae* (Lund, 1949), and online at http://penelope.uchicago.edu/Thayer/L/Gazetteer/Places/Europe/Italy/Lazio/Roma/Rome/_Texts/Regionaries/text*.html.

9. Ostia provides archaeological evidence for well-appointed, spacious apartments. In his youth, the future first-century BCE dictator Sulla lived in an apartment in Rome. His means were limited at the time, but the 3,000 sesterces he paid in rent was considerably more than most Romans could earn in several years; the dwelling was humble only considering that he came from an ancient and noble family (Plutarch, *Sulla* 1.4).

10. William D. McNulty, "Eminent Domain in Continental Europe," *Yale Law Journal* 21.7 (May 1912): 555–558.

11. Augustus also transformed the city substantially. No catastrophe had prompted his innovations, but he was responding to a disaster of sorts: neglect due to decades of intermittent political turmoil and civil war had left much of Rome in desperate need of renovation and reorganization.

12. On why the Italians finally found the will and a way to erect the embankments, see Gregory Aldrete, *Floods of the Tiber in Ancient Rome* (Johns Hopkins UP, 2007—hereafter cited as *Floods*), 247–252.

13. National Weather Service (http://www.srh.noaa.gov/tsa/?n=hydro_TADD).

14. 39.61. On Dio, see Appendix A.

15. *Julius Caesar* 58.

16. Aldrete, *Floods*, 192–198.

17. Many other factors likely contributed to the ancient Romans' failure to build embankments or to take any other definitive measures to eliminate flood; see Aldrete, *Floods*, 232–239.

18. The father and son emperors responsible for building the Colosseum in the late first century CE.

19. Hurricane Sandy (2012) provides an instructive example. Immediately after the event, much thought and determination were invested in preparing for the next hurricane. Over time, however, Sandy fell off people's radar, apprehension about the future dissipated, and attention shifted to more immediate concerns, with the result that years later the northeastern United States is almost as vulnerable today to the next major hurricane as it was to Sandy in 2012 (http://www.motherjones.com/environment/2013/10/how-were-failing-to-prepare-for-the-next-sandy/).

20. 5.3.7.

21. 21.33.7.

22. Suetonius (on him, see Appendix A) says that around twenty thousand people were killed (*Tiberius* 40); Tacitus estimates the number of casualties at fifty thousand (*Annals* 4.63). More on this tragedy pp. 73–74.

23. 2.53.

24. *Satires* 3.225.

25. *Satires* 3.190–196. Translated by Peter Green, *Sixteen Satires* (Penguin, 1999).

26. *Letters to Atticus* 14.9; 14.11.

27. The first two passages are from private correspondence and thus most likely represent his actual view of the lower classes (*Letters to Atticus* 1.19.4; 1.16.11). The last is from a trial speech, delivered in public and then published by Cicero; so, even if it did not represent his actual view and was a response to a rhetorical need of the moment, it must have represented a view many in his listening audience, propertied people like Cicero, held (*pro Flacco* 18; cf. *de Domo* 5).

28. Augustus—Strabo 5.3.7; Trajan—Aurelius Victor (late fourth century CE) 13.13.

29. Propertius (born c. 50 BCE) 16.5–6.

30. Suetonius, *Nero* 16.

31. Suetonius, *Nero* 26.

32. *rerum rusticarum* 1, epilogue.

33. *Roman Antiquities* 4.24.4.

34. 5.42.

35. 19.59.

36. Suetonius, *Nero* 33.

37. Elder Pliny (23/24–79 CE), *Natural History* 35.164.

38. Suetonius, *Augustus* 56.

39. Suetonius, *Augustus* 43.

40. Benjamin Kelly argues that the authorities were involved in the investigation, pursuit, and suppression of day-to-day, person-against-person crime ("Policing and Security," in Erdkamp, *AR*, 410–416), but he concedes that there is no evidence whatsoever for this in the sources and that even if the authorities tried, their efforts were largely ineffective. Passages such as Varro, *de lingua latina* 5.81, which suggest that the authorities

conducted investigations, do not indicate what sort of illegal activities they investigated, and everything else we know of the Roman authorities suggests that they investigated only illegal activities that threatened stability and order. Escaped and criminal slaves, for example, were not pursued to defend the rights of their specific victims and owners but rather to preserve the (in Roman eyes) essential but vulnerable institution of slavery.

41. *Annals* 6.11.

42. Roman law was so vast, intricate, and influential on subsequent law that even today some law schools offer courses in it. But those courses focus primarily on civil law—disputes about property, wills, contracts, divorce, and the like—with which the corpus of surviving Roman law is principally concerned.

43. Kelly, "Policing and Security," in Erdkamp, *AR*, 423.

44. Martial 7.61.

45. 12.57.3–6.

46. *Letters* 56.1–2. Whether the letter recounts Seneca's own personal experience or the experience a Roman *might* have had is irrelevant; the letter made sense only if the account of the activities and noisiness of bathhouses was credible.

47. Among many sources: Horace (65–8 BCE), *Epistulae* 2.2.79; Juvenal, *Satires* 3.231–238; Elder Pliny, *Natural History* 26.111.

48. Suetonius, *Caesar* 39.

49. 3.269–277.

50. The number of pets, service animals, and those intended to provide food may have equaled that of the human population. In addition, many uninvited creatures added their evacuations to the mix. For an idea of the extent and variety of Rome's animal population (including bibliography), see Michael MacKinnon, "Pack Animals, Pets, Pests, and Other Non-Human Beings," in Erdkamp, *AR*, 110–128.

51. *Satire* 3.247–248. Complaints about mud were common: e.g., Martial 3.36, 10.10; Seneca, *de ira* 3.35.

52. Suetonius, *Vespasian* 5.

53. Ray Laurence, "Traffic and Land Transportation in and near Rome," in Erdkamp, *AR*, 251–252.

54. Suetonius, *Nero* 51.

55. In the fourth century CE, there were 11 imperial bath complexes and 856 smaller establishments. See pp. 21–22, 36–37. The number in our period was likely smaller, but still in the many hundreds.

56. The more empire-wide pollution Roman mining and other activities generated for the Mediterranean world and beyond is not the issue here. For a brief introduction to those issues, see https://farrington1600.wikispaces.com/file/view/HowRomePolluted.pdf.

57. *fumum et opes strepitumque Romae*; harsh clouds: *nubibus arduis*, which in its context suggests something more like London's Great Smog of 1952 than overcast weather (Horace, *Carmina* 3.29.10–12).

58. *Vitellius* 13.

59. *Claudius* 18.

60. Elder Pliny, *Natural History* 9.77.

61. In 2 BCE, for example, Augustus distributed the grain dole to only slightly more than two hundred thousand residents of Rome (*Res Gestae* 15)—a large number, but a small percentage of the city's million or so inhabitants.

62. On the vexed issues surrounding assessing the extent of hunger and malnourishment in Rome, see P. Garnsey, "Mass Diet and Nutrition in the City of Rome," in *Nourrir la plebe*, ed. A. Giovannini (Friedrich Reinhardt, 1991), 67–101.

63. *Letters to Family and Friends* 7.26.

64. 14.72.

65. It is no accident that the Latin word Martial used for sausage, *botulus*, has given us the word *botulism*, an often foodborne disease.

66. Ancient descriptions of illnesses and diseases do not always correspond neatly to diseases we have today, and the archaeological evidence that human remains provide is limited. This means that speculation about precisely which disease a given ancient source is describing at a given point is frequently unavoidable. Too often our sources do not even provide a description of the symptoms of a disease or an epidemic, or they provide only a cursory one. As is usual with ancient sources, moreover, literary and rhetorical conventions make depictions of illnesses suspect.

67. 11.328 (Kühn).

68. "Disease and Death," in Erdkamp, *AR*, 52.

69. Plague of 65: Suetonius, *Nero* 39 (for number of casualties); Tacitus, *Annals* 16.13 (for the date). That casualty figure has struck some as suspiciously high and/or too neat. On ancient estimates of epidemic casualties, see Walter Scheidel, "Germs for Rome," in *Rome the Cosmopolis*, ed. Catharine Edwards and Greg Woolf (Cambridge UP, 2003), 171–172, esp. n. 57. Plague fifteen years later: Suetonius, *Titus* 8; the number comes from Jerome, *Chronography* 272, although Jerome has the wrong date. This number too is doubted, and with better reason, I believe. In any event, round and exaggerated numbers from antiquity are always suspect, but even when imprecise and inflated, they indicate that a serious and deadly outbreak occurred.

70. For details, see Aldrete, *Floods*, 141–154.

71. Plutarch, *Tiberius Gracchus* 1.3–5.

72. 18a.347 (Kühn).

73. *Natural History* 28.238.

74. *Natural History* 29.85.

75. *Natural History* 30.26.

76. 1.47.

77. The city's voracious appetite for wood had largely deforested central Italy (Aldrete, *Floods*, 74–77).

78. *Crassus* 2. Perhaps a bit of grim come-uppance, in the view of some of the property owners he had victimized, at any rate: Crassus wound up losing his head—literally—in his disastrous campaign to conquer Parthia, roughly modern-day Iran. The slumlord millionaire's head then served as a prop in the performance of a Greek tragedy at the Parthian court.

79. The authorities did not entirely neglect fire, of course. Some sources suggest that the consuls, the Roman Republic's highest elected officials, were supposed to address the danger (e.g., Cicero, *In Pisonem* 11.26). Still, none of the evidence we have suggests a permanent, professional unit of firefighters, and much evidence, like that concerning Crassus, suggests something of a free-for-all. A useful survey of the complicated issue: Olivia F. Robinson, "Fire Prevention at Rome," *Revue internationale des droits de l'antiquité* 24 (1977): 377–378.

80. This text will refer to the fire department as a whole as the *Vigiles*, with a capital V, and the firefighters themselves as *vigiles*, with a lower-case *v*.

81. Although much of the evidence for these tools is later than the Great Fire, there is no reason to assume that they did not exist in Nero's day.

82. The closest thing we have to a description of what *vigiles* did tells us that they stayed up all night patrolling the city with axes (*dolabris*) and buckets (*hamis*) (*Digest* 1.15.3).

83. Vegetius, *Epitoma rei militaris* II.25.

84. For a scholarly but accessible treatment, see the middle section ("During") of Philip Fradkin's *The Great Earthquake and Firestorm of 1906: How San Francisco Nearly Destroyed Itself* (U of California P, 2006).

85. For the most comprehensive list of attested fires in ancient Rome, see Robert Sablayrolles, *Libertinus Miles: Les Cohortes de Vigiles* (École Française de Rome, 1996—hereafter cited as *Cohortes*), 771–802.

86. Modern refugees from natural and political disasters present a different case, of course.

87. From the Regionaries, on which see p. 138, n. 8. The number of bathhouses in Nero's day was smaller, but there were undoubtedly already hundreds in the city.

88. See pp. 116–118.

89. Martial is our principal ancient source (text and commentary in *Martial: Liber Spectaculorum*, ed. Kathleen Coleman [Oxford UP, 2006]).

90. Suetonius, *Caesar* 39; *Augustus* 43.

91. Much of the discussion here, and specifically some of the professions mentioned, are from Wim Broekaert and Arjan Zuiderhoek, "Industries and Services," in Erdkamp, *AR*, 317–319.

92. The author is a resident of Baltimore and engages in the ritual complaining about the city. Still, he loves living there.

93. On the authorities' responses to disasters, see Jerry Toner, *Roman Disasters* (Polity, 2013), 45–46.

94. The encounter between Croesus and Solon: *Histories* 1.29–33. The Greek *olbiotaton*, translated above as "fortunate," is a more complicated term than that and suggests happiness and prosperity as well as good fortune. According to Herodotus, Croesus later learned the wisdom of Solon's words when he suffered a disaster of his own making: he lost his kingdom and even his freedom by attacking and then being defeated by Cyrus the Great, the founding king of the Persian Empire.

CHAPTER II: INFERNO

1. The narrative that follows is based primarily on Tacitus's account, and secondarily on Suetonius's. Our third principal source, Dio, is employed sparingly. Tacitus provided the most detailed and reliable account, and the fire actually occurred in his lifetime. Tacitus can be a slippery character and a master of insinuation, but he tends to get his facts right. Other materials, such as the archaeological record and what we know about life in ancient Rome and the behavior of fires, also inform this narrative. For discussion of the sources, particularly Tacitus, Suetonius, and Dio, see Appendix A. I have not hesitated to fill in blanks where it seemed warranted and necessary to convey a sense of what happened and how Rome's residents experienced the fire. Although Tacitus's account of the Great Fire is one of antiquity's longest and most detailed accounts of a disaster, it is still spare and

lacking in specifics by modern standards. For a suggested day-by-day chronology of the Great Fire, see Appendix B.

2. Dio has Nero sending men out to different sections of the city to start a series of fires that evolved into the Great Fire. He says that these multiple points of origin bewildered Romans, who saw fires in different places, "as in a military camp" (62.16). This is most likely a reflection of how the Great Fire, as it spread, was in many locations simultaneously—raging here, igniting there, spending itself in yet other places. Moreover, the controlled fires the *vigiles* set would have added to the number of locations ablaze. It might offer an appealing tableau for the imagination, but at no moment was the city entirely engulfed in flames.

3. This is surely how the powerful navigated the streets of Rome amidst the mayhem—the great mass of Romans were expected or forced to give way in even the best of times—though neither Tacitus nor our other sources mention this. For them: not worth mentioning, however outrageous and newsworthy we might find such behavior; our sources belonged to the classes that had such retinues and felt entitled to use them to make their own lives easier and, in emergencies, safer.

4. Dio 62.16.

5. The second is discussed on pp. 71–72.

6. Paul Zanker, *The Power of Images in the Age of Augustus*, trans. Alan Shapiro (U of Michigan P, 1988–90), 201–210.

7. Dio depicts the *vigiles* as out-of-control villains who completely abrogated their duty and exacerbated the situation. They rush to the fire, but instead of fighting it, set more fires to facilitate their plundering of Rome. Dio's *vigiles* behave, essentially, like a conquering army sacking a city (62.17). Suetonius does not mention *vigiles* but claims that Nero's "personal staff" were setting fires with tow and torches (*Nero* 38), and even former consuls were afraid to confront them. Was this another reflection of misunderstanding of the *vigiles*' strategy? See Gregory N. Daugherty, "The *Cohortes Vigilum* and the Great Fire of 64 AD," *Classical Journal* 87.3 (1992): 233 (hereafter cited as "Great Fire"). Some *vigiles* may have taken the opportunity to loot. We cannot know for certain. I suggest below, however, that other *vigiles* may have performed effectively in some locations, although our sources do not describe this.

8. Suetonius, *Nero* 38.

9. Suetonius, *Claudius* 18.

10. In Throop, New York, extreme atmospheric heat apparently caused horse manure to burst into flame (https://www.washingtonpost.com/news/morning-mix/wp/2016/07/29/dry-hot-american-summer-horse-manure-spontaneously-catches-fire-in-upstate-new-york/); the article also explains how and why such ignitions occur.

11. Suetonius (*Nero* 38) explicitly places refugees among the tombs.

12. Modern firefighters mostly scoff at the personification of fire as a living being fighting for survival, but the Great Fire's behavior and course, so vast a conflagration in an environment like that of ancient Rome, resembled that of an animal desperately and ruthlessly doing all that it could to sustain itself. In societies like ancient Rome's, where scientific explanations of natural phenomena are rare and no more than unsubstantiated guesswork, people process fires through metaphors and narratives, not science. In his description of the Great Fire, Tacitus used language and images that suggest both the ravenous beast and the pitiless invader (for detailed commentary on the pervasive invader imagery, see Rhiannon Ash, *Tacitus* Annals *Book XV* [Cambridge UP, 2018—hereafter cited

as *Book XV*]), 177-212. This strategy complements broader themes of his work, but it also likely reflects how the ancient city's beleaguered inhabitants perceived and made sense of the fire. To convey *their* experience and processing of that experience, I describe the fire's behavior employing Tacitus's metaphors. For Tacitus and his contemporaries, the fire was more an actor than a mere catalyst.

13. *alitur* (*Annals* 15.38.2—in the passive voice in the Latin).

14. See Appendix B for a hypothetical day-by-day chronology for the fire's spread.

15. *et Palatium et domus et cuncta circum haurirentur* ("the Palatine and the home(s) and everything in the vicinity were consumed" [*Annals* 15.39]); again, Tacitus depicted the fire as a voracious beast. The context suggests that Tacitus here may have been thinking of the palace, not the Palatine Hill, but it comes down to essentially the same thing: by that time, the palace had enveloped the heights of the hill.

16. On the "logistical and administrative" shortcomings that may have contributed to the *Vigiles'* inability to contain the Great Fire early on, see Daugherty, "Great Fire," 234-240.

17. *Annals* 15.38: *antiit remedia velocitate mali*.

18. The other military and quasi-military units stationed in the city likely joined the *vigiles* in confronting the emergency (Daugherty, "Great Fire," 254).

19. Filippo Coarelli, *Rome and Environs: An Archaeological Guide* (U of California P; updated English edition, 2014), 28-41.

20. Edward Champlin, *Nero* (Harvard UP, 2005—hereafter cited as *Nero*), 123-125.

21. On the nexus among Nero, Augustus, and Apollo/Sol, see Champlin, *Nero*, 138-144.

22. Suetonius, *Augustus* 73.

23. If these "stands" against the Great Fire occurred, why does Tacitus not mention them? Later in his account of the fire he does mention a stand at the base of the Esquiline Hill, in the vicinity of Nero's own Esquiline property. Why mention only that one? One of Tacitus's priorities was to show how appallingly self-absorbed Nero was—Nero's Esquiline stand took place only after the fire had been ravaging Rome for days, and the emperor was on the spot only to save his own palace—and so including the Esquiline stand fits Tacitus's agenda perfectly. If the *vigiles* scored other victories against the fire, as I posit they did, their inclusion would not have contributed to this thematic priority, nor do they fit the *Annals'* broader themes of corruption and degeneration. Tacitus would not have viewed his omission as concealment, but rather as the elision of material less vital to the communication of the Great Fire's meaning, what it revealed about the emperor and the state of the Roman people at that time. In his frustratingly brief (by our standards) account, he omitted the vast majority of occurrences in the nine days of the Great Fire because his principal concern was not to provide a thorough account of *everything* that transpired, but to make sure his readers understood the *significance* of the disaster.

24. If the 8 was not entirely complete, it was likely nearly so.

25. Modern Anzio, site of the major battle in World War II in which, among many others, the father of Pink Floyd's Roger Waters died.

26. *Annals* 15.37-38. I have taken considerable liberties with this translation to make the implications of Tacitus's terse Latin clear and to avoid having to go into the complicated particulars of Roman weddings. The Latin: "inditum imperatori flammeum, missi auspices, dos et genialis torus et faces nuptiales, cuncta denique spectata quae etiam in femina nox operit. sequitur clades, forte an dolo principis." This travesty of a Roman marriage may have actually been a parodic performance of a religious initiation (J. Colin, "Juvénal et le

mariage mystique de Gracchus," in *Atti della Accademia delle Scienze di Torino*. 2, *Classe di Scienze Morali, Storiche e Filologiche* 90 [1955/56]: 186–192), but Tacitus does not consider or portray it as such, and that is the issue here. For interpretation of the salacious details of the orgy, see Ash, *Book XV*, 171–177.

27. *flagitia*, a word that plays an important role in our discussion of Nero's scapegoating of the Christians for the Great Fire.

28. 62.15.

29. Philip Waddell ("Eloquent Collisions: The *Annales* of Tacitus, the Column of Trajan, and the Cinematic Quick-Cut," *Arethusa* 46 [2013]: 471–497) characterized this juxtaposition as "collision quick-cut," intended to influence readers' construction of the events.

30. *Annals* 15.39: "He did not return to the city until the fire was approaching his home" (*ante + quam* ["until"] + *propinquaret* ["was approaching"]).

31. The Domus Transitoria was considerably more than a passageway linking two wings of the palace; the archaeological remains suggest that it had its own assemblage of elegant suites (Maria Antonietta Tomei, "Nerone sul Palatino," in *Nerone*, ed. Maria Antonietta Tomei and E. Rossella Rea [Electa, 2011], 118–135; for a précis of the earlier findings and evidence for the Domus Transitoria, see Mariette de Vos, in *Lexicon Topographicum Urbis Romae*, ed. Eva Margareta Steinby, 5 vols. (Edizioni Quasar, 1993–1999), 2: 199–202.

32. Much of this derived from Jerry Toner, *Roman Disasters* (Polity, 2013), 49–57.

33. *Titus*, 8.

34. What follows is my best conjecture of what actually transpired.

35. Dio 62.29; Juvenal, *Satire* 8.221. For fragments of Nero's poetry, including the very few remains of his *Songs of Troy*, see Edward Courtney, *The Fragmentary Latin Poets* (Oxford UP, 1993), 357–359. On the Roman habit of employing Troy to make sense of later disasters, see Ash, *Book XV*, 186–187.

36. The most useful survey and analysis of Nero's musical, dramatic, and equine ambitions and performances: Champlin, *Nero*, 53–82; Mathew Owen and Ingo Gildenhard, *Tacitus*, Annals, 15.20–23, 33–45 (Open Book, 2013—hereafter cited as *Tacitus*), provide a précis of Champlin's material, including a chart of the stages of Nero's career (30–32).

37. *Letters to His Brother Quintus* 3.7.1. On Homer's "validity": *viget illud Homeri*.

38. *praesentia mala vetustis cladibus adsimulantem* (Annals 15.39.3); the standard translation of *adsimulantem* is "compare" (e.g., Ash, *Book XV*, 187), but something both stronger and subtler than mere comparison is going on.

39. 62.17.

40. For our purposes, the best translation of *infamia* might be "lack of respectability," which for the Romans was more than just one's reputation. Or, to put it differently, for the Romans, reputation and respectability were indispensable and defining elements of the social, political, and even legal order.

41. Tacitus, *Annals* 15.67.3.

42. http://www.history.com/news/ask-history/did-nero-really-fiddle-while-rome-burned.

43. Suetonius, *Nero* 38; Tacitus *Annals* 15.39; Dio 62.18.

44. This is how we get the English word *palace*—originally just the name for the hill, then for the hill that became all palace, then simply for the Roman emperors' palace/home (because that is what the hill had become), and finally, for any grand imperial or royal residence.

45. Tacitus may not have even intended the term to be taken literally.

46. Champlin, *Nero*, 49.

47. Champlin, *Nero*, 49; Owen and Gildenhard, *Tacitus*, 204.

48. The cithara is in the lyre family of instruments.

49. On how later traditions put a fiddle into Nero's hands, see Mary Francis Gyles, "Nero Fiddled while Rome Burned," *Classical Journal* 42.4 (1947): 211–217.

50. *Annals* 15.50.

51. *Annals* 15.40: "vast tract of land"—*per immensum*; "plain"—*campus*.

52. Tacitus's narrative suggests that the fire had been extinguished at this point, which surely reflects the perception of many if not most of Rome's inhabitants, including the authorities. It is likely, however, that minor fires were still burning here and there in the city, and they were to contribute to the Great Fire's second surge (see Appendix B).

53. *Annals* 15.40.2; Dio 62.18. For a consensus view concerning which of Rome's fourteen districts fell into which level of destruction, see Lawrence Richardson Jr., *A New Topographical Dictionary of Ancient Rome* (Johns Hopkins UP), 1992, 332.

54. The assessment of Hurricane Maria's 2017 death toll in Puerto Rico provides a recent case (https://www.nytimes.com/interactive/2017/12/08/us/puerto-rico-hurricane-maria-death-toll.html).

55. Although the Roman authorities did not keep official casualty counts for disasters, that did not stop ancient writers from providing estimates, as Tacitus himself did for the tragic collapse of the amphitheater at Fidenae (fifty thousand—*Annals* 4.63); that is, it would have been perfectly in line with the standards of ancient writers for Tacitus to have provided a casualty count, even if based on no actual data. Tacitus wanted his readers to focus on other things.

56. In what follows, I employ elements of Kelly Shannon's stimulating and detailed discussion of the significance of these buildings in Tacitus's narrative ("Memory, Religion and History in Nero's Great Fire: Tacitus, *Annals* 15.41–7," *Classical Quarterly* 62.2 [2012]: 749–765); Shannon explores the Tacitean nexus among memory, "religious correctness" (756), piety, depravity, and Nero's behavior.

57. *Annals* 15.41.1. For a brief rundown on the controversies regarding the identities and identifications of these structures, see Ash, *Book XV*, 190–191.

58. Cicero provides the *locus classicus* for this sentiment (*pro Rabirio perduellionis reo* 5).

59. 8.102–307.

60. Livy, *History of Rome* Preface 6–9.

61. *Annals* 15.41.

62. *Annals* 15.41.

63. For a précis of the issues, see Owen and Gildenhard, *Tacitus*, 216–218.

64. On the complex intersections among the Gallic sack, Livy's narrative of it, the fall of Troy, Tacitus's narrative of the Great Fire and of Nero's reconstruction of the city, and Rome's changing configurations, see Christina S. Kraus, "'No Second Troy': Topoi and Refoundation in Livy, Book V," *Transactions of the American Philological Association* 124 (1994): 267–289.

65. *immensum numerum insularum*, where *insularum* could be translated as "city blocks" instead of "apartment houses."

66. All *Nero* 38.

CHAPTER III: THE DAY AFTER

1. Suetonius, *Nero* 38; Tacitus, *Annals* 15.43.
2. In 27 BCE (*Annals* 4.63).
3. All: *Nero* 38.
4. On the complexities of employment in Rome's construction industry: P. A. Brunt, "Free Labour and Public Works at Rome," *Journal of Roman Studies* 70 (1980): 81–100; Wim Broekaert and Arjan Zuiderhoek, in *The Cambridge Companion to Ancient Rome*, ed. Paul Erdkamp (Cambridge UP, 2013—hereafter cited as *AR*), 325–328.
5. When someone told the emperor Vespasian that he could move columns onto the Capitoline Hill through an engineering innovation, that is, with very few laborers, the emperor said, essentially, "No thanks," that he preferred to feed Rome's poor (*plebiculam*) through the employment such tasks provided (Suetonius, *Vespasian* 18).
6. Attempts to express the worth of ancient sums of money in modern currencies are more art than science and are always misleading, and in this case we do not actually have a figure. Two considerations that suggest we should conceive of the cost of the cleanup and rebuilding of Rome as something in the billions: (1) imagine damage on a similar scale to a great modern city and what cleanup and reconstruction would cost—in the many billions (New York's comptroller's office, for example, reckoned just the property losses [including cleanup] of 9/11 at $55,000,000,000 [*New York Times* 9/8/11: http://www.nytimes.com/interactive/2011/09/08/us/sept-11-reckoning/cost-graphic.html?_r=0]); (2) the scale of Nero's exactions and their impact on the entire empire suggest an astoundingly large sum.
7. *Annals* 15.45; *Nero* 38.
8. *Description of Greece* 10.7.1.
9. 31.149. Late first/early second century CE.
10. Elder Pliny, *Natural History* 34.84. Neither Pausanias nor Pliny asserts explicitly that Nero acquired these statues in the aftermath of the fire, and Nero surely acquired works of art at other times. Still, the aftermath of the Great Fire is a likely context for a significant portion of the wholesale plundering, and Pliny explicitly connects the pillaging to Nero's Domus Aurea, built in the wake of the fire on land the fire had cleared.
11. All Tacitus, *Annals* 15.45; see, too, Suetonius, *Nero* 38.
12. The Books were a collection of old and often cryptic oracular utterances in verse. Consultations, then, consisted largely of interpretation of how those texts illuminated the gods' will regarding a specific event or crisis. As happens so often with such interpretations, those consulting the Books very likely found in them what they wanted or needed to find; once emperors had replaced the Republic, the interpretations came to reflect the desires of the sitting emperor.
13. Tacitus, *Annals* 12.43.
14. For links to these and other such claims: https://en.wikipedia.org/wiki/Natural_disasters_as_divine_retribution.
15. *Annals* 15.44.
16. *Nero* 38.
17. *Annals* 15.38.1. I have translated Tacitus's word *dolo* as "machinations"; the word suggests trickery and carries more than a whiff of malice.
18. See *Identifying the Culprit. Assessing Eyewitness Identification*, by the Committee on Scientific Approaches to Understanding and Maximizing the Validity and Reliability of

Eyewitness Identification in Law Enforcement and the Courts et al. (National Academies Press, 2015), which can be accessed free online at: http://www.nap.edu/catalog/18891/identifying-the-culprit-assessing-eyewitness-identification.

19. An accessible account of the fire: Joshua Hammer, *Yokohama Burning* (Free Press, 2006), 149–179, on the scapegoating of Koreans.

20. A complete list of arguments, pro and con, with analyses of their virtues and flaws would require dozens of pages, unfortunately well beyond the scope of this book.

21. Suetonius, *Nero* 38; Dio 62.16; Elder Pliny, *Natural History* 17.5; pseudo-Seneca, *Octavia* lines 826ff.

22. The relevant passages in chronological order: *Annals* 15.33 (plan to travel to Greece), 15.36 (trip cancelled/postponed; plan to travel to Egypt; trip cancelled/postponed), 15.37 (orgy), 15.38 (Great Fire). This necessarily brief account does not do justice to all the elements of Champlin's argument; for his entire case, see Edward Champlin, *Nero* (Harvard UP, 2005—hereafter cited as *Nero*), 186–191.

23. Theater collapse, Tacitus, *Annals* 15.34; panic attack, *Annals* 15.36.

24. Dio 62.16; Suetonius, *Nero* 38; *Annals* 15.38.

25. When four years later it was apparent that Nero would fall, Tigellinus betrayed him. In early 69 CE the unpopular and disloyal prefect was forced to kill himself.

26. Daugherty, "Great Fire," 234–235, 240.

27. *Nero* 38.

28. Dio 58.23.4.

29. G. B. Townend, "The Sources of the Greek in Suetonius," *Hermes* 88 (1960): 112.

30. The Pisonian Conspiracy, named after Calpurnius Piso, the man the conspirators would have made emperor.

31. Tacitus claimed that he was quoting Subrius's exact words (*Annals* 15.67.3).

32. Champlin, *Nero* 186.

33. For the opposing view that social cruelty and dehumanization actually result from the victimizers' recognition of the victims' humanity, see Alan Fiske and Tage Rai, *Virtuous Violence: Hurting and Killing to Create, Sustain, End, and Honor Social Relationships* (Cambridge UP, 2014).

34. The level to which Christians could engage in the aspects of the society around them that (in their view) paganism had tainted was already an issue for Christians at this time, as Paul's First Epistle to the Corinthians indicates. The issue had not been settled more than 140 years later, when the African Christian writer Tertullian addressed it in his *On the Spectacles* (*de spectaculis*). We can only speculate on the number of Christians in the '60s CE who avoided the games and the number who attended.

35. On the charge of human sacrifice in antiquity, particularly in the context of religious tensions, see James Rives, "Human Sacrifice among Pagans and Christians," *Journal of Roman Studies* 85 (1995): 65–85; recently on the charges against the early Christians: Bart Wagemakers, "Incest, Infanticide, and Cannibalism: Anti-Christian Imputations in the Roman Empire," *Greece and Rome* 57 (2010): 337–354.

36. *Annals* 15.44.

37. The authenticity of the passage has been doubted (most recently: Richard Carrier, "The Prospect of a Christian Interpolation in Tacitus, Annals, 15.44," *Vigiliae Christianae* 68.3 [2014]: 264–283), as has the historicity of the Neronian persecution (most recently: Brent Shaw, "The Myth of the Neronian Persecution," *Journal of Roman Studies* 105 [2015]:

73-100). I do not share these doubts. (Shaw himself characterizes his argument as "deliberately framed as a provocative hypothesis," 74).

38. This question is connected to the broader issue of Nero's popularity, a vexed and debated issue. For an introduction to the approaches and evidence, see Egon Flaig, "Wie Kaiser Nero die Akzeptanz bei der Plebs urbana verlor: Eine Fallstudie zum politischen Gerücht im Prinzipat," *Historia* 52.3 (2003): 351–372. My reading of the issue is that responses to Nero were always mixed and frequently fluctuated, across but also within classes. The best we can do is to identify moments when "some" people, at any rate, felt certain ways, but the number and percentage of such people elude us. It is always iffy to assert that "The Romans thought X," or even more narrowly, "The senatorial class thought X" and "The urban plebs thought Y," as it would be to assert that "Americans think X" or "Working-class Americans think X" about any issue. Some Americans of all classes, for example, are wildly enthusiastic about Donald Trump, others are quite the opposite, and the opinions of yet others mixed and evolving. Later generations' fascination with Nero is a different issue.

39. Robert Wilken, *The Christians as the Romans Saw Them* (Yale UP, 1984), 17–21.

40. The Latin word translated above as "gather," *confluunt*, literally means "flow together."

41. Representative of the doubters: Erich Koestermann, "Ein Folgenschwerer Irrtum des Tacitus (Ann. 15, 44, 2ff.)?," *Historia* 16.4 (1967): 456–469.

42. *Claudius* 25.

43. The author's wife's first name is Gayla. When she meets people, they tend to assume her name is the more common Gail. No one, on the other hand, hears Gail and assumes the rarer Gayla.

44. On which, with bibliography, T. D. Barnes, *Early Christian Hagiography and Roman History* (Tria Cordia 5; Mohr Siebeck, 2010), 331–337.

45. *Martyrdom of Pionius* 21, in *Acts of the Christian Martyrs*, ed. Herbert Musurillo, vol. 2 (Oxford UP, 1972).

46. Robert E. A. Palmer, "Severan Ruler-Cult and the Moon in the City of Rome," *Aufstieg und Niedergang der römischen Welt* II.16.2 (Berlin, 1978—hereafter cited as "Severan Ruler-Cult"): 1107–1110. Varro (116–27 BCE) tells us that the temple "shines by night" (*lucet noctu* [*On the Latin Language* 5.68]). This is not the temple of Luna that Tacitus mentions in his accounting of the Great Fire's destruction.

47. Such as Seneca experienced watching executions in a largely empty arena (*Letters* 7).

48. Kathleen M. Coleman, "Fatal Charades: Roman Executions Staged as Mythological Enactments," *Journal of Roman Studies* 80 (1990—hereafter cited as "Executions"), 44.

49. *Nero* 12.

50. Much of what follows relies on Champlin's shrewd reading of the mythological elements of the Christians' punishments (*Nero* 121–126). For further commentary on the executions and the issues Tacitus's depiction of them raises, see Rhiannon Ash, *Tacitus Annals Book XV* (Cambridge UP, 2018), 207–209.

51. 1 Clement 6.2. The Roman Catholic Church counts this Clement as the fourth Pope.

52. A persecution under the emperor Domitian has been suggested as the context for Clement's martyrs. The evidence for such a persecution is meager and suspect, however (T. D. Barnes, *Tertullian* [Oxford UP, 1971], 150); Barnes, "Legislation against the Christians," *Journal of Roman Studies* 58 (1968): 32–36.

53. The standard interpretation is that the Christian women appeared in some way or other with jugs, a prop that would indicate to the audience who they were meant to represent, and that is where the correspondence between the Danaids' and Christians' fates ended (Coleman, "Executions," 65–66).

54. On the variety of aquatic spectacles and the trouble the Romans would take to stage them: Kathleen M. Coleman, "Launching into History: Aquatic Displays in the Early Empire," *Journal of Roman Studies* 83 (1993): 48–74; on adapting existing dry venues for aquatic shows, 56–60.

55. *What Would You Die For? Perpetua's Passion*, ed. Joseph J. Walsh (Apprentice House, 2006), 92.

56. Argument for damage to the Palatine Temple of Apollo: Champlin, *Nero*, 123–125.

57. Circuses were *the* venues for chariot-racing, but the Romans put other shows on in them as well. Tacitus does not specify which circus and gardens served as the venues for the executions. The standard view is that they took place on the western side of the Tiber in the Vatican Valley, in the imperial gardens located there, and in the nearby Circus of Caligula. As we see in Chapter 5, the early Christians' *belief* that they took place there was to have a profound impact on Rome's future. Some have advocated the Gardens of Sallust and the track located there for the persecutions (Palmer, "Severan Ruler-Cult," 1109); these gardens were located on the northeastern fringes of the city and were for the most part or entirely spared by the fire (E. Nash, "Obelisk und Circus," *Mitteilungen des Deutschen Archäologischen Instituts: Römische Abteilung* 64 [1957]: 232–259, on the track, its obelisk, and the gardens). In any event, soon after the Great Fire, the Circus Maximus was in no condition to host any event.

58. Suetonius, *Nero* 24. Nero toured the four great Panhellenic Festivals (Olympic, Pythian, Nemean, Isthmian), at which he "won" all the chariot-racing and musical competitions he entered.

59. This is not to say that Nero thought of himself as or was claiming to be Apollo incarnate; rather, that he was claiming elements of Apollo's identity and significance as his own. Apollo and his associations served as a kind of shorthand to convey who Nero was and what he represented. On the Nero/Apollo nexus in this and other contexts, see Champlin, *Nero*, 112–144.

60. Elder Pliny, *Natural History* 8.20–21.

CHAPTER IV: NEROPOLIS

1. The rubble that was not hauled away or leveled probably wound up as aggregate for the tons of concrete the rebuilding of Rome would require.

2. Everything we know about Nero suggests that the new city reflected his vision and intentions, but his advisors, architects, and engineers must also have played a significant role in the deliberations concerning the cleanup and reconstruction of the city.

3. *Nero* 16.

4. *Annals* 15.43; *Nero* 16.

5. It is not out of the question, however, that when Tacitus referred to fire-resistant stone he was also thinking of that stone's employment as aggregate in concrete.

6. This is not to suggest the elimination of timber from Roman architecture. For one thing, the areas unaffected by the fire continued to have the older form of architecture, and

for another, the upper floors of apartment houses continued to be allowed to have the old post-and-lintel timber-dependent configuration. So little Neronian-era private architecture survives in Rome that we are reduced to speculation. See below, pp. 116–117.

7. Frontinus, *de aquis* 75–76.
8. All: Tacitus, *Annals* 15.43.
9. All: Tacitus, *Annals* 15.43.
10. Gaius, *Institutiones* 1.33.
11. *Attic Nights* 15.1.
12. For a survey of fires subsequent to the Great Fire, Robert Sablayrolles, *Libertinus Miles: Les Cohortes de Vigiles* (École Française de Rome, 1996), 771–802.
13. *Annals* 15.43.
14. 3.254–259.
15. 5.22.
16. *Nero* 39; Tacitus, *Annals* 16.13.
17. Much of the discussion that follows is based on R. F. Newbold, "Some Social and Economic Consequences of the A.D. 64 Fire at Rome," *Latomus* 33 (1974): 858–869.
18. Suetonius, *Tiberius* 48; Suetonius, *Caligula* 16.
19. Suetonius, *Nero* 55; Tacitus, *Annals* 15.40.2 (although Tacitus did not explicitly say "Neropolis").
20. See above, p. 57.
21. *Nero* 31.
22. *Annals* 15.42.
23. *Natural History* 34.45–46. The bibliography on the Colossus is considerable, as are the scholarly controversies regarding the statue. For introduction to the debates and further bibliography, see R. R. R. Smith, "Nero and the Sun-God: Divine Accessories and Political Symbols in Roman Imperial Images," *Journal of Roman Archaeology* 13 (2000): 536–548 (review article of M. Bergmann, *Die Strahlen der Herrscher: Theomorphes Herrscherbild und Politische Symbolik im Hellenismus und in der Römischen Kaiserzeit* [Mainz, 1998], which is also of great value); E. R. Varner, *Mutilation and Transformation: Damnatio Memoriae and Roman Imperial Portraiture*, vol. 10, *Monumenta Graeca et Romana* (Leiden, 2004), 66–67.
24. *Natural History* 34.41.
25. *liber de spectaculis* 2.
26. What we call the area today. In Nero's day, the Colosseum had not yet been built.
27. The Domus Aurea was unfinished when Nero committed suicide less than four years after the Great Fire. We simply do not know for certain which elements of the estate were completed before his death and which were still under construction, although our sources and the archaeological evidence (the considerable remains of the Oppian pavilion, for example) suggest that the better part of the complex was up and running. The description of the views from the Oppian pavilion that follows here, then, is close to the state of the Domus Aurea at Nero's death, that is, what Nero actually would have seen, although some of these elements (like the Colossus) may have still been works in progress. This description, then, more precisely reflects what Nero *would have seen* upon completion of the palace, had he lived to see to it and to see it.
28. Madurodam, the Netherlands' popular 1:25 scale model of the country's cities and landmarks (https://www.youtube.com/watch?v=ofGXKSCbtpU).

29. Pliny, *Natural History* 33.54; verses: Suetonius, *Nero* 39.

30. *liber de spectaculis* 2.

31. Tacitus, *Annals* 15.52.

32. Françoise Villedieu, "Une Construction néronienne mise au jour sur le site de la Vigna Barberini: La *cenatio rotunda* de la *Domus Aurea*?," *Neronia Electronica*, 2011, https://hal.archives-ouvertes.fr/file/index/docid/704698/filename/Villedieu_Neronia-Electronica-1.pdf, 38–53. The famous octagonal dining room of the Oppian complex has generally been considered the best candidate for the rotating dining room, although some archaeologists believe we simply have not yet found remains of the room, if any remains have survived to be found (Villedieu provides bibliography).

33. *liber de spectaculis* 2.3.

34. Pliny, *Natural History* 33.54.

35. *Natural History* 35.51. The painting may have depicted the colossal statue of the Domus Aurea, or, if the statue was not yet complete, a painting of what it was going to look like. It was eventually struck by lightning and burned.

36. Third founder/refounder of the city; fourth founder/refounder of the Roman people—Aeneas played no role in the foundation of the city.

37. *Nero* 55.

38. Aeneas was *the* model of *pietas*; in Virgil's *Aeneid*, fulfilling his obligations to destiny, family, people, and gods trumps personal indulgence of pretty much any kind. Despite the occasional lapse, his was a life of unrelenting sacrifice.

CHAPTER V: LEGACY

1. Of course, there are many more (though less consequential and less widely shared) Romes of the postclassical imagination—almost as many as there have been imaginations.

2. A recent example: Edward Watts, *Mortal Republic: How Rome Fell into Tyranny* (Basic Books, 2018).

3. Such as Stanley Kubrick's *Spartacus* (1960) and William Wyler's *Ben-Hur* (1959). Not just films: Aram Khachaturian's ballet *Spartacus* (1954) provides an example from another genre.

4. Tinto Brass and Bob Guccione's *Caligula* (1979) provides a telling example in film—plenty shocking and weird, at least in the days before the everything-goes internet, although not particularly inventive. Even the rebel gladiator Spartacus proved himself to be adaptable to the prurient appetites of today's era, as the sex-and-violence drenched New Zealand–American television series *Spartacus* (2010–13) showed.

5. E.g., Jeet Heer, "Are We Witnessing the Fall of the American Empire?," *New Republic*, March 7, 2018—https://newrepublic.com/article/147319/witnessing-fall-american-empire.

6. Ancient Romans like Tacitus would of course recognize and appreciate this reemployment of the past.

7. Suetonius's *Caligula* is replete with the emperor's outrages; among the choicest sections: 11–12, 22–42, 48, 55. Dio (59) is the other principal extant source for Caligula's outrageous behavior. Unfortunately, the better part of Tacitus's treatment of Caligula's life and reign is lost.

8. Not just among emperors: Edward Champlin, *Nero* (Harvard, 2005), 235, notes of Nero that "of all the non-Christian men and women of classical antiquity, his name surely arouses the widest interest today."

9. Superstar—Giuseppe Pucci ("Nerone Superstar," in *Nerone*, ed. Maria Antonietta Tomei and E. Rossella Rea [Electa, 2011]), 62–75, enumerates thirty-seven nondocumentary movies and television shows in which Nero has played a role, usually a starring one; many more could be added: Martin M. Winkler, "Nero in Hollywood," in *The Cambridge Companion to the Age of Nero*, ed. Shadi Bartsch, Kirk Freudenburg, and Cedric Littlewood (Cambridge UP, 2017—hereafter cited as *Age of Nero*), 318–332. Exhibition—various locations around Rome (2011); the exhibition had a double catalogue: Tomei and Rea, *Nerone* (cited in and an invaluable resource for this text; a series of beautifully illustrated scholarly essays), and a second that can be found online (http://gallery.electaweb.it/albums/userpics/10002/cartellastampa_def.pdf). Reassessments and rehabilitations—the "Neronian Age" has garnered two significant scholarly "Companions" in just the last few years, for example (see "Further Reading"); it is no surprise that Nero has a society dedicated to studying him and "the Neronian era" (International Society for Neronian Studies: http://www.sien-neron.fr/the-sien/?lang=en). Scholars have also assigned to Augustus his own era (normally designated the "Augustan Age"), but Caligula has failed to garner one. For another view, principally in terms of literature, of why Nero has earned his own "Age," see Martin Dinter, "Introduction: The Neronian (Literary) 'Renaissance,'" in *A Companion to the Neronian Age*, ed. Emma Buckley and Martin Dinter (Wiley-Blackwell, 2013—hereafter cited as *Neronian Age*), 1–14.

10. For an attempt to identify reasons for Nero's popularity and particularly his rehabilitation in recent scholarship, see Miriam Griffin, "Nachwort: Nero from Zero to Hero," in Buckley and Dinter, *Neronian Age*, 467–480. The reconsideration of Nero can even take on a life of its own, to the point where *constructions* of "Nero," entirely independent of the historical Nero, can be employed to probe and criticize academics' attitudes and assumptions. One essay dedicates considerable energy to employing ancient writers' and modern scholars' processing of Nero to process the processors (Erik Gunderson, "The Neronian 'Symptom,'" in Bartsch, Freudenburg, and Littlewood, *Age of Nero*, 335–353).

11. See p. 7.

12. Remnick: https://www.newyorker.com/magazine/2018/01/15/the-increasing-unfitness-of-donald-trump (January 15, 2018). This does not mean that other emperors are not employed in this project: e.g., Nicholas Kristof on Caligula and President Trump, "There Once Was a Great Nation with an Unstable Leader" (https://www.nytimes.com/2017/08/26/opinion/sunday/caligula-roman-empire.html; *New York Times*, August 26, 2017). An example of Barack Obama as Nero: James Taranto, "American Nero" (https://www.wsj.com/articles/SB10001424052748704312104575298550188788086; *Wall Street Journal*, June 10, 2010).

13. Available at http://www.dailymotion.com/video/x22waxw; the Nero scene starts at the 34.28 mark. For further analysis of the scene, see Winkler, in Bartsch, Freudenburg, and Littlewood, *Age of Nero*, 320–321.

14. This section's emphasis on the spotlight Nero has recently been enjoying should not be taken to suggest that he ever truly went away. From his death, through late antiquity, into the Middle Ages and the Renaissance, through the Early Modern period, and well into the nineteenth and early twentieth centuries, poets, historians, painters, sculptors, political theorists, composers, choreographers, novelists, and others have found Nero's life and character an abiding source of creative inspiration and an object of consideration for their thought and art. This is a vast topic, but good places to start one's exploration (also

providing bibliographical help) are: Donatien Grau, *Néron en Occident* (Gallimard, 2015); W. B. Gwyn, "Cruel Nero: The Concept of the Tyrant and the Image of Nero in Western Political Thought," *History of Political Thought* 12.3 (1991): 421–454; Harry Maier, "Nero in Jewish and Christian Tradition from the First Century to the Reformation," in Buckley and Dinter, *Neronian Age*, 385–404; Peter Stacey, "The Image of Nero in Renaissance Political Thought," and Elena Russo, "Resurgences of Nero in the Enlightenment," both in Bartsch, Freudenburg, and Littlewood, *Age of Nero*, 290–317.

15. Still the best assessment of Nero's urban and architectural policies and practice and their impact, including on Rome's port city Ostia, whose extensive archaeological remains today likely provide the closest notion of what the Neronian reconfigured sections of Rome may have looked like: André Balland, "Nova urbs et 'Neapolis': Remarques sur les projets urbanistiques de Néron," *Mélanges de l'école française de Rome. Antiquité* 77 (1965): 349–393.

Only a very few archaeological remains of domestic architecture in Rome can plausibly be tied to the Neronian reconstruction, and what those remains can tell us is limited (e.g., S. Priester, *Ad summas tegulas: Untersuchungen zu vielgeschossigen Gebäudeblöcken mit Wohneinheiten und Insulae im kaiserzeitlichen Rom* [*Bulletino della Commissione archeologica communale di Roma*, suppl. 11 (2002)]: 129–132, 214–216). For the revolutionary creativity of the Domus Aurea, see esp. Larry Ball, *The Domus Aurea and the Roman Architectural Revolution* (Cambridge UP, 2003). Caroline Quenemoen, "Columns and Concrete: Architecture from Nero to Hadrian," in *A Companion to Roman Architecture*, ed. Roger Ulrich and Caroline Quenemoen (Wiley-Blackwell, 2014), 63–64, for a sample of scholars who consider Neronian architecture a revolutionary turning point, and others who are more reserved in their assessment.

16. *Vespasian* 8; see too *Corpus Inscriptionum Latinarum* VI.931. Principal among the "earlier fires" Suetonius alludes to was certainly the Great Fire.

17. Flavian dynasty: 69–96 CE. For the scale of the construction, restoration, and urban reconfiguration under the Flavians, see Filippo Coarelli, "I Flavi e Roma," in *Divus Vespasianus: Il Bimillenario dei Flavi*, ed. Filippo Coarelli and Letizia Abbondanza (Mondadori Electa, 2009—hereafter cited as *Vespasianus*), 68–97, esp. 68–69, 86–88, on the connection to the Great Fire and Nero's urban projects; Robin Haydon Darwall-Smith, *Emperors and Architecture: A Study of Flavian Rome* (Collection Latomus 231; 1996), passim, but esp. 35–41, 55–68, 70–74, 236, and 257 on the connection to Nero.

18. *de spectaculis* 2; the "Caesar" of the poem is Domitian, third and last of the Flavian emperors.

19. On the Flavians' "careful recalibration of the Neronian visual program," see Eric Varner, "Nero's Memory in Flavian Rome," in Bartsch, Freudenburg, and Littlewood, *Age of Nero* 237–257, esp. 250–257, on architecture.

20. On the collection and its presentation, Alessandra Bravi, "Immagini adeguate: Opere d'arte greche nel *Templum Pacis*," in Coarelli and Abbondanza, *Vespasianus*, 176–183; in the same volume, other useful and up-to-date essays on the Temple of Peace: 158–201.

21. Or "accusation," a translation of the word *crimen* that would not change the issue.

22. On this issue and its relation to the persecutions, see G. E. M. de Ste. Croix, "Why Were the Early Christians Persecuted?," *Past and Present* 26 (Nov. 1963—hereafter cited as "Why Persecuted"), 12.

23. For the most part, this reading of the earliest persecutions follows de Ste. Croix's ("Why Persecuted," 6–38); see "Further Reading" for other bibliography.

24. This book has already addressed some of those controversies (see above, pp. 88–95).

25. For (1) Interpolation: Richard Carrier, "The Prospect of a Christian Interpolation in Tacitus, *Annals* 15.44," *Vigiliae Christianae* 68.3 (2014): 264–283; for (2) Tacitus retrojecting: Brent Shaw, "The Myth of the Neronian Persecution," *Journal of Roman Studies* 105 (2015—hereafter cited as "Myth"), 73–100; for (3) Christians guilty: Carlo Pascal, *L'incendio di Roma e i primi cristiani* (1900; Mimesis, 2011), 32–40; in a somewhat related vein, Adalberto Giovannini, "L'interdit contre les Chrétiens," *Cahier Glotz* 7 (1996): 121–129. The internet has kept the accusation alive, as it has, sadly but predictably, offered a platform for the accusation that Rome's Jews started the Great Fire.

26. Early Christian enthusiasts for martyrdom, on the other hand, could view the blood spilled in bearing witness as a powerful recruiting tool, the inspirational "seed" of the religion, as Tertullian famously put it around 200 CE (*semen est sanguis Christianorum*: *Apology* 50).

27. Tertullian's expression *institutum neronianum* (*ad nationes* 1.7.9) has been taken to suggest confirmation of a law forbidding Christianity, but the best translation of the phrase is "thing Nero started," that is, a precedent. The bibliography on this topic is immense, but Shaw provides a representative survey ("Myth," 73–74, n. 2). For one of the most reasonable discussions, see J. W. Ph. Borleffs, "*Institutum Neronianum*," *Vigiliae Christianae* 6.3 (1952): 129–145.

28. An "axial event in Christian history," according to Shaw ("Myth," 72), if historical.

29. Insightful on the role and status of martyrs in early Christianity: Robin Lane Fox, *Pagans and Christians in the Mediterranean World from the Second Century AD to the Conversion of Constantine* (Viking, 1986; repr., Penguin, 2006), 419–492; with particular attention to the roles memory and gender played in embedding martyrdom in the Christian imagination, Elizabeth Castelli, *Martyrdom and Memory: Early Christian Culture Making* (Columbia UP, 2004); also, and like Castelli going beyond antiquity, the essays in Johan Leemans, ed., *More than a Memory: The Discourse of Martyrdom and the Construction of Christian Identity in the History of Christianity* (Peeters, 2005); on the broader ancient context, Glen Bowersock, *Martyrdom and Rome* (Cambridge UP, 1995).

30. *History of the Church* 1.1.2 (early fourth century).

31. To give just one, but a famous and influential example: John Foxe's depiction of the English Protestant martyrs as the spiritual descendants of the early Christian martyrs (the text has a complicated history; all editions plus commentary available at *John Foxe's The Acts and Monuments Online* [https://www.johnfoxe.org]; first publication: 1563).

32. https://www.catholicnewsagency.com/news/pope-francis-martyrs-are-still-the-life-blood-of-the-church-77537.

33. All Eusebius, *History of the Church* 2.25. The dating of Dionysius and Gaius depends on other information Eusebius provides in the passage.

34. *de viris illustribus* 1, although Jerome seems to suggest that Peter perished towards the end of Nero's reign. By Jerome's day, the first St. Peter's Basilica stood on the spot. Variations in the story of Peter's life and death, including the precise year, circulated among early Christians, and it can be difficult to discern the extent to which the narratives are completely fabricated or if, among the clearly fanciful and fantastic material, authentic memories of his life are preserved; the extent to which even authentic tradition became imprecise, garbled, or embellished is debated.

35. Explicitly stated in the *New Advent/Catholic Encyclopedia* entry on St. Peter (http://www.newadvent.org/cathen/11744a.htm#IV); although the entry accepts that Peter died in the persecution Tacitus described in connection to the Great Fire, it allows for the possibility that Peter met his fate a few years after the Great Fire. Though somewhat dated, the entry provides a relatively clear, thorough, and useful English-language assessment of the ancient literary evidence.

36. The sources regarding Peter's later life and death are extremely complicated and vexed, and thus their interpretation is as well. Little is certain, and much is disputed. Even a cursory analysis of the issues would require another volume. For a balanced and accessible nonscholarly treatment of some of the controversies, though one more focused on the questionable authenticity of Peter's putative bones (as the title suggests) than on other issues concerning his death, see Thomas Craughwell, *St. Peter's Bones* (Image, 2013). See too Francesco de Stefano, in *The Atlas of Ancient Rome*, ed. Andrea Carandini (Princeton UP, 2017—hereafter cited as *Atlas*), 583–587, with particular focus on the evolution of the Vatican area's topography in antiquity. The most complete and persuasive argument against Peter's death in Rome, and the most thorough and recent assessment of the evidence: Otto Zwierlein, *Petrus in Rom: Die literarischen Zeugnisse* (*Untersuchungen zur antiken Literatur und Geschichte* 96 [2010]); Zwierlein returned to the issue and refined some of his readings of the sources in 2012, "Petrus in Rom? Die literarischen Zeugnisse," in *Petrus und Paulus in Rome: Eine interdisziplinäre Debatte*, ed. Stefan Heid (Herder, 2012), 444–467; cumulatively, the essays in Heid provide a comprehensive and up-to-date appraisal of the state of the debate regarding most of the issues related to Peter in Rome, including, of course, the controversies surrounding his martyrdom. On the engrossing intrigue surrounding the putative tomb and bones of Peter, see Craughwell, *St. Peter's Bones*; T. D. Barnes, *Early Christian Hagiography and Roman History* (*Tria Cordia* 5; Mohr Siebeck, 2010), 397–406; Tom Mueller, "Inside Job," *Atlantic*, October, 2003, https://www.theatlantic.com/magazine/archive/2003/10/inside-job/302801/. Despite Protestants', Roman Catholics', Orthodox Christians', and non-Christians' investment in the debate, one can believe that Peter was martyred in Rome and not be Roman Catholic, and one can believe that Peter died elsewhere and peacefully and still be Roman Catholic. Whatever one's religious convictions, one can of course be convinced that Peter was among Nero's victims in the wake of the Great Fire but reject his burial on the site where St. Peter's Basilica now stands.

37. Alienation: 34–41; dog: 9–12; fish: 13.

38. Even if Peter was martyred in the surrounding Vatican gardens rather than in the Circus—we should recall that Tacitus describes two stages and locations for the Christian executions, the first in unspecified imperial gardens, and the second in an unnamed circus (*Annals* 15.44)—the Via Cornelia was nonetheless among the closest places to inter his body, and so that is likely where his remains would have wound up anyway.

39. The identification of the Vatican gardens (not to be confused with the "Vatican Gardens" of today's Vatican City; the ancient ones were originally designated the Gardens of Agrippina, after Caligula's mother, who owned them at an earlier date—Filippo Coarelli, "Il Circo di Caligola in Vaticano," *Atti della Pontificia Accademia Romana di Archeologia. Rendiconti* 81 [2009]: 6–8 and on the circus more generally, 3–13]) and their associated Circus of Caligula as the sites of the persecution is contested, although the scholarly consensus inclines towards the Vatican identification. Regardless, the issue here is what the early Christians believed, not where the executions had actually occurred.

40. The tombs that have been uncovered so far along the Via Cornelia date to after the first century CE, that is, to after the period of the Great Fire and the Neronian persecution. They represent, however, only a fraction of the tombs and graves that lined the road in antiquity, and nearby (and recently uncovered and opened to the public) burials date to as far back as the early first century CE. The most up-to-date and accessible English description of the Vatican necropoleis: P. Liverani, G. Spinola, and P. Zander, *The Vatican Necropoles* (Brepols, 2010; translation of *Le Necropoli Vaticane* [Jaca, 2010]).

41. Also known as the Circus of Nero or the Circus of Gaius and Nero. For its history, see Coarelli, *Rome*, 355–356. On the topography of the area and of its gardens and circus, see Paolo Carafa and Paola Pacchiarotti, in Carandini, *Atlas*, 558–559.

42. http://www.vaticanstate.va/content/vaticanstate/en/ricerca.html?q=obelisk. The obelisk was originally on the Circus's spine (*spina*, a kind of island that ran down the middle of the track and around which the chariots raced), just as the obelisk standing today in Rome's Piazza del Popolo stood on the Circus Maximus's spine. Only fragments of the Circus remained by the time the first St. Peter's Basilica was completed. The statement quoted reflects the Roman Catholic Church's conviction that Peter died in the Neronian persecution associated with the Great Fire and that the persecution Tacitus described took place in the Circus of Caligula.

43. The demolition of the old and construction of the new was such a massive and complicated undertaking that the whole process lasted over a century.

44. http://stpetersbasilica.info/Exterior/Obelisk/Obelisk.htm.

45. Since everything regarding the sources for Peter's death is messy, Rome offers another option for the location of Peter's martyrdom, where San Pietro in Montorio stands (site of Bramante's famed Tempietto), a choice that garnered much support during the Renaissance (discussion with bibliography: Philipp Fehl, "Michelangelo's Crucifixion of St. Peter: Notes on the Identification of the Locale of the Action," *Art Bulletin* 53.3 [1971]: 326–330).

46. As for Paul's "trophy," Constantine had a church built on that spot as well, and that church evolved into San Paolo fuori le Mura, which fire mostly destroyed in the nineteenth century and which was reconstructed. No St. Peter's Basilica, of course, but it is one of Christianity's grandest and most historic churches and, along with St. Peter's, St. John Lateran, and Santa Maria Maggiore, one of Rome's four papal basilicas. For the church's convoluted history, see Marina Docci, *San Paolo fuori le mura* (Gangemi, 2006). On the claim that Paul's tomb has been uncovered there: http://news.bbc.co.uk/2/hi/europe/6219656.stm.

47. At the very latest, Trajan's baths had ceased to function in the early sixth century, when the Ostrogoths cut off Rome's aqueducts.

48. In his *Life of Giovanni da Udine*, Georgio Vasari says that the grottoes were discovered when the ruins of Titus's palace, right around San Pietro in Vincoli, were being excavated to find ancient statues. Renaissance elites were hungry for classical art and artifacts to enrich their collections and enhance their reputations, and Renaissance artists were eager to use uncovered antiquities for models and inspiration. Scientific archaeology, with its disciplined attempt to elucidate and preserve the past, did not yet exist. Vasari was the influential biographer of Renaissance artists, and as writer, painter, and architect, quite the Renaissance man himself.

49. For an early statement on the nature of the frescoes, see Vasari, in his *On Painting*, 27. The earliest explorers tended to identify the underground chambers with the emperor

Titus, not Nero; they did not realize that they were visiting the Domus Aurea, which did not lessen the impact of what they saw.

50. *de architectura* 7.5.3. In his famous and influential *Ars Poetica*, Horace made clear that he was no fan, either, of painters who blended birds with snakes and lambs with tigers, and that sort of thing (lines 1–13). In the nineteenth century, John Ruskin curmudgeonly characterized Raphael's employment of Neronian grotesques as "an unnatural and monstrous abortion"! (*The Complete Works of John Ruskin*, ed. E. T. Cook and Alexander Wedderburn, vol. 11 [George Allen, 1904], 171).

51. Raphael's own role would most likely have been confined to approval of the employment of Neronian grotesques, which we know he saw, and to overall design.

52. The excavation and discovery of frescoes in Pompeii gave Roman grotesques a fresh tailwind and influenced the American embrace of Neronian-style painting and decoration.

APPENDIX A: Sources

1. Tacitus more reliable than Suetonius: Keith Bradley, *Suetonius' Life of Nero: An Historical Commentary* (Collection Latomus 157; 1978): 226–236.
2. *Annals* 15.38.

APPENDIX B: Proposed Timeline of the Great Fire

1. Six days: Tacitus, *Annals* 15.40. Nine days: a Flavian-era inscription specifies that the fire burned for nine days—"urbs per novem dies arsit neronianis temporibus" (*Corpus Inscriptionum Latinarum* VI.1.826); on which, see Virginia Closs, "*Neronianis Temporibus*: The So-Called *Arae Incendii Neroniani* and the Fire of A.D. 64 in Rome's Monumental Landscape," *Journal of Roman Studies* 106 (2016): 102–123; Robert E. A. Palmer, "Jupiter Blaze, Gods of the Hills, and the Roman Topography of CIL VI 377," *American Journal of Archaeology* 80 (1976): 43–56. Domus Transitoria: Tacitus, *Annals* 15.39.

2. In *Nerone*, ed. Maria Antonietta Tomei and E. Rossella Rea (Electa, 2011), 79–91; simulation: 87–89; Panella's reconstruction also provides the best assessment of the archaeological evidence and the most useful and complete bibliography (250).

3. Although no archaeological trace of this temple has been uncovered, our literary sources indicate that it was located on the lower slopes or at the base of the western edge of the Aventine (Lawrence Richardson Jr., *A New Topographical Dictionary of Ancient Rome* [Johns Hopkins UP, 1992—hereafter cited as *Dictionary*]), 238.

4. Or just the Temple's courtyard of the Danaids.

5. Excavations in the Valley of the Colosseum have even turned up rare archaeological evidence of the Great Fire's destruction. On this evidence and on other issues related to the fire and its aftermath, the essays in *Meta Sudans I: Un'area sacra in Palatio e la valle del Colosseo prima e dopo Nerone*, ed. Clementina Panella (Libreria dello Stato, 1996); of particular relevance are the contributions of Panella (27–91 passim), G. Schingo (145–158), and M. Medri (165–188, on the Domus Aurea).

6. Since the Temple of Luna Noctiluca's precise location on the Palatine is unknown, it is impossible to say when the fire would have reached it, if in fact the Great Fire did reach it. (The Temple of Luna Noctiluca is a different temple from the Aventine Temple of Luna, destroyed on Day 1.) Placing Nero's return on this day is neither an endorsement nor a rejection of Tacitus's view that Nero returned to Rome only because his Domus Transitoria was threatened.

7. Although the temple's precise location is debated (Filippo Coarelli, *Il Foro Romano* [Quasar, 1983], 26–33, *Rome and Environs: An Archaeological Guide* [U of California P; updated English ed., 2014], Richardson, *Dictionary*, 225), it was certainly about halfway into the forum.

8. In this chronology, these measures to succor victims of the fire immediately follow Nero's return to Rome, although it is just as likely that Roman officials on the spot began to take these steps before Nero returned.

9. Its precise location is uncertain and debated: Eva Margareta Steinby, ed., *Lexicon Topographicum Urbis Romae*, 5 vols. (Edizioni Quasar, 1993–99), 4: 158–159; Richardson, *Dictionary*, 3; and Filippo Coarelli, *Il foro boario dalle origini alla fine della repubblica* (Quasar, 1988), 147–155.

10. The northern Campus Martius and the other more northerly parts of the city correspond reasonably well to Tacitus's description of the places destroyed at this phase as "the more open parts of the city" (*patulis magis urbis locis*) and ones with porticoes dedicated to pleasure (*porticus amoenitati dicatae* [both: *Annals* 15.40]). Much of the northern fringes of the city consisted of landscaped parklands.

SUGGESTED FURTHER READING

Notes in the text are primarily focused on ancient sources and specific issues related to them. This means that I have employed many secondary sources that have not received the acknowledgment they deserve. The range of issues, people, places, and institutions this book considers is so broad—from life in the city of Rome, to Nero, to the nature and narratives of early Christianity, to modern approaches to understanding disasters, to the Great Fire itself and beyond—that even a simple list of significant readings is beyond its scope. What follows, then, are the works to which I am most indebted and the ones that would be of most use for further exploration of the events and controversies this book addresses. Where possible, I have provided English-language texts.

Life in Rome
For introductions to many topics and for surveys of the contemporary state of scholarly debates regarding life in ancient Rome, the essays in *The Cambridge Companion to Ancient Rome*, ed. Paul Erdkamp (Cambridge UP, 2013), are hard to beat. The most useful introductions to daily life in Rome are Gregory Aldrete, *Daily Life in the Roman City* (U of Oklahoma P, 2009), and Peter Connolly and Hazel Dodge, *The Ancient City: Life in Classical Athens and Rome* (Oxford UP, 2000). Jérôme Carcopino's *Daily Life in Ancient Rome* is still valuable and engaging, but it is essential to use the second edition, with the Mary Beard introduction and bibliography, trans. E. O. Lorimer (Yale UP, 2003). On the legal, social, and physical obstacles poor tenants confronted in navigating life in Roman *insulae*, see Rena van den Bergh, "The Plight of the Poor Urban Tenant," *Revue internationale des droits de l'antiquité* 50 (2003): 443–477. On specific topics: floods—Gregory Aldrete, *Floods of the Tiber in Ancient Rome* (Johns Hopkins UP, 2007); crime—J. A. Crook, *Law and Life of Rome* (Cornell UP, 1967), Wilfried Nippel, *Public Order in Ancient Rome* (Cambridge UP, 1995), and Jill Harries, *Law and Crime in the Roman World* (Cambridge UP, 2007); pollution—Alex

Scobie, "Slums, Sanitation, and Mortality in the Roman World," *Klio* 68 (1986): 399–433; disease—Mirko D. Grmek, *Diseases in the Ancient Greek World*, trans. Mireille Muellner and Leonard Muellner (Johns Hopkins UP, 1989), and Ralph Jackson, *Doctors and Diseases in the Roman Empire* (British Museum, 1988); city planning—Olivia F. Robinson, *Ancient Rome: City Planning and Administration* (Routledge, 1994).

Firefighting and the Great Fire

Although our sources are full of references to fires, these sources and the archaeological record are relatively sparse on details, particularly on firefighting. We have no account of a unit of Rome's *Vigiles* actually fighting a fire, and so we are reduced, as so often happens with the ancient world, to speculation. The most comprehensive treatment of fires in Rome and of Roman firefighting and firefighters in our period is Robert Sablayrolles's *Libertinus Miles: Les Cohortes de Vigiles* (École Française de Rome, 1996). I have used this excellent study extensively. Among the most useful English-language studies: P. K. B. Reynolds, *The Vigiles of Imperial Rome* (Ares, 1996); Olivia F. Robinson, "Fire Prevention at Rome," *Revue internationale des droits de l'antiquité* 24 (1977): 377–388; J. S. Rainbird, "The Fire Stations of Imperial Rome," *Papers of the British School at Rome* 54 (1986): 147–169; and Lucas Rubin, *De Incendiis Urbis Romae: The Fires of Rome in their Urban Context* (PhD diss., State University of New York, Buffalo, 2004). See Gregory N. Daugherty, "The *Cohortes Vigilum* and the Great Fire of 64 AD," *Classical Journal* 87.3 (1992): 229–240, for speculation on the leadership of the *Vigiles* in 64 and on the reasons for the failure to nip the fire in the bud.

For analysis of the literary sources on the reconstruction of Rome (including the Domus Aurea), see Rhiannon Ash, *Book XV* 193–196, 198–203 (with bibliography; see below in "Literary Sources"); for the continued reconstruction of Rome after Nero's death, Filippo Coarelli and Letizia Abbondanza, eds., *Divus Vespasianus: Il Bimillenario dei Flavi* (Mondadori Electa, 2009). For the Roman construction industry, Janet DeLaine, "Building the Eternal City: The Construction Industry of Imperial Rome," in *Ancient Rome: The Archaeology of the Eternal City*, ed. J. C. Coulston and Hazel Dodge (Oxford UP, 2000), 119–141; Coulston and Dodge offers a series of first-rate contributions on what we know about life in Rome and how we know it. For the state of modern knowledge regarding the behavior and control of fires, see James G. Quintiere, *Principles of Fire Behavior*, 2nd ed. (CRC Press, 2016), and Vytenis Babrauskas, *Ignition Handbook: Principles and Applications to Fire Safety Engineering, Fire Investigation, Risk*

Management, and Forensic Science (Fire Science, 2003). On ancient disasters and the Romans' responses to them, Jerry Toner, *Roman Disasters* (Polity, 2013), *the* book on Roman disasters and one I have relied upon throughout this text. Every book-length treatment of Nero addresses the Great Fire and its aftermath.

City of Rome
This text's depictions of life in ancient Rome and of the Great Fire and its aftermath and legacy depend on what we know about the physical city. Useful introductions to the configuration, topography, and archaeology of ancient Rome and to the structures discussed in this book are Filippo Coarelli, *Rome and Environs: An Archaeological Guide* (U of California P; updated English ed., 2014), and Amanda Claridge, *Rome*, 2nd ed. (Oxford UP, 2010). These are the guides to bring on your next trip to Rome. Two indispensable reference works are Lawrence Richardson Jr., *A New Topographical Dictionary of Ancient Rome* (Johns Hopkins UP, 1992), and Andrea Carandini, ed., *Atlante di Roma antica* (Mondadori Electa, 2012), now in English translation by Andrew Halavais, *The Atlas of Ancient Rome* (Princeton UP, 2017). Copiously and beautifully illustrated, the translation occasionally differs from the original Italian text, however, and the notes in particular would have profited from more careful proofreading. The most comprehensive, accessible, and reliable treatment of Rome's remains, however, is Eva Margareta Steinby, ed., *Lexicon Topographicum Urbis Romae*, 5 vols. (Edizioni Quasar, 1993–99), most entries in Italian; with other editors, supplemental editions, 2005–7, 2012, 2014. My utilization of these texts is apparent on almost every page of this book. For an up-to-date bibliography on and introductions to issues regarding Roman architecture, see Roger B. Ulrich and Caroline K. Quenemoen, eds., *A Companion to Roman Architecture* (Wiley-Blackwell, 2014).

Nero
Nero and his age have proved irresistible to scholars and non-scholars alike, and as I suggest in the chapter "Legacy," there has recently been an explosion of interest in him and therefore of publications about him. The result is that far too many authors have commented on his life, career, era, and connection to the Great Fire to be included here. The majority of the suggestions that follow are in English. The essays included in Emma Buckley and Martin Dinter, eds., *A Companion to the Neronian Age* (Wiley-Blackwell, 2013), and in Shadi Bartsch, Kirk Freudenburg, and Cedric Littlewood, eds., *The Cambridge Companion to the Age of Nero* (Cambridge UP, 2017), provide accessible introductions to the many

issues and controversies scholars wrestle with; the two texts together also offer a comprehensive and current bibliography.

I have made extensive use of Edward Champlin's excellent *Nero* (Harvard UP, 2005) and Miriam Griffin's classic *Nero: The End of a Dynasty* (Yale UP, 1985). Anthony Barrett, Elaine Fantham, and John Yardley, eds., *The Emperor Nero: A Guide to the Ancient Sources* (Princeton UP, 2016), provides translation and some commentary on the principal (and some less familiar) sources and yet another useful bibliography, and it serves as an introduction to Nero's life and impact. Donatien Grau, *Néron en Occident* (Gallimard, 2015), provides a stimulating reading of Nero and the ancient sources for him, but focuses principally on the *idea* of Nero, particularly after his death and in postclassical times. The images and Italian-language essays in Maria Antonietta Tomei and E. Rossella Rea, eds., *Nerone* (Electa, 2011), address Nero's life, impact, and afterlife; they are also, for the most part, accessible, illuminating, and lively; Clementina Panella's essay on the Great Fire (76–91) is by far the most useful attempt to plot out the course of the fire; first-rate bibliography, too, particularly on the relevant archaeology and on the Domus Aurea. Add the essays by Maria Wyke, Joan-Pau Rubiés, Tamsyn Barton, and Jaś Elsner, in *Reflections of Nero: Culture, History, and Representation*, ed. Jaś Elsner and Jamie Masters (U of North Carolina P, 1994).

Christians and Executions

The bibliography on the Neronian persecution of the earliest Christians and the role it may have played for subsequent generations of ancient Christians is immense. Accessible and evenhanded and yet scholarly and thorough, John Granger Cook, *Roman Attitudes toward the Christians* (Mohr Siebeck, 2010), provides the best introduction to the issues and debates surrounding the interpretation of the Neronian persecution and Tacitus's account of it. Among issues possibly of interest to readers of this book, Cook addresses textual complications in Tacitus's account (40, 49, 59–60, 69–76), Tacitus's sources (41–42), hypotheses on the precise legal procedures the Roman persecutors employed (43–45, 57–62), the Christians' "abominations" (47–49, 51–54), the Chrestos/Christos debate (49), textual and historical issues regarding the gruesome executions (69–79), including a variety of telling and disturbing examples of Roman cruelty and creativity in punishing criminals, and the location of the executions (79–81). Cook also assesses what Suetonius and other sources have to offer (83–98) and the evidence and arguments for and against Peter's and Paul's martyrdoms in Rome (98–105). The book of Revelation raises such thorny issues of interpretation that I have for the most part ignored it in my account, but Cook offers an excellent introduction to the possible connection between Revelation and the Neronian persecution (105–111); his bibliography on Nero and Revelation is as thorough and up-to-date as any bibliography can be when dealing with a topic to which so many pages have been dedicated.

The most important exploration of the shifting logic of the persecutions is still G. E. M. de Ste. Croix, "Why Were the Early Christians Persecuted?," *Past and Present* 26 (Nov. 1963): 6–38. In essential agreement with de Ste. Croix, but adding to and updating the argument somewhat: T. D. Barnes, "Legislation against the Christians," *Journal of Roman Studies* 58 (1968): 32–50; "Pre-Decian Acta Martyrum," *Journal of Theological Studies* 19 (1968): 509–531; and *Tertullian* (Oxford UP, 1971), 143–186. For a contrarian view, Brent Shaw, "The Myth of the Neronian Persecution," *Journal of Roman Studies* 105 (2015): 73–100. See, too, Timothy D. Barnes, *Early Christian Hagiography and Roman History* (Tria Cordia 5; Mohr Siebeck, 2010). The classic study of the nature of executions as spectacles is Kathleen M. Coleman, "Fatal Charades: Roman Executions Staged as Mythological Enactments," *Journal of Roman Studies* 80 (1990): 44–73. Accessible and full of insight are Jerry Toner, *The Day Commodus Killed a Rhino* (Johns Hopkins UP, 2014), in the same series as this book, and Keith Hopkins and Mary Beard, *The Colosseum* (Harvard UP, 2005). Alison Futrell, *The Roman Games: A Sourcebook* (Wiley-Blackwell, 2006), provides translation and brief commentary on some of the most revealing ancient sources.

Domus Aurea and Grotesques

The classic study of the Domus Aurea is Axel Boethius, *The Golden House of Nero* (U of Michigan P, 1960), which is still valuable. Much work and rethinking have been done since, however, and of particular interest is Larry Ball, *The Domus Aurea and the Roman Architectural Revolution* (Cambridge UP, 2003). For the rediscovery and impact of the Domus Aurea's grotesques, Nicole Dacos, *Le découverte de la Domus Aurea et la formation des Grotesques couverte de la Domus Aurea et la formation des Grotesques à la Renaissance* (Studies of the Warburg Institute 31; Brill, 1969); see, too, Dacos's *The Loggia of Raphael: A Vatican Art Treasure* (Abbeville, 2008). On the grotesque in antiquity, E. Walter-Karydi, "Die Enstehung der Grotteskenornamentik in der Antike," *Mitteilungen des Deutschen Archäologischen Instituts (Römische Abteilung)* 97 (1990): 137–152. For an accessible English-language introduction with up-to-date bibliography, Michael Squire, "'Fantasies so Varied and Bizarre': The Domus Aurea, the Renaissance, and the 'Grotesque,'" in Buckley and Dinter, *Neronian Age*, 444–464. On the grotesque in general, Wolfgang Kayser, *The Grotesque in Art and Literature*, 1981 ed. (Columbia UP, 1981).

Literary Sources

Barrett, Fantham, and Yardley, *The Emperor Nero,* provides translation, some annotation, and bibliography for key sources. For Tacitus, Rhiannon Ash's scholarly but accessible commentary, *Tacitus* Annals, *Book XV* (Cambridge UP, 2018), is the place to start. Ash's annotations to Tacitus's account of the Great Fire (177–212) supersede earlier commentaries, and her introduction to Tacitus's employment of sources (2–9) and bibliography (326–350) are current and useful. Her annotations to his account of the fire, moreover, also comment copiously on Suetonius's and Dio's accounts, and elucidate the fire itself, and her commentary explores Tacitus's language of invasion and his narrative's engagement and dialogue with earlier events and historiography. Mathew Owen and Ingo Gildenhard, *Tacitus*, Annals, 15.20–23, 33–45 (Open Book, 2013), provides a handy, lively, and occasionally funny student-oriented commentary to Tacitus's Latin (bibliography included) and, like Ash, offers insightful analysis of Tacitus's language of invasion. Still useful are the classic commentaries on Tacitus's account of the fire and Nero: Henry Furneaux, *Cornelii Taciti Annalium Ab Excessu Divi Augusti Libri*, vol. 2, ed. H. F. Pelham and C. D. Fisher (Oxford UP, 1907), and Erich Koestermann, *Cornelius Tacitus,* Annalen, *erläutert und mit einer Einleitung versehen*, vol. 4, bks. 14–16 (Winter, 1968).

For introduction to the scholarship on Tacitus with up-to-date bibliographies, see the essays in *The Cambridge Companion to Tacitus*, ed. A. J. Woodman (Cambridge UP, 2009), particularly Griffin's and Keitel's contributions; add those in *A Companion to Tacitus*, ed. Victoria Emma Pagán (Wiley-Blackwell, 2012), particularly Benario's and Potter's. For greatest hits of Tacitean scholarship, Rhiannon Ash, ed., *Tacitus*. Oxford Readings in Classical Studies (Oxford UP, 2012). Two accessible introductions to Tacitus and his *Annals*: Ronald Mellor, *Tacitus' Annals* (Oxford UP, 2006), and Rhiannon Ash, *Tacitus*. Ancients in Action (Bristol, 2006). For Suetonius's *Life of Nero*, most useful is Keith Bradley, *Suetonius' Life of Nero: An Historical Commentary* (Collection Latomus 157; 1978). For a more general introduction to Suetonius, Andrew Wallace-Hadrill, *Suetonius*, 2nd ed. (Bristol, 1995; Bloomsbury, 2013). The starting point for Cassius Dio remains Fergus Millar's *A Study of Cassius Dio* (Oxford UP, 1966); for exhaustive bibliography, and for more recent research regarding Dio's life, work, and influence, see the essays in Valérie Fromentin, Estelle Bertrand, Michèle Coltelloni-Trannoy, Michel Molin, and Gianpaolo Urso, eds., *Cassius Dion: Nouvelles lectures:*

Scripta antiqua, 94, 2 vols. (Ausonius, 2017); most are in French, but a smattering are in English, Italian, and German. For English translations of Tacitus and Suetonius: Tacitus—*The Annals*, ed. Anthony Bartlett, trans. J. C. Yardley (Oxford UP, 2008); Suetonius—*The Twelve Caesars*, trans. Robert Graves; rev. ed. with introduction and notes by James Rives (Penguin, 2007).

INDEX

Page numbers in *italics* refer to figures.

Acratus, 76
Acta Diurna, 6
Actaeon, 91
Aeneas, 46–47, 68, 110
Aeneid (Virgil), 46–47, 71
Agrippina, 114
air pollution, 25–26
Allen, Irwin, 116
Amphitheater of Taurus, 54–55, 93, 134
Annals (Tacitus), 63, 131
Antium, 56
Anzio, 56–57, 134
apartment houses (*insulae*), 10, 49, 99, 101, 134
Apollo, 54, 94
aqueduct system, 12, 97–98
Ara Maxima, 67, 68, 134
archaeological record: for Domus Aurea, 104, 105; for embankment, 14; for Great Fire, 50, 132–33, 134; for pumps, 34
architecture of buildings, 6, 30
art: display of, 118; of Domus Aurea, 104–5; legacy of Great Fire on, 126–28; plunder of, 76–77; of St. Peter's Basilica, 125
Augustus: Aeneas and, 46–47; Campus Martius and, 55; crime and, 19–20; fire department established by, 33; as first emperor, 111, 115; house of, 54, 135; reforms of, 17, 40, 138n11; Temple of Apollo and, 54
Aullus Gellius, 98, 99
Aventine Hill, 50, 134

ballistae, 34–35
bathhouses: public, 24, 25, 36–37; of Trajan, 105–6, 118, 126
Bernini, Gian, 125
bodyguards for wealthy people, 45

Britain, views of martyrdom in, 121–22
buildings: collapses of, 15–17, 45, 73; construction of, 16, 17, 97, 99, 100, 117; materials for, 30; purchase of, while ablaze, 32; role of, 6. *See also* dwellings; public projects; reconstruction
burials along Via Cornelia, 124, 124–25

Caelian Hill, 55, 107
Caligula, 25, 114–15
Campus Martius: Augustus and, 55; open spaces of, 49; path of fire and, 51; significance of, 54
Capitoline Hill: path of fire and, 49, 51, 134–35; significance of, 53; view of, from Domus Aurea, 107
Carrinas Secundus, 76
Catholicism, Roman, 121–22, 123, 125, 126
cause of fire, 77–85
character, as revealed by disasters, 2–3
Christ/Christos/Chrestos, 89–90
Christians: martyrdom in identity of, 121–22; martyrdom of Peter and, 122–23, 124, 125–26; persecution of, 5, 118–21; as scapegoats, 86–95, 92
Cicero: on building collapses, 17; on floods, 60; on food safety, 28; on Herodotus, 40; on streets and housing, 10
Circus Maximus: description of, 2; as origin of fire, 42, 50
Circus of Caligula, 123, 124, 124, 125
Cispian Hill, 98, 99
city planning, rectilinear, 8–9
class: escape from fire and, 45–46; Nero and, 56, 94; poor, employment for, 74–75; poor, views of, 17; professional performers and, 61; rewards for rebuilding by, 98

Claudius: as expelling Jews, 89; food supply and, 26–27; temple to, 107
cleanup after fire, 73–75, 76–77, 96, 101–2
Clement of Rome, 92
climate of Rome in July, 43
Coleman, Kathleen, 91
Colosseum: as anti-Neronian, 117–18; as built over Domus Aurea, 126; celebratory opening of, 37; construction of, 7, 125; as public project, 11, 15
Colossus of Rhodes, 104
Commodus, 55
communication, modes of, 6–7
configuration of Rome, 8–9
conspiracy against Nero, 85
Constantine, 121, 125
construction practices, 16, 17, 97, 99, 100, 117. *See also* reconstruction
Cornelia, 28–29
costs of cleanup and reconstruction, 76–77, 101–2
Crassus, 32
crime: Christians and, 119; looting, 45, 47, 74; as peril, 17–20; punishment of, 90–91
Croesus, 40–41
crucifixion, 91
culture, loss of, 67–71

damage done by fire, 65–72, 66
Danaids, 92, 93
Day 1: origins and path of fire on, 42, 50–51; overview of, 134
Day 2: damage done on, 66; map of, 44; overview of, 134–35
Day 3, 135
Day 4: damage done on, 66; map of, 52; overview of, 135
Day 5, 135
Day 6, resurgence of fire on, 65, 83, 135
Day 7, 136
Day 8, 136
Day 9, 66, 136
Dio Chrysostom, 76
Dio Cocceianus, Cassius: on fire, 51, 82; on flooding of Tiber, 13; on Nero and performance, 60, 61, 62–63, 64; on orgy, 56; as source, 129–30
Dionysius, Bishop of Corinth, 122
Dionysius of Halicarnassus, 18
Dirce, myth of, 92, 92–93
disasters: divine discontent and, 77; experience of, 128; impact of, 7; as levelers, 40–41; moralizing perspective on, 4, 5; noblesse oblige and, 57–58; processing of and control over, 80–81; response of society to, 3; as revealing character of individuals, 2–3; urban planning after, 11; vulnerability to, 3, 4–5, 39–40; worldview and, 14–15, 39–40
disease, 28–30, 101
Domitian, 10, 117
Domus Aurea (Golden House): art for, 76, 83, 104–5; construction of, 5, 102; as country estate within city, 103–4; grotesques of, 127–28; legacy of, 126; opinions of, 108–9; Oppian pavilion of, 105–7, 118, 126; rediscovery of, 126–27; sightlines of, 107; as stage, 110; Suetonius on, 103
Domus Transitoria (Passage Palace), 57, 62, 102–3, 135
duration of fire, 65, 134–36
dwellings: availability of, after land seizure, 109; fire as spreading to, 43; porticoes or porches for, 96–97; rebuilding of, 99, 101; types of, 10–11

economic losses, 75
emperors: as benefactors, 57–58; Palatine Hill and, 9; as *Pater Patriae*, 58. *See also specific emperors*
entertainments, 37. *See also* executions; spectacles
epidemics, 28
equipment for fighting fires, 33–35, 47–48, 97
Esquiline Hill: fire and, 2, 55, 135; firebreak at base of, 64–65; Tower of Maecenas on, 59, 62–63
Eusebius, 121, 122
executions: as engaging senses, 95; methods of, 87, 90–93; Nero's performance at, 93–94
eyewitness testimony, reliability of, 79–80

facts of events, as difficult to ascertain, 5–6, 119–20
fascination with Romans, 128
fatal charades, 91, 93
festivals, 22
Fidenae, collapse of theater at, 16, 73
fire: air pollution and, 25; building collapses and, 16; frequency of, 32–33; as peril, 30–31; set by Gallic Senones, 71–72; subsequent to Great Fire, 98–99; techniques for fighting, 34–35, 47–48, 97; in Troy, 46–47, 59, 110–11

firebreaks: anticipatory, 97; creation of, 34–35, 47–48, 64–65
firefighters (*vigiles*): as appearing to start or abet fires, 82–83; crime and, 19; equipment of, 34–35, 47–48, 97; first municipal, 33; numbers of, 35; priorities of, 36, 51, 53, 54–55
Flavians, 117–18
floods: building collapses and, 16; disease and, 28; frequency and impact of, 12–15
folk medicine, 29
food poisoning, 19
food supply, 12–13, 26–28, 40, 96, 101
fountain room of Oppian pavilion, 106
Francis (pope), 122

Gaius, 122
Galen, 28
Gallic Senones, burning of Rome by, 71–72
gods, appeasement of, 77–78
Golden House. *See* Domus Aurea
Great Chicago Fire, 65
Great Kanto Earthquake and Fire, 65, 80
Great London Fire, 65
Great San Francisco Earthquake and Fire, 35, 65
Greece: appropriation of culture of, 70–71; attack on Troy by, 46–47, 59, 110–11
grotesques, 127–28

Hadrian, 130
health issues, 12, 28–30, 101
Herodotus, 40–41
history: interpretations of, 119–20; literary tradition and, 129; Livy on, 69–70; morality and, 69; mythology and, 5–6, 60; relationship to, 4
Homer, 60, 71, 106
Horace, 26, 158n50
Hurricane Katrina, 66, 77

Icarus, 91
ignitions, spontaneous, 48
impact of Great Fire: on art, 126–28; on belief in martyrdom of Peter, 122–26, 124; on images of Nero, 112–16, 113; on persecution of Christians, 118–22; on public projects, 116–18
imperialism, Roman, 38, 113–14
infant mortality, 28–29
injury, 29

Jerome, 28, 122
Julio-Claudians, 131

Julius Caesar: ballistae and, 34; descendants of, 131; floods and, 14; on population diversity, 38; spectacles of, 22
Juvenal, 16–17, 23, 100, 132

latrines, public, 24
Library of Congress, Thomas Jefferson Building, 127–28
Livy, 15, 69–70
looters, 45, 47, 74
lower classes, views of, 17
Lucusta, 19

Maecenas, villa and gardens of, 57
Martial: on Colosseum, 117; on crime, 18; on doctors, 30; on Domus Aurea, 109; on food safety, 28; on noise, 21; on overcrowding, 9; on reconstruction, 100; on shops in streets, 10
martyrdom: in Christian identity, 121–22; of Peter, 122–26, 124
materials, flammable, 50, 51
medical remedies, 29–30
Michelangelo, 125
military equipment in firefighting, 47–48
monsters/monstrosities, depictions of, 127–28
morality: of Domus Aurea construction, 108–9; historians and, 4, 5; history and, 69; *pietas*, 46–47, 152n38; theater and, 61, 63
mosaics, 106
mythology: of Domus Aurea, 106; history and, 5–6, 60; reenactments of, 91–93. *See also specific characters*

neighborhoods of Rome: Augustus and, 40; fire as spreading to, 42–43; moral obligation in, 46–47; overview of, 11
Nero: Apollo and, 54, 94; birthplace of, 56; character and personality of, 4, 108, 114; as charioteer, 93–94; contemporary mentions of, 116; crime and, 18; death of, 111, 117; as exploiting tragedy for gain, 109; as fiddling while Rome burned, 58–64, 84; legacy of, 7, 112, 113; in martyrdom of Peter, 122–23; mythological narrative of, 5; noblesse oblige and, 57–58; orgy of, 56–57; persecution of Christians by, 86–95, 92, 120; plunder of art by, 76–77; poisoners of, 19; portrait of, 109; rebuilding of city by, 6, 96–98, 110–11, 116–17; remedies and, 29; residences of, 43, 53, 57, 62–63; return to

Nero (*cont.*)
　Rome of, 57, 58, 84, 134; as starting fire, 78–79, 80–85; statue of, 103, 104; Tacitus account and, 68–69; theater and, 54–55, 59–61, 81–82, 102–3, 110, 115. *See also* Domus Aurea
Neropolis, 102, 111
New York City, Rome compared to, 9
noblesse oblige, 57–58
noise pollution, 21–22
Nonius Asprenas, 19
Numa Pompilius, 67–68

obelisk, Egyptian, 125
Odysseus, 106
Oedipus, 39, 40–41
oil lamps, 30–31, *31*
Oppian Hill, pavilion on, 105–7, 118, 126
orgies, 56–57, 83
Ostia: archaeological remains of, 138n7, 138n9, 154n15; as port city, 57
Ostian Way, 122

Palatine Hill: emperors and, 9; fire as spreading to, 43, 50–51, 53, 134–35; summit of, 51; Temple of Apollo on, 54, 93
Panella, Clementina, 134
Pasiphae, 91
Passage Palace (Domus Transitoria), 57, 62, 102–3, 135
Pater Patriae, 58
Paul, martyrdom of, 122, 157n46
Pausanias, 76
pax deorum, 67, 77
people: destinations of, 48–49; fleeing fire, 43–47; psychological impact on, 65, 80; reports and imaginations of, 47–48. *See also* class; rumor; slaves; urban experience of residents of Rome
perfumes, 25
perils in Rome: building collapses, 15–17; crime, 17–20; diseases and injuries, 28–30; fires, 30–36; floods, 12–15; food supply, 26–28; overview of, 2, 8, 39; pollution, 20–26; reconstruction and, 99–101
Peter: burial of, 123, 124, 125; martyrdom of, 122–23, 125–26
pickaxes, 34
pietas, 46–47, 152n38
Pionius, 90
Piso, 109
plague, 28, 101

Pliny the Elder: on crime, 18; on Domus Aurea, 108; on folk medicine, 29; on plunder of art, 76; on portrait of Nero, 109; on statue of Nero, 104; Tacitus and, 131; on Temple of Peace, 37
Pliny the Younger, 130, 131
Plutarch, 14, 32
poisoning, 19
politics in Roman Republic, 33
pollution: air, 25–26; noise, 21–22; smell, 23–25; water, 12, 13
Pompeii: destruction of, 131; frescoes in, 126, 158n52; streets of, 24; townhouses of, 10
Pompey, 95
Poppaea, 114
population of Rome, 9, 38
post-fact world, 7
post hoc propter hoc fallacious reasoning, 83
public projects: architecture of, 37–38; of Flavians, 117–18; heritage and grandeur of, 55; impact of Great Fire on, 116–18; oversight of, 11; views of, 15; workers for, 74–75
pumps, 34
punishment of criminals, 90–91

Quirinal Hill, 55, 135–36
Quo Vadis (film), poster for, *113*

rags to smother fires, 34
Raphael, 127
reconstruction: costs of, 76–77, 101–2; economic and social impact of, 101; efficacy of, 98–100; incentives for, 98; legacy of innovations of, 116–17; principles of, 96–98
Regia, 67, 68, 135
Remnick, David, 116
restoration of order, 93
resurgence of fire on Day 6, 65, 83, 135
Roman Forum: fire as spreading to, 51, 135; purpose and importance of, 53; view of, from Domus Aurea, 107
Roman History (Dio), 129
Rome: burning of, by Gallic Senones, 71–72; Christianization of, 125; climate of, in July, 43; decadent, 114; images of, 8; imperial, 38, 113–14; politics in, 33; population of, 9, 38; republican, 112–13; theater district of, 54; as vast and complex, 1–2. *See also* neighborhoods of Rome; perils in Rome; streets of Rome; urban experience of residents of Rome

Romulus, 67, 68, 111
rumor: role of, 6–7, 44–45; slander and, 86; Tacitus and, 63
Rushdie, Salman, *The Golden House*, 116

San Paolo fuori le Mura, 157n46
San Pietro in Montorio, 157n45
scapegoats: characteristics of, 85–86; Christians as, 86–95, 92
Scheidel, Walter, 28
Scipio Africanus, 28
Seneca, 21–22, 37
Servius Tullius, 67, 68
sewer system, 14
shops: under arches of Circus Maximus, 42, 50; destruction of, 75; in neighborhoods, 11
Sibylline books, 77
Siemiradski, Henryk, *Christian Dirce*, 92
Sixtus V (pope), 125
slaves: as blocking streets, 45; economy based on, 35; as skilled labor, 74
Solon, 40–41
Sophocles, 39
sources, 129–33
spectacles: of Augustus, 19–20; as benefit of life in Rome, 37; Nero and, 4, 60; noise of, 22; as transactions between sponsor and audience, 95; venues for, 9. *See also* executions
Story of Mankind, The (film), 116
St. Peter's Basilica, 7, 122–25
Strabo, 15
streets of Pompei, 24
streets of Rome: condition of, 23–24; escape from fire on, 43–44; perils of, 9–10; private property and, 101; reconstruction of, 96–97
Subrius Flavus, 85
Suetonius Tranquillus, Gaius: biography of Nero by, 130; on Caligula, 115; on Christians, 89–90; on Claudius, 27; on cleanup crews, 74; on damage done, 72; of diet of Vitellius, 26; on Domus Aurea, 103, 108; on fire, 51, 82; on Nero, 60, 61, 62, 64, 78–79; on plague, 28, 101; on porticoes or porches, 97; on reenactments of myths, 91–92; as source, 129, 130–31; on Titus, 58

Tacitus, Publius Cornelius: on Agrippina, 114; on Augustus, 20; on cause of fire, 77–78, 79, 81; on Christians as scapegoats, 87–89, 95, 119; on collapse of theater of Fidenae, 73; on damage done, 65–69, 71; on destruction of Rome by Senones, 72; on Domus Aurea, 103, 108; on Great Fire, 2; as historian, 3; morality, history, and, 70; moral logic of, 111, 132; on Nero and performance, 60, 61, 62, 63–64; on orgy, 56–57; on origins of fire, 50, 82; on path of fire, 50, 51; on plunder of art, 77; on reconstruction, 98; on resurgence of fire, 65; on return to Rome by Nero, 84, 134; as source, 129, 131–32; on Subrius Flavus, 85; themes of work of, 144n23
taxes for costs of cleanup and reconstruction, 76–77
Temple of Apollo, 54, 93, 135
Temple of Claudius, 107
Temple of Jupiter Stator, 67, 68
Temple of Luna, 67, 68, 91, 134
Temple of Peace, 37, 76, 118
Temple of Vesta, 53, 67, 68, 82, 135
Tertullian, 122, 155nn26–27
theater: district for, in Rome, 54; morality and, 61, 63; Nero and, 54–55, 59–61, 81–82, 102–3, 110, 115
Theater of Fidenae, collapse of, 16, 73
Theater of Marcellus, 109
Tiberius, 84, 87, 101, 114
Tiber River: barges on, 96; flights across, 49; flooding of, 12–15; Ostia and, 57; pollution of, 28; west side of, 75
Tigellinus, reignition of fire on property of, 83, 134
timeline of Great Fire, 134–36
Titus, 58, 117
townhouses, 10
trades, specialized, 38
Trajan, 105, 118
Troy, fire in, 46–47, 59, 110–11
Trump, Donald, 116
Twelve Caesars, The (Suetonius), 130–31

urban experience of residents of Rome: benefits of, 36–39; landscape and, 9; overcrowding and, 10; overview of, 4; perils of, 11–12. *See also* disasters; perils in Rome

Valley of the Colosseum, 53, 107, 108, 117, 158n5
Varro, 18
Vatican City, 123, 126
Vatican Hill, 122–23
Vedius Pollio, 27
Vespasian, 15, 25, 117
Via Cornelia, 123–25, *124*

vigiles. See firefighters
Viminal Hill, 55, 135, 136
Virgil, *Aeneid,* 46–47, 71
Vitellius, 26
Vitruvius, 127
vulnerability to disaster, 3, 4–5, 39–40

waste disposal, 23–25
water buckets, 34

water supply, security of, 97–98
wealth, confiscation of, 76–77
winds and direction of fire, 43, 50
workplace quarters, 10–11
worldview about disasters, 14–15, 39–40

Xiphilinus, 129–30

Zenodorus, 104